# America's Songs

This book continues to tell the stories behind popular songs in our country's history, serving as a sequel to the bestselling *America's Songs: Stories Behind the Songs of Broadway, Hollywood, and Tin Pan Alley*. Organized in short easy-to-read essays, this collection provides historical context to specific songs but also demonstrates how certain songs facilitated the popularity of particular genres, subsequently reshaping the landscape of American popular music. *America's Songs II: Songs from the 1890s to the Post-War Years* will appeal to American popular music enthusiasts but will also serve as an ideal reference guide for students or as a supplement in American music courses.

**Michael Lasser** is a lecturer, writer, broadcaster, critic, and teacher. Since 1980, he has been the host of the nationally syndicated public radio show, *Fascinatin' Rhythm*, winner of a 1994 Peabody Award.

# America's Songs II

## Songs from the 1890s to the Post-War Years

*For Marcia & Harry —
Who will, I hope,
keep singing the songs.
With affection.*

**Michael Lasser**

*6/2/14*

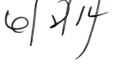

Routledge
Taylor & Francis Group

NEW YORK AND LONDON

First published 2014
by Routledge
711 Third Avenue
New York, NY 10017

and by Routledge
2 Park Square, Milton Park
Abingdon, Oxon OX14 4RN

Routledge is an imprint of the Taylor & Francis Group, an informa business

© 2014 Taylor & Francis

The right of Michael Lasser to be identified as author of this work has been asserted by him in accordance with sections 77 and 78 of the Copyright, Designs and Patents Act 1988.

### Library of Congress Cataloging-in-Publication Data

Lasser, Michael L., author.
    America's songs II: songs from the 1890's to the post-war years / Michael Lasser.
        pages cm
    1. Popular music—United States—History and criticism. 2. Songs—United States—History and criticism. I. Title. II. Title: America's songs two. III. Title: America's songs 2.

ML3477.L37 2014
782.421640973—dc23                                                                          2013021293

ISBN: 978-0-415-81007-4 (hbk)
ISBN: 978-0-415-81008-1 (pbk)
ISBN: 978-0-203-07120-5 (ebk)

Typeset in Minion Pro
by Apex CoVantage, LLC

Senior Editor: Constance Ditzel
Editorial Assistant: Elysse Preposi
Production Manager: Mhairi Bennett
Marketing Manager: Cedric Sinclair
Copy Editor: Nikky Twyman
Proofreader: Jane Canvin
Cover Design: Jayne Varney

Printed and bound in the United States of America by Sheridan Books, Inc. (a Sheridan Group Company).

*For the generations:*

*Celia & Evelyn*
*Carol & Bobby*
*& Alison*

# Table of Contents

# Table of Figures

# Table of Songs

# Foreword

A few years ago, when Michael Lasser and I collaborated on *America's Songs: The Stories Behind the Songs of Broadway, Hollywood, and Tin Pan Alley*, we started with what we thought was a modest list of about 700 songs. As we researched and wrote about the stories behind those songs, however, it became clear that we had to cut the number of songs drastically if the book was to be smaller than an unabridged dictionary. Each cut was painful. We were cutting a great song—and a great story. We haggled, we argued, and finally we horse-traded: "I'll cut 'How About You?' if you'll cut 'At Last.'" At the end of the regimen, more than half the songs were on the cutting-room floor.

After the book came out, we heard from readers who liked the book but wondered, sometimes with some vehemence, "How could you not include . . . [naming one of their favorite songs]?"

Therefore I'm delighted that Michael has taken on the task of writing about these songs in a second book. The songs are just as good; the stories of how they were written are just as fascinating; the reading will be just as much fun.

These songs have done what popular songs are not supposed to do: stayed popular. The very idea of "popular song," after all, is based on transience. One song is popular for a few weeks or months, then is displaced by newer songs, remembered, if at all, by its original listeners as a "golden oldie."

But in the first half of the twentieth century, about 700 songs have endured and still sound as fresh today as when they were first heard seventy, eighty, even a hundred years ago. We call them "standards" (the British, who love them as much as we do, call them "evergreens").

One reason these songs have lasted is that many of them were written for Broadway musicals, and as musicals such as *Show Boat* and *Kiss Me, Kate* are regularly revived in Broadway, regional, and amateur productions, their songs reach a younger audience. Many were also written for Hollywood films, and as we continue to watch Fred and Ginger, Gene and Judy, we continue to hear the songs of Irving Berlin, the Gershwins, Cole Porter, and other great songwriters. Musician friends tell me that the chord progressions of these songs are so much more intriguing than blues songs such as "I Got Rhythm," "Body and Soul," and other classics that have become the bedrock of jazz improvisation.

But these songs have lasted simply because they are just so good. They were composed by *songwriters*, which may sound tautological, but increasingly in the latter half of the twentieth century, songs have been composed by the same people who perform them. But the Gershwins, Rodgers and Hart, and Kern and Hammerstein were not performers but songwriters. Their trade was usually further divided into two other specializations: composers and lyricists. Most of those composers (with the major exception of Irving Berlin) were classically trained; George Gershwin, Richard Rodgers, and Cole Porter brought the intricacies of classical music to the simple formulas of Tin Pan Alley songs. Plus, they composed melodies on the piano rather than the more musically limited guitar.

Lyricists such as Lorenz Hart and Ira Gershwin were trained in the rigors of light verse. In school, they composed villanelles and rondeaux, sonnets and triolets. When they set words to music, they knew where accents fell, what syllables could be fitted to musical notes. They listened to the way Americans talked and found that an ordinary catchphrase—"You Do Something to Me," "How Long Has This Been Going On?," "You Took Advantage of Me"—sounded great when wedded to a musical phrase. They would never rhyme "sunshine" with "sometime."

Finally, they all knew each other—mostly New Yorkers, immigrants or the children of Jewish immigrants. On Broadway or in Hollywood, they hung out together, demonstrating their latest songs. You would never play a dull chord with Jerome Kern in the room, never use a clichéd lyric with Johnny Mercer at your shoulder.

The songs they have left us have become known, collectively, as "The Great American Songbook," the closest thing America has to a body of classical song that is reinterpreted, year after year, generation after generation, by singers and musicians. In recent years, these standards have been sung by singers as diverse as Rod Stewart, Meat Loaf, Carly Simon, Sheena Easton, Paul McCartney, Willie Nelson, Brian Wilson, and *Glee*'s Matthew

Morrison. Appropriately, such singers "vote" with their voices for the songs that make it into the canon.

And, in this book, Michael Lasser with wit, wisdom, and extensive research, gives you the stories behind those songs and how they reflect the America of their time—and of ours. It's his way of keeping these great songs alive and kicking.

Philip Furia
June 2013

# Preface

*America's Songs II: Songs from the 1890s to the Post-War Years* is a companion to *America's Songs: The Stories Behind the Songs of Broadway, Hollywood, and Tin Pan Alley,* published by Routledge in 2006. I set out to finish the job that Philip Furia and I began together in 2005. We knew from the start that we were collaborating on a book about the sometimes-elusive game of collaboration that songwriters played so well during the first half of the twentieth century. Whether Ira Gershwin was asking George to add a few more notes to a musical phrase or George was suggesting a necessary word to Ira, the division of labor was often more ambiguous than that. The creative key was the partnership between the composer and the lyricist; everything else derived from that.

At the heart of this book is a rich trove of anecdotes that reveals how and why the songwriters did their work; it also relies on some selective close reading, mainly of lyrics, to illuminate just how good the songs are. I hope that the anecdotes and the commentary will be useful to those engaged in the study of songs and the men and women who wrote them, but also satisfying for those who know, enjoy, and love this unequaled body of song, and might be tempted to hum along as they read. Some will want to read the entries selectively, to search out songs they remember fondly, but those who read it from beginning to end will have a chance to see how the nature of the anecdotes changed over the years, even though many songwriters had developed similar ways of collaborating. As Robert Frost wrote in "A Tuft of Flowers": " 'Men work together,' I told him from the heart, / 'Whether they work together or apart.' "

The first volume begins in 1910 and ends in 1977, while this new one covers the years between 1891 and 1951. The choice of years may sound arbitrary, but isn't. The first song in *America's Songs II: Songs from the 1890s to the Post-War Years* is "After the Ball," because its success was instrumental in transforming music publishing into an enormously profitable national business known as Tin Pan Alley. Eventually located on West 28th Street in Manhattan, the Alley was popular music's home from the 1880s until the 1930s, when phonograph records and radio left sheet music sales in their dust, and when movie studios, eagerly gobbling up everything they could turn into Talkies, purchased many of the publishing houses and moved their centers of power to the West Coast. By that time, though, Tin Pan Alley had become a generic name that meant the entirety of commercial popular music in America.

The book ends with "Too Young," just before the eruption of rock 'n' roll changed the game in the early 1950s. It established a powerful new cultural force that we later began to call "youth culture." "Too Young" was one of the first ballads to capitalize on the emergence of young people as a market. Although it precedes rock 'n' roll, the song was one of the first signs that the culture was changing.

The trick, in a book that moves chronologically from song to song, is to find a way to convey a sense of history and authorship. Even standards are artifacts of their own time. Like this book, they came about because there was a task to perform—a score to complete, a star to write for, an image or scrap of melody that stuck in the mind. If nothing else, the men and women who wrote for Broadway, Hollywood, and Tin Pan Alley did not wait around for inspiration. They had work to do. Sammy Cahn's answer, when someone asked him which came first, the music or the words, has become a cliché. "The phone call," he'd say. It was practical work, usually performed with one eye on the clock and another on the bank account, but the songwriters succeeded and achieved beyond anyone's imagination. In retrospect, and not incorrectly, we call the thousands of songs from the first half of the twentieth century the Great American Songbook.

The best way to understand these collaborations is through anecdotes, because they make the experience of songwriting recognizable and under-standable. This is how these people did their work—a familiar mix of intent and intuition, hard work and good luck, and, beneath it all, an implicit sense of mastery. I have limited the songs largely to standards, those relatively few extraordinary songs that outlast their initial popularity. They are songs whose mere mention from a stage can make an audience murmur with an-ticipatory delight. Some important songs are not included, because there is no anecdote to tell; the songwriters sat down, wrote a song, and then stood up. End of story. In the few cases where a song is not quite a standard, I've included it because its story is unusually entertaining and revealing, and because it fits especially well with a standard from the same time.

Where do all the stories come from, especially since nearly all the songwriters have died? As you might expect, from histories and critical studies, biographies and memoirs, and newspaper and magazine interviews. Surprisingly, a large number of anecdotes came from obituaries, and, less surprisingly, more and more material came from the Internet. Online sources are more reliable than they used to be. I was especially fortunate to have a number of fine libraries to work in and found most of what I needed at the Central Branch of the Rochester (NY) Public Library, a fine collection for a public library in a slightly out of the way city; the Sibley Music Library of the University of Rochester's Eastman School of Music; and the Special Collections Department of the New York Library of the Performing Arts at Lincoln Center, the source of most of the clippings I found. I'm grateful to the librarians in all three places for their patience, knowledge, and guidance. They do their often-undervalued profession proud. I also want to thank Constance Ditzel and Elysse Preposi for their patience and clarity, and my wife, who understands the kind of solitary concentration the task requires.

Even though Tin Pan Alley is long gone, I was very glad to learn that the same kinds of stories about songwriting persist even though the music business continues to change dramatically. Here's one I learned about the wrong kind of music and from the wrong time: in 1964, Willie Nelson was broke, living with his wife and three children in a Texas trailer park stuck between a cemetery and a used car lot. In a recent interview, country singer Kinky Friedman said that, "in the car lot, there's a sign that says, 'Trailers for sale or rent,' and Roger Miller pulls up to Willie's place and sees that sign."[1] There are so many good stories that shed light on how and why important songs came to be written that it was impossible to fit them all in one book. Even a second volume doesn't entirely finish the task.

Michael Lasser
2013

# Introduction

*"There is, of course, some kind of tale behind every song, but mostly songs are written because one is a songwriter and there is a reason to write particular songs."*[1]

— Irving Berlin, in a letter to Abel Green, Editor of *Variety*

When Gene Lees met Harold Arlen near the end of the composer's life, he asked him a question that apparently no one had asked before: "Mr. Arlen, when you and George Gershwin and Rodgers and Hart and the others were writing for the theater in the thirties, were you consciously aware that what you were writing was art music?" Lees remembered that Arlen "looked at me for what seems in memory a long moment and then said, softly, 'Yes.'"[2]

Lees and Arlen were talking about the Great American Songbook, the unequalled popular songs written between 1920 and 1950, but anticipated by the arrival of ragtime, jazz, and especially Tin Pan Alley in the preceding two decades. Writing almost exclusively about love—some mix of romance, sex, and marriage—the songwriters of the Great American Songbook combined rich melodies, sophisticated harmonies, and smart rhythms with lyrics derived from the slangy vitality of American speech. The results were striking, especially in the ways they wove sentiment and wit together within the limits of a single song. Although this sounds complicated, most songwriters were devoted to simplicity. Despite their clever wordplay, accessibility was a virtue and Irving Berlin was its greatest master. Novelist Anita Loos once had a chance to watch him work: "He would go over and over a lyric until it seemed perfect to my ears. Then he'd scrap the whole thing and begin over again. When I asked Irving what was wrong, he invariably

**FIGURE 0.1**   Two kids from the Lower East Side, George Gershwin and Irving Berlin. Courtesy of Photofest.

said, 'It isn't simple enough.'"[3] What John F. Baker said of Sammy Cahn is equally true of all the good lyricists: they possess "an uncanny ability to fit shapely, singable words to almost any tune written . . . and make them sound inevitable."[4]

That inevitability often lay in the songwriters' ability to maneuver within the unyielding conventions and conservative public taste that made innovation difficult. Despite the slavish commitment to a single subject, the repetition of the same old imagery, and the frequency of clichés both musical and verbal, the best songwriters' gift for innovation is at the heart of *American Popular Song: The Great Innovators*, Alec Wilder's book about composers, and *Poets of Tin Pan Alley: A History of America's Great Lyricists*, Philip Furia's about lyricists. Despite the temptation to settle for banality, each songwriter had to make a song work on his—and its—own terms. Berlin said, "I've always despised that constant effort in the theater and pictures to be unique and original. A picture or a play is good or bad. So is a song. If they're also different, okay . . . but it's a great mistake to set out with no objective but being unusual."[5]

Using no more words than it took to match thirty-two bars of music, a good lyric could spark what was tired and lift what was flat. Just as good songwriting combined sentiment and wit in a single song, so it had to be both familiar and fresh at the same time. But the men and women who wrote these songs didn't sit around waiting for inspiration to strike. They went out looking for it or fought their way through its absence. Johnny Mercer compared songwriters to baseball players: "A ballplayer gets up there and he has to produce. Bam! He whacked it! Then he's done for the day; and they have to get ready for the next game. It might be two or three days, but remember, even though he's not in the lineup, he's constantly practicing. However, they still have to concentrate on one game at a time, and they don't think about how far the ball's going to fly. We do the same thing with songs . . . How do you write a song, how do you hit a ball? Don't think about it, just write it, just hit it. It's the same thing."[6]

As they learned that ragtime and jazz provided enough edge to keep things interesting, composers capitalized on the looseness and drive of syncopation, while lyricists created a lively up-to-date language given shape by their playfulness with sound and rhyme in songs that gave voice to everyone, especially the young. We identified as standards those songs that were so good they refused to disappear after their initial popularity. They continued to buzz along just under the surface until new singers emerged to perform them, thereby confirming that what we'd been singing in the shower all along was worth remembering, even if it was as simple, sweet, and sad as this:

I long to rest my weary head on somebody's shoulder,
I hate to grow older
All by myself.[7]

The reasons elude me, but the history of songwriting is dense with anecdotes about the songwriters and the songs: the serendipitous moment—or was it dumb luck, the way somebody worked, why and how a song came to be written, and then the recognition that it worked—what Herman Melville called "the shock of recognition." Songwriting—the completed song—stands at the confluence where collaboration and history meet, along with art and commerce. With the exception of Berlin, Cole Porter, and a few others who wrote both words and music, nearly all these songs were the result of collaboration. It was something like a marriage, shaped by affection and conflict, common understanding but seething tension—not only as a result of personality but often in terms of the work as well. Even George and Ira Gershwin, who loved each other beyond measure, occasionally argued sharply. Because the music usually came first, the task of setting words to it was no mean feat, especially if the collaborators heard a melody from different emotional perspectives. As Johnny Mercer put it, "Writing music takes more talent, but writing lyrics takes more courage."[8] Mercer's mentor E.Y. Harburg said of being a lyricist, "You've got to be a euphoric masochist."[9]

Attitudes toward love, sex, and marriage changed rapidly and dramatically through the twentieth century, and songwriters had to keep up. They weren't poets and they certainly weren't sociologists, but the moment when the lyric and the music became one—a new third thing—could be thrilling. Yip Harburg said that "the greatest romance in the life of a lyricist is when the right words meet the right notes."[10] To stay in the game, songwriters needed to live in their own time with their antennae aquiver for the newest catchphrase, the sharpest rhythms of the day, the hottest gossip, and the latest changes in what people wanted and what they were doing. While some of the songs were autobiographical, more often than not the songwriters' subject was not themselves, but us. We remember a song, we attune ourselves to its emotional vibe, and we're able to say, "Yes, that's it. That's how it was; that's how it feels." The songwriters would never have said so, but they were democratic populists who told us our own stories in our own time, and then the best of those songs continued to speak to other times. To see how they did it, song by song, is the purpose of this book.

# Chapter 1
## 1891–1895

**"After the Ball"** [*A Trip to Chinatown*] (1892)
Lyrics and music by Charles K. Harris (1867–1930)

The business of American popular music began in a storefront in Milwaukee. Charles K. Harris, a small-time vaudeville performer, wrote songs for any performers he could finagle into singing them. Eventually, he opened his own publishing house and hung a sign over the door: "Songs Written to Order."

No song is more important to the history of Tin Pan Alley than "After the Ball," a lugubrious strophic (verse–chorus–new verse–repeat chorus, etc.) waltz of unrequited love that records its main character's lifetime of bitter disappointment. They wept; we yawn. They embraced grand emotions; we prefer irony.

In 1891, Harris attended a dance during a visit to Chicago. He watched a young couple argue and then separate. A line came to him: "Many a heart is aching after the ball." When he got back to Milwaukee, he finished the ballad in which an old man explains to his niece why he never married and why his former sweetheart soon died of a broken heart. He had seen the woman he loved kiss another man but learned only years later that the man was the young woman's brother. Of such unsubtle melodramatic plot lines were Sentimental Ballads often made.

The first time a performer sang "After the Ball" in a Milwaukee vaudeville house, he forgot the words and the song flopped. Harris then paid a well-known theater performer named J. Aldrich Libbey $500 and a percentage of the sheet music sales to sing it in full evening dress during a San Francisco performance of the hit musical, *A Trip to Chinatown*. At the end of the first verse and chorus, and then the second, the audience was silent.

Harris wrote, "I was ready to bolt but my friends . . . held me tightly by the arms. For a full minute the audience remained quiet, and then broke loose with applause . . . the entire audience arose and, standing, wildly applauded for five minutes."[1] "After the Ball" soon became the most successful song of its time, partly because Harris promoted it shamelessly. It also didn't hurt that John Philip Sousa's Orchestra played it at the Chicago World's Fair. In 1892 alone it sold over two million sheet music copies. Its remarkable success taught publishers and songwriters alike that a single song could make huge profits if it was properly written and promoted. Harris soon moved to New York City, as did most of the major music publishers. The American popular music business re-established itself in a single place—in the shadow of Manhattan's Union Square, the home of beer halls, dance halls, concert halls, and vaudeville houses, soon to be renamed Tin Pan Alley.

Harris never wrote another song that was anywhere near as successful. But thirty-five years later, when Jerome Kern and Oscar Hammerstein were writing *Show Boat* and needed a song to exemplify the music of the 1890s, they revived "After the Ball" rather than writing a song of their own.

## "The Bowery" [*A Trip to Chinatown*] (1892)
Lyrics by Charles H. Hoyt (1859–1900), music by Percy Gaunt (1852–1896)

As he watched the rhinoceros in P.T. Barnum's famous menagerie, a young playwright named Charles H. Hoyt said to nobody in particular, "No man ought to write a play unless he has a skin as thick and tough as that fellow wears."[2] Yet Hoyt soon achieved great success with a series of musical farces he wrote with composer Percy Gaunt. The shows were fast-paced and outrageously plotted, and the addition of singing, dancing, and acrobatics to a farcical story made them even more frenzied and fantastical. The public soon started to call Hoyt the "Father of American Farce." The most important of his musicals, *A Trip to Chinatown*, had so thin a plot that Hoyt revised and rewrote it throughout its 650-performance run. His efforts paid off: *Chinatown* was the longest-running American musical of the nineteenth century and the first musical whose score included three hit songs: "Reuben and Cynthia" and "After the Ball," as well as "The Bowery," which Hoyt added to the show to help buoy it up after the opening.

Despite the show's San Francisco setting, Hoyt included "The Bowery," a song set in New York—a widely known but disreputable street in Lower Manhattan. Its comic lyric tells the story of a hayseed, who explains how he loses his way on The Bowery and is conned by the locals. As he says at the end of each of the song's six choruses, "I'll never go there anymore." Although legitimate theaters had flourished on The Bowery before 1875, by the next decade it was a pretty rough place. Flophouses, dance halls, and pawnshops had replaced most of the theaters, but because of its fame it appeared in a number of songs during the last years of the nineteenth century and the first years of the twentieth.

## "Daisy Bell" (1892)
Lyrics and music by Harry Dacre (1860–1922)

With the decline of the Sentimental Ballad, songs just before and after the turn of the century replaced melancholy with optimism and introspection with action. Whatever appealed to the public also appealed to the characters inside song lyrics. Bicycles caught on in the 1890s because they had become safer and more comfortable, especially for women, who took to wearing bloomers so they could preserve their modesty while they pedaled. Thousands of cyclists clogged the streets of New York City all day and into the night because ordinary people loved the new mobility that bicycles gave them. The bike fad faded quickly, though, with the coming of the automobile in the next decade. Between 1900 and 1905, the number of American bicycle manufacturers dropped from 312 to 101.

During the years of their greatest popularity, bicycles were the subject of many popular songs. Vaudeville artists performed bicycle rags, marches, and two-steps, and people danced to them at cotillions. E.T. Paull wrote the "New York and Coney Island Cycle March Two-Step"; Dave Reed, Jr. wrote "A Satiric Coon Song" entitled "Ridin' on de Golden Bike," and M. Florence dedicated "Bloomer 2 Step March" to the "cycling women of America." The sheet music cover depicted a perfectly attired Gibson Girl seated on her bicycle. Yet only one cycling song has survived: Harry Dacre's "Daisy Bell," often called "A Bicycle Built for Two."

Dacre left England for America in 1891, and brought his bicycle with him. When immigration officials charged duty for it, lyricist William Jerome said to him, "It's lucky you don't have a bicycle built for two, otherwise you'd have to pay double duty." The phrase "bicycle built for two" stuck with Dacre, who wrote the song during his visit.[3] When he had trouble finding a publisher, an American singer named Kate Lawrence said she would perform it during her upcoming tour in England.

Like other songs about technological change—telephone songs, automobile songs, movie songs, airplane songs—the lyrics set references to the bike in the context of a love song. "Daisy Bell," with its plea to "give me your answer, do," depicts a young man who agonizes as he waits for Daisy to reply to his proposal. To persuade her, he describes the marriage he anticipates: they will be poor and their married life will not be "stylish," but they will be a modern couple: "you'll look sweet upon the seat / Of a bicycle built for two."

### "The Sidewalks of New York" (1894)
Lyrics by James W. Blake (1862–1935), music by Charles B. Lawlor (1852–1925)

Small-time vaudevillian Charles B. Lawlor couldn't sleep after a night of carousing. "Suddenly," he remembered, "the idea for this song came to me. 'The sidewalks of New York.' The name stuck to me. Often I had watched the children dancing on the sidewalks. I woke up my wife, and told her I had a hit, and I got up immediately and wrote the name and some of the words on a slate that belonged to my children." The next morning, he sought out a friend, haberdashery salesman James W. Blake. "He helped me put the words together," Lawlor said, "and I put the music to them standing right up in that hat store."[4] Another version of the story says that, as Lawlor wandered into John Golding's store on Third Avenue at Fifteenth Street to buy a new derby hat, he was humming a slow but lilting waltz. Blake listened for a while and said, "You get the music on paper, Charlie, and I'll write the words."[5]

In 1900, New York had a population of three and a half million people, seventy percent of them born elsewhere. For the ever-changing city, where ethnic groups carved out their turf and defended it virtually to the death, the song provided an idealized view of life in the neighborhoods, with Tony playing the organ for dancing and Jakey Krause the baker just down the street. On Blake's block, though, everyone was Irish. His lyric looked back nostalgically to the childhood friends he had grown away from. The children played "ring a-rosie" and the older kids—especially "pretty Nellie Shannon"—danced "the waltz step on the sidewalks of New York." A Mr. Higgins owned the house with a brown stoop next door, but Blake changed his name to Casey because he thought it sounded better. His best friends were Johnny Higgins and Jimmy Crowe, and after another neighbor named Mamie Rorke taught him the slow waltz, the two of them would "trip the light fantastic" along the sidewalk. It sounds as if he had a crush on her.

After audiences began to sing the chorus with vaudevillian Lottie Gilson when she introduced the song at the Old London Theater down on The Bowery, a publisher bought the rights for $5,000, and that was all the money the two writers ever got from it. Lawlor died penniless in 1925.

## "The Band Played On" (1895)
Lyrics by John F. Palmer (1870–?), music by Charles B. Ward (1865–1917)

Even though ragtime was about to sweep away nearly every other kind of music in the first years of the new century, waltzes kept coming. One morning in 1895, an unknown actor named John F. Palmer was standing by an upstairs window in his sister's house, listening to an itinerant German street band. His sister called him down to breakfast, but he hollered back, "I'll be down in a second. I want to hear the band play on." He realized almost immediately that he had uttered a title for a song. The next day he wrote a lyric about his friend Matt Casey. The real Casey had had an affair with a strawberry blonde who eventually became his wife. Palmer set the words to a tune but no publisher would take it, even though nothing was more popular than an Irish waltz about winsome Irish lasses. After vaude-villian Charles B. Ward helped with the melody, he bought the rights from Palmer and published the song. The first printing of the sheet music gave Palmer credit for the lyrics but named Ward as the composer (in much larger type). Ward earned a fortune from its success, but Palmer got nothing more than his original small fee. Their falling out over the money became a personal feud that they never resolved.

Like the influential "After the Ball," "The Band Played On" was an Irish waltz whose lyric combined the romantic with the suggestive, though here the lyric treats sexuality in a comic way. Casey's waltz with the "strawberry blonde" is a graceful glide, and Casey adores her, but their dancing together arouses them: "his brain . . . nearly exploded" and she shook with alarm. Fear not, the ending is happy: he pledges his heart to "the girl with the strawberry curls" as they dance together while "the band played on." The repeated title phrase helps to tie the song's tripping melody together.

# Chapter 2
## 1896–1900

**"A Hot Time in the Old Town Tonight"** (1896)
Lyrics by Joe Hayden (1845–1916), music by Theodore A. Metz
(1848–1936)

Founded within twenty years of one another, Tin Pan Alley and ASCAP imposed some rules on the tough, competitive men (and the few women) in the music business. Charles K. Harris ("After the Ball") was one of the first to realize that writing and publishing popular songs could be a very profitable business. By the mid-1890s, he and his fellow publishers and song writers had opened offices in New York City within a few blocks of one another to create what had come to be called Tin Pan Alley. In 1914, Victor Herbert, along with such fellow songwriters as Irving Berlin, Otto Harbach, James Weldon Johnson, Jerome Kern, and John Philip Sousa, founded the American Society of Composers, Authors, and Publishers (ASCAP) to protect the copyrights of its members' songs. Before that, songwriters were strictly on their own. They invented, adapted, borrowed, and stole, but from now on they made sure they copyrighted their songs as quickly as they could, regardless of a song's source.

In 1896, Theodore A. Metz, the bandmaster for McIntyre and Heath Minstrels, copyrighted "A Hot Time in the Old Town Tonight." Joe Hayden, a singer in the company, helped Metz with the lyrics, but the song's original sheet music does not mention him, although his name appeared on the cover soon after that. Metz allegedly wrote "Hot Time" after seeing several young African Americans energetically fighting a fire in Old Town, Louisiana. When one of his fellow minstrels said, "There'll be a hot time in Old Town tonight," Metz knew he had an idea for a rousing minstrel song and asked Hayden to collaborate with him. More likely, he appropriated the melody from one he had heard often at Babe Connor's, a popular St. Louis whorehouse. When he saw the fire, everything came together.

Earlier that same year, the sheet music for Cad L. Mays' "In Old Town To-night" described it as "an up to date hot stuff coon song."[1] Mays' publisher and Metz's soon combined the two songs into one with sole credit to Metz for the music and Hayden for the words.[2]

The McIntyre and Heath troupe used the number as a march in street parades but it never caught on until Hayden finished the lyric. He ignored the fire but created a sense of the joyful anticipation to be found in a Southern revival meeting. The song's raggy syncopation eventually made it one of the most popular songs among the American troops in Cuba during the Spanish-American War. They sang it so often that the Spanish troops were convinced it was America's National Anthem. A French newspaper correspondent reported that the Rough Riders sang it when they reached the top of San Juan Hill even though Teddy Roosevelt disliked it because, he said, it was coarse.[3]

## "In the Baggage Coach Ahead" (1896)
Lyrics and music by Gussie Davis (1863–1899)

When the Nelson Musical College in his native Cincinnati rejected him because of his color, Gussie Davis worked as a janitor in exchange for private music lessons. Although he died at 36, he became one of the first important African American songwriters in the decades after the Civil War. He wrote his first hit song, "The Lighthouse by the Sea," at the age of 18, and when the printer featured the sheet music in his store window, Davis stood outside for days, pointing out the display to passers-by. "See that?" he'd say. "That's me."[4] He wrote many of his songs for his own company, the Davis Operatic and Plantation Minstrels, but, more importantly, he was the first African American to succeed in Tin Pan Alley. When he died thirteen years after moving to New York, he had published over 200 songs, yet he remains known for only two of them: "Irene, Good Night," reappearing a half-century later in heavily revised form as "Goodnight, Irene", and an unusually morose Sentimental Ballad, "In the Baggage Car Ahead."

Before his success in Tin Pan Alley, Davis had worked as a Pullman porter. One night, a crying child told him that his mother was in a coffin in the train's baggage car. He told the story to a fellow porter, who wrote a poem about the incident and gave it to Davis. Some years later, when songs about death were especially popular, he set it to music but then sold it outright to a publisher for a few dollars. A few years earlier, Charles K. Harris wrote "Is

Life Worth Living," a song with an almost identical plot, and at least four other songs are about dead bodies on trains, all written before "Baggage Coach." Davis probably did not borrow directly from these other songs but he had to be aware of them. The tragic story of a weeping child, distraught father, and deceased young mother was exactly the kind of melodramatic narrative fitting for a Sentimental Ballad.

**"My Gal Is a High Born Lady"** (1896)
Lyrics and music by Barney Fagan (1850–1937)

**"Darktown Is Out Tonight"** (1898) [*Clorindy, or The Origin of the Cakewalk*]
Lyrics by Paul Laurence Dunbar (1872–1906), music by Will Marion Cook (1869–1944)

"Coon songs" were syncopated in the style of the popular ragtime songs of the day. Their ragged rhythms were irrepressible and their caricatures of African American behavior and speech were considered amusing. Everyone wrote them, even blacks. Barney Fagan was a Boston Irishman, a minstrel show performer and clog dancer who was often identified as the "Father of Tap Dance," and the writer of the cakewalk, "My Gal Is a High Born Lady." Will Marion Cook was a serious African American violinist and a composer of Broadway musicals when such things were unusual in America, and Paul Laurence Dunbar was an African American poet, novelist, and playwright who collaborated with Cook on "Darktown Is Out Tonight," one of the most important of all "coon songs."

The story of Fagan's strutting cakewalk is one of many examples of a song's origin that sounds as if it comes from a bad movie, especially since Fagan may have invented the story to tell about himself. Down to his last 25c on his wife's birthday, he took a bicycle ride along Lake Michigan in Chicago. When he broke a pedal, he became aware of a persistent tapping as the dangling piece clicked against the wheel with each revolution. The words "My gal is a high born lady" fit the pedals' syncopated rhythm—perfect for a ragtime song. He stopped to write down the main theme and, when he got home, he finished the song about a man who pursues his "dark Venus." A publisher paid him $100 for it. He never earned a nickel from sheet music sales, but with the money he got that day he bought his wife a dress and held a big party to celebrate her birthday.

In 1898, Cook and Dunbar collaborated on *Clorindy, or The Origin of the Cakewalk*, a musical consisting of comic and musical sketches, including "Darktown Is Out Tonight." Dunbar was a well-known poet, so Cook pursued him about collaborating. Once Dunbar agreed, Cook described their working session: "We got together . . . one night about eight o'clock. We had two dozen bottles of beer, a quart of whiskey, and we took my brother's porterhouse steak, cut it up with onions and red peppers and ate it raw. Without a piano or anything but the kitchen table, we finished all the songs, all the libretto and all but a few bars of the ensembles by four o'clock the next morning. By that time Paul and I were happy, so happy that we were ready to cry 'Eureka!' only we couldn't make any noise at that hour so both of us sneaked off to bed, Paul to his house three blocks away and I to my room."[5]

About a month before the show opened, Cook told the major music publisher Isadore Witmark that if Witmark helped to get *Clorindy* produced, Cook would give him the publication rights to the songs plus all the royalties. It was that difficult for a black to get a show on Broadway. Witmark agreed to help but said that Cook could keep the royalties. Cook remembered the incident differently: Witmark told him that no Broadway audience would pay to hear "Negroes" sing. When the hour-long show opened triumphantly, Cook said of the evening, "I was so delirious that I drank a glass of water, thought it wine and got glorious drunk. Negroes at last were on Broadway, and there to stay . . . We were artists and we were going a long way. We had the world on a string tied to a runnin' red-geared wagon on a down-hill pull."[6]

### "Sweet Rosie O'Grady" (1896)
Lyrics and music by Maude Nugent (1873?–1958)

A lot of the female songwriters during the early days of Tin Pan Alley were vaudevillians who wrote an occasional song to use in their acts. Among them was Maude Nugent, who supposedly wrote both the words and music to this quintessential Irish waltz ballad about an innocent but spirited colleen named Rosie O'Grady. The first generation of Irish songs had looked longingly back to Ireland, but half a century after the first wave of immigration, the children and grandchildren of the immigrants thought of themselves as Americans first. Rather than missing the Emerald Isle, they preferred songs about young Irish men and women who had become American or else had been born there.

Nugent took her song to music publisher Edward B. Marks. He turned it down because "there had been a whole cycle of 'name' waltz songs . . . We thought this cycle was on the wane."[7] She stormed out of the office, heading for another publisher, but Marks chased her down the street to say he had changed his mind. "I'll buy it," he kept shouting at her, "I'll buy it." On the spot, he gave her $100.[8] Another story says that several publishers turned it down until her performance made it into a hit. Then Joseph W. Stern bought and published it.

Nugent wrote a number of other songs, none of them anywhere near as successful, and then retired from the stage at 28 to raise a family. Her husband was the successful lyricist William Jerome, who occasionally wrote lyrics to her tunes. Some skeptics have suggested that Jerome wrote "Rosie" rather than his wife.

### "At a Georgia Camp Meeting" (1897)
Lyrics and music by Kerry Mills (1869–1948)

Frederick Allen Mills was a classically trained performer and head of the violin department at the University of Michigan School of Music. When this white composer began to write "coon songs" under the name of Kerry Mills, he soon became convinced that they were insulting to black people. He set out to write songs that were syncopated but portrayed African Americans in less cartoonish ways. For "At a Georgia Camp Meeting," he borrowed his musical theme from a Civil War song, "Our Boys Will Shine Tonight,"[9] and added a lyric about a religious gathering in the South when he realized he had a hit on his hands. When the team of Genaro and Bailey introduced the song in vaudeville, they added a cakewalk. It was a high-stepping, strutting dance in which the performers bent their bodies back as they held their hats high and twirled their canes.

The cakewalk originated on plantations during slavery, probably as a mocking imitation of white masters. A former slave repeated a story he had heard from a black nanny:

> Us slave watched white folks' parties where the guests danced a minuet and then paraded in a grand march, with the ladies and gentlemen going different ways and then meeting again, arm in arm, and marching down the center together. Then we'd do it too, but we used to mock 'em every step. Sometimes the white folks noticed it, but they seemed to like it; I guess they thought we couldn't dance any better.[10]

An ex-ragtime entertainer named Shepard Edmonds told stories he heard from his parents:

> It was generally on Sundays, when there was little work, that the slaves both young and old would dress up in hand-me-down finery to do a high-kicking, prancing walk-around. They did a takeoff on

the manners of the white folks in the "big house," but their masters, who gathered around to watch the fun, missed the point. It's supposed to be that the custom of a prize started with the master giving a cake to the couple that did the proudest movement.[11]

## "On the Banks of the Wabash Far Away" (1897)
Lyrics and music by Paul Dresser (1857–1906)

"On the Banks of the Wabash Far Away" has been one of the most beautiful, most beloved American songs since the day that Paul Dresser wrote it in a hotel room in Chicago. It has also been one of the most profitable. Its success earned the songwriter the equivalent of $2.5 million. Max Hoffman, the orchestrator for music publisher Isadore Witmark, was in the hotel room when Dresser wrote it. His memory illuminates the way a songwriter teases out a song. "It was summer," Hoffman remembered:

all the windows were open and Paul was mulling over a melody that was practically in finished form. But he did not have the words. So he had me play the chorus over and over again at least for two or three hours, while he was writing down the words, changing a line here and a phrase there until the lyric suited him . . . When Paul came to the line "Through the sycamores the candlelights are gleaming," I was tremendously impressed . . . I have always felt that Paul got the idea from glancing out of the window now and again as he wrote, and seeing the lights glimmering on Lake Michigan.[12]

Dresser's brother, novelist Theodore Dreiser, also claimed, less believably, to have played a role in writing the song. In later years, he downplayed his contribution but never denied that he had written the song's first verse and chorus. Dreiser wrote after his brother's death that they were talking casually on a Sunday morning when Dresser asked, "What do you suppose would make a good song these days? . . . Why don't you give me an idea for one once in a while, sport?" Dreiser replied, "Me? . . . I can't write those things. Why don't you write something about a State or a river . . . something that suggests a part of America? People like that. Take Indiana— what's the matter with it—the Wabash River? It's as good as any other river, and you were 'raised' beside it." Dresser replied, "That's not a bad idea, but how would you go about it? Why don't you write the words and let me put the music to them? We'll do it together?" Although Dreiser begged off after struggling to write a few lines, he had a strong reaction when he first heard the song a year later: "I jumped up. They were my words! It was Paul's song!"[13] Dreiser's retelling feels disingenuous, especially since he also wrote,

"I know absolutely whereof I speak when I say that the words . . . were written in less than an hour on an April Sunday afternoon, and that the music did not require a much longer period. The whole deed was pleasurable and easy, while the reward was proportionally great."[14]

The song's two verses are characteristic of a Sentimental Ballad in their reminiscence of the singer's home "along the Wabash." As in so many others, the theme of returning is at its heart. The first verse portrays a loving mother "standing in the doorway," and the second a beloved Mary who rejected his love and has since died. Because his memories are so sad, he feels he cannot return. Only the tenderness of the chorus provides any emotional uplift, especially the imagery of "the breath of new mown hay" and the candlelight gleaming through the sycamores.

### "When You Were Sweet Sixteen" (1898)
Lyrics and music by James Thornton (1861–1938)

Years after they met, a man assures his beloved that he still loves her as he did long ago, "when you were sweet sixteen." James Thornton found the song's inspiration in his wife, Bonnie. When he came home after a night of drinking, she asked him if he still loved her. He answered, "I love you like I did when you were sweet sixteen."[15] Thornton used the line as the basis of his most famous song.

The Thorntons' marriage was more complicated than this glib romanticism suggests. In addition to being a songwriter and a performer, James was an alcoholic. Bonnie, who appeared in vaudeville, used to wait at the stage door to collect his pay each week before he could head for the nearest saloon. Eventually, after more than fifteen years of marriage, she left him.

"Sweet Sixteen" has the feel of a sweet Irish melody, even though it was written in America for American audiences. As tastes changed in the 1920s, Thornton gave up songwriting. The success of a song like "Yes! We Have No Bananas" made him feel as if he had lost touch with the public. He told an interviewer, "When those things click, I don't know anything."[16]

### "Hello, Ma Baby" (1899)
Lyrics and music by Joseph E. Howard (1878–1961) and Ida Emerson (1876–1964)

### "Hello, Frisco" [*Ziegfeld Follies of 1915*] (1915)
Lyrics by Gene Buck (1885–1957), music by Louis A. Hirsch (1887–1924)

"Hello, Ma Baby" was one of the earliest important ragtime songs, shaped by the syncopated "hello" that opens the chorus. It was a "coon song," a cakewalk, and a telephone song about two lovers who conduct their love affair by telephone. They talk every day so he can tell her how much he loves her. Joe Howard and Ida Emerson wrote songs together, performed in vaudeville together, and were husband and wife. They met when the already-married Howard was only 17. He divorced his wife and married her—she was the second of his nine wives!

In the 1890s, the telephone was considered little more than a gadget of no particular importance, though it soon began to gain popularity. Large numbers of households soon considered it a necessary part of daily life. Reflecting that shift in attitude, in the next decade Tin Pan Alley songwriters produced almost as many telephone songs as they did automobile songs. Perhaps the most important was "Hello, Frisco," written by Louis A. Hirsch and Gene Buck in 1915 to celebrate the opening of telephone service from the East all the way to the Pacific. The service actually began with a brief conversation between Alexander Graham Bell in New York and his old colleague Thomas Watson in San Francisco, but Buck supposedly got the idea for the lyric from overhearing producer Florenz Ziegfeld yell into a telephone, "Hello—Frisco? Hello?" Using an impatient young man who is trying to telephone his girl in San Francisco, Buck recreates an early call, complete with an operator: "Please, long distance, do connect me, / Get her on the telephone." When the young man finally reaches his girl, who just happens to be named Frisco, the song becomes a conversational duet.

Theatrical revues, which first reached Broadway just before the turn of the century, parodied recent events, popular fads, and other hit shows. They were perfect settings for TPA songs that combined the state of the heart with the state of the nation. In the years before the Great Depression, though, "extravagant revues"—Florenz Ziegfeld's *Follies*, George White's *Scandals*, and Earl Carroll's *Vanities*—dominated Broadway. They turned the fads and fancies of the moment into opulent theatrical effects featuring glamorous stars, extraordinary sets, and equally glamorous and extraordinary (and scantily dressed) showgirls. For the "Hello, Frisco" production number near the end of *The Follies'* first act, a man and woman sat at opposite sides of the stage, singing into prop telephones. Behind them, a string of tiny light bulbs on a huge map of the United States showed the lovers' cross-country connection. The number also featured showgirls dressed as various cities to salute the latest miracle of modern technology.[17]

### "A Bird in a Gilded Cage" (1900)
Lyrics by Arthur J. Lamb (1870–1928), music by Harry Von Tilzer (1872–1946)

In his day, nobody wrote as many songs, as many kinds of songs, or as many successful songs as composer Harry Von Tilzer. He was the Irving Berlin of his time, but without the genius. "A Bird in a Gilded Cage," his first major hit and the song he called "the key that opened the door of wealth and fame,"[18] was a stylistic leftover from the previous century. With its reliance on elevated emotion and melodramatic stories, and with a peculiar affection for the suffering and death of the innocent, the Sentimental Ballad was the most important song form of the nineteenth century. "A Bird in a Gilded Cage" is a variation on its central theme of early death. It tells the story of a lovely young woman who chooses, fatefully, to marry "for wealth not for love."

Years later, Von Tilzer explained that Arthur Lamb, who had previously written the words to "Asleep in the Deep," approached him with a lyric about an unmarried young woman and her aged companion. Von Tilzer liked what he read but insisted that Lamb revise the lyric so the two characters were man and wife rather than man and mistress. "Why, you've written a song about a whore," he said. Lamb scribbled the changes in a few minutes, and Von Tilzer, with who knows what sense of irony, took the lyrics with him to a party in a nearby brothel. Ignoring the boisterous goings-on, he sat at a piano, composing a suitable melody. When he sang what he'd written, several of the girls began to cry. He said, "Now I know I have a hit, if even these ladies can weep over my song."[19]

In a ballroom "filled with fashion's throng," a young woman "to her lover then softly sighed." She tells him the story of the wasted life of one who "married for wealth not for love." The lyric that Von Tilzer set to music possesses the inversions and other clumsy structures that characterize the inexpert lyric writing of the nineteenth century, but also gives the song its typical formality. Despite its forced rhetoric and cloying emotionalism, the tale rings true, if only within the confines of the Sentimental Ballad.

# Chapter 3
## 1901–1905

**"Bill Bailey, Won't You Please Come Home?"** (1902)
Lyrics and music by Hughie Cannon (1877–1912)

Tin Pan Alley songwriters were out to make a buck. At the turn of the twentieth century, that meant writing syncopated "coon songs." Similar to the minstrel songs of the nineteenth century, they were written by whites to be performed by whites, often in blackface. The words were a crude parody of Southern black dialect, and the characters were stereotypes. Most "coon songs" were also ragtime songs, including Hughie Cannon's "Bill Bailey, Won't You Please Come Home?" Although he was black, Cannon wrote "coon songs" because all songwriters wrote what the market would bear. A piano player, vaudeville performer, and occasional songwriter, Cannon began drinking and using drugs soon after he wrote his most important song. His career collapsed and ten years later, at the age of 35, he died.

The real Bill Bailey was a black vaudeville performer and a friend of Cannon's who arrived home after a night of revelry to find that his wife had locked him out. Cannon paid for Bailey's hotel room and assured him that in the morning, "She'll be begging you to please come home."[1] The problem with the story is that Cannon didn't meet Bailey until after he wrote and published the song. Although traditional jazz musicians still perform it, their vocals frequently omit the verse, even though it makes clear who Bailey was and why he wasn't home:

> She married a B & O brakeman that took and throw'd her down.
> Bellering like a prune-fed calf with a big gang hanging 'round;

A more likely explanation is that Cannon's "Bill Bailey" is one of a half-dozen songs deriving from the famous folk song, "Frankie and Johnny."

Together, they form a loose narrative that begins earlier in 1902, when Walter Wilson and John Queen wrote "Ain't Dat a Shame" about a Bill Bailey who angrily leaves his lady friend but later begs to return. Cannon's song makes the woman his wife but flips the point of view so she begs him to return. In that same year, in "Since Bill Bailey Came Home," Bailey returns home, and in the final song, "Bill, You Done Me Wrong," Mrs. Bailey grieves after her husband dies. This song has the closest connection to "Frankie and Johnny."

"Bill Bailey" was also the basis for a number of other songs unrelated to the "Frankie and Johnny" sequence, including Cannon's 1904 sequel, "He Done Me Wrong," as well as Rozier Daughtry's "Bill Bailey Left His Happy Home Again" (1903), Frank Fogerty, Matt C. Woodward, and William Jerome's "I Wonder Why Bill Bailey Don't Come Home" (1904), and Charles McCarron and Nat Vincent's "When Old Bill Bailey Plays the Ukulele" (1915).

## "Come Down, Ma Evenin' Star" [*Twirly Whirly*] (1902)
Lyrics by Elmer Smith and Robert B. Smith (1875–1951), music by John Stromberg (1853–1902) and W.T. Francis (1859–1916)

By 1902, Lillian Russell had become a major star through a combination of beauty and notoriety. A biographer wrote, "Her voice, while never rich, was at least a clear, full-throated lyric soprano . . . of impressive quality."[2] She was a temperamental blue-eyed blonde with a hefty hourglass figure, whose size reflected her "roaring passion for food, especially rich-buttered corn."[3] She also had a reputation for not paying bills or honoring contracts, and for walking out on both shows and husbands. But her long relationship with the equally notorious financier (and gourmand) Diamond Jim Brady is what made her a national celebrity.

Later in her career, when her star had begun to fade, Russell became a permanent member of the Broadway company put together by the comedy team of Joe Weber and Lew Fields. Before they began rehearsals for their 1902 show, *Twirly Whirly*, songwriter John Stromberg promised Russell "the prettiest song you ever sang."[4] He was supposed to write an entire score for Weber and Fields' newest show, but pain from rheumatoid arthritis incapacitated him. "Ma Evenin' Star" was the only song he completed.

After he finished the melody, Stromberg changed his mind and told Russell the song was not ready. A few days later, he committed suicide by swallowing a fatal dose of insecticide. Someone found the completed manuscript in his coat pocket, and Robert B. Smith quickly wrote a lyric for what became Russell's signature song, "Come Down, Ma Evenin' Star."

A story that says Russell burst into tears when she sang it on opening night is probably the invention of a press agent.

Stromberg's last song was Robert Smith's first hit. He spent the next two decades writing lyrics for Broadway shows, including Victor Herbert's operetta, *Sweethearts*, and later worked in Hollywood, turning stage musicals into movies. The lyric that Smith dashed off to Stromberg's melancholy melody is a strange hash of nineteenth-century formality combined with the conversational style of "coon songs." Here, an unhappy lover portrays his absent beloved in elevated language, but Smith insists on turning the word "my" into "ma" each time he uses it: "I recognize ma true love / Underneath the tiny orbs of light." Because "ma love is unabating" even though he is earthbound, the lover calls on her, touchingly, to "come down from there, ma evenin' star."

## "In the Good Old Summertime" (1902)
Lyrics by Ren Shields (1868–1913), music by George Evans (1870–1915)

## "On a Sunday Afternoon" (1902)
Lyrics by Andrew B. Sterling (1874–1955), music by Harry Von Tilzer (1872–1946)

Ragtime was so exciting and irreverent that it is easy to overlook how love songs were changing. Most importantly, the tearjerker gave way to what David Jasen calls "the pleasant love song."[5] Many of the best examples of this new style are light, lilting waltzes with straightforward melodies, helped along by a good-spirited conversational lyric that discards the elevated diction of the Sentimental Ballad. Instead of the formality of "Beautiful dreamer, wake unto me," lyrics were adapting the everyday talk of ordinary people: "On a Sunday afternoon / You can see the lovers spoon."

America feasted on a rich musical stew at the start of the century: millions of people, especially in cities, were singing and dancing in new ways to the rhythms of African American music, and each ethnic group that crossed the Atlantic brought its own music to be absorbed and "Americanized" by Tin Pan Alley tunesmiths. The versatile Harry Von Tilzer was writing Dixie songs, "coon" songs, moon songs, "Egyptian" songs, Irish songs, Southern songs, dance songs, comic songs, Mother songs, dialect songs, Sentimental Ballads, waltzes, and even the best known of all the beer songs, "Under the Anheuser Busch." It was a sign of his adaptability that he wrote "A Bird in a Gilded Cage," one of the last of the tearjerkers, and then, two years later, one of the most appealing "pleasant love songs,"

"On a Sunday Afternoon." Watching working people enjoy the sun and the sea at Brighton Beach on a summer weekend, he thought of the line, "The one day that's fun day is Sunday," although he did the actual composing on a rainy day when he could not go to a ballgame. He then persuaded Andrew Sterling to write the lyric that would invite young lovers in New York City to spend their day off taking "a trip on the Hudson" or riding the trolley together. Because the lovers who spoon on Sunday will be back at work on Monday, they are entitled to "one day that's fun day."

The successful "pleasant love songs" include "By the Light of the Silvery Moon," "Wait Till the Sun Shines, Nellie," "I Wish I Had a Girl," and "Let Me Call You Sweetheart," but none was more important than "In the Good Old Summertime." One afternoon, lyricist Ren Shields suggested some rhymes in response to George Evans' passing remark about "the good old summertime," and Evans quickly provided a tune. Because he was unable to write music, he hummed it to singer Blanche Ring, who notated it and eventually sang it on Broadway. Despite the serendipitous moment with Shields, and despite the fact that Evans ran the well-known minstrel troupe the Honey Boy Minstrels, the collaborators had trouble convincing a major music publisher to buy their song. They thought that having a chorus begin "In the good old summertime, / In the good old summertime" meant that sales would plummet right after Labor Day. When Ring added it to the score of her new show, *The Defender*, audiences took to it immediately and often joined her in singing the chorus that ended, "she's your tootsie-wootsie, / In the good old summertime." For the first time, a song about a season became a hit.

### "Under the Bamboo Tree" (1902)
Lyrics by James Weldon Johnson (1871–1938) and J. Rosamond Johnson (1873–1954), music by Bob Cole (1861–1911)

### "Aba Daba Honeymoon" (1914)
Lyrics and music by Arthur Fields (1888–1953) and Walter Donovan (1888–1964)

Black entertainers did not often perform in mainstream vaudeville. No more than one African American act ever appeared on a white bill. Bob Cole was one of the few who crossed over. He was an important early African American composer whose act consisted of some of the two hundred songs he wrote, usually with his co-lyricists, the Johnson brothers, James Weldon and J. Rosamond. Because they were concerned about the dignity of blacks only four decades after Emancipation, their songs for Broadway musicals

**FIGURE 3.1 and 3.2**   Lyricists and brothers, James Weldon and J. Rosamond Johnson. Courtesy of Photofest.

often avoided the stereotypes common to "coon songs" and used Standard English rather than dialect. James Weldon Johnson described the songs they heard all around them:

> The Negro songs then the rage were known as "coon songs" and were concerned with jamborees of various sorts and the play of razors, with the gastronomical delights of chicken, pork chops and watermelon, and with the experiences of red-hot "mammas" and their never too faithful "papas." These songs were for the most part crude, raucous, bawdy, often obscene.[6]

Rosamond Johnson added, "We wanted to clean up the caricature.[7]

In 1900, 28-year-old Weldon worked as the principal of an African American public school in Jacksonville while he studied for a law degree. He wrote the words, and his brother the music, for a song, "Lift Every Voice and Sing," that the students were to sing on the ninety-first anniversary of Abraham Lincoln's birth. A few years later, after seeing the pleasure Rosamond took from studying and then teaching music, Weldon wrote, "His enthusiasm roused my curiosity about this new world." They decided to write songs together; Rosamond would write the music and they would collaborate on the words. After some success locally, off they went to New York City, propelled by "invincible faith" in themselves.

Weldon soon returned to Jacksonville, but when he received two large royalty checks from Rosamond, he moved to New York for good. Rosamond remembered that after a performance at the Winter Garden in Manhattan, Cole and the Johnsons walked uptown:

> As we strolled pensively northward, Bob and I wondering about our next booking, and Jim deciding whether or not to go back and teach school, I hummed one of the sacred songs of our ancestors, one of the spirituals which alone enabled the Negro to live during the dire days of slavery, the immortal "Nobody Knows the Trouble I See."
> "Wait a minute," says that scalawag Bob. "That's the song we need for our act."
> "No you don't," I said. "That is a sacred song, which is not to be desecrated on the vaudeville stage."
> "What kinder musician are you?" says Bob. "Been to the Boston Conservatory and can't change a little old tune around."[8]

When they took their revised tune to publisher Edward B. Marks, he refused to release it until Cole and the Johnsons changed the title from "If You Lak-a Me" to "Under the Bamboo Tree" because, he said, their title didn't mean anything.[9] The success of "Under the Bamboo Tree" inadvertently began a twenty-year rage for "jungle songs," some of which were also "monkey songs." Just what are you supposed to make of a musical tale about a monkey and a chimpanzee who fall in love and find a baboon to marry them, especially when these songs are actually humorous (and racist) treatments of African life and, by implication, sexuality. "Aba Daba Honeymoon" was the most popular of a whole troop of "monkey songs" that began in 1907 with Theodore F. Morse and Jack Drislane's "In Monkey Land," and continued with Morse and lyricist Edward Madden's "Down in Jungle Town" in 1908 and "On a Monkey Honeymoon" by Morse and Drislane again in 1909. The most popular of these songs was one of the last, Arthur Fields and Walter Donovan's, "Aba Daba Honeymoon." Tin Pan Alley was never shy about exploiting fads.

"Under the Bamboo Tree" also led more directly to a second strain that portrayed African natives who, like monkeys, fall in love and marry, but often speak a mumbo-jumbo that makes a mockery of African life:

> If you lak-a-me lak I lak-a-you
> And we lak-a-both the same,
> I lak-a-say,
> This very day,
> I lak-a change your name.

Cole and the Johnsons wanted to dignify African American life by illuminating African traditions, but they knew very little about them and soon fell back on Tin Pan Alley formulas.

Whether the characters were simian or uncivilized, the point was the same. Songs that mocked those that inhabited the jungle may have been entertaining, but they were fueled by racism. The chimpanzees and the ridiculous natives alike were clearly inferior to the white audiences who found them so amusing. A decade later, Duke Ellington and one of his musicians, trumpeter Bubber Miley, exploited the term by labeling Miley's peculiar style of using a plunger mute and growling into his horn. They called it "jungle music," and the all-white audiences at the Cotton Club ate it up. To get the point in the songs, all you have to do is substitute "baboon" for "coon." Other songs of the time made similar allusions, especially about the sexual prowess of African Americans, bluntly in a song like Ida Cox's "Wild Women Don't Get the Blues" that sings about peaceful wives wondering where their wandering husbands are, while these "monkey men" pursue "wild women" because "wild women don't worry, / Wild women don't get the blues."

## "Ida, Sweet as Apple Cider" (1903)
Lyrics by Eddie Leonard (1870–1941), music by Eddie Munson (?)

Sometimes a song has no flash of inspiration; it comes from hard work. In this case, the stories start after the fact with Al Jolson, whose emergence as a performer is linked, probably apocryphally, to a song that was linked in turn to another great star, Eddie Cantor. There's a well-exercised tale that says Jolson's first job in show business involved sitting in the balcony of a vaudeville house during a singer's performance. When the singer invited the audience to join in, the young man, so carried away by the song he can't help himself, stood to sing in an especially sweet voice, turning a routine tune into a surprise smash hit and virtually guaranteeing an increase in sheet music sales. Young Jolson would do exactly the same thing, afternoon and evening, for the duration of the run. The onstage singer responsible for Jolson's twice-a-day outburst was reputed to be blackface minstrel and song-and-dance man, Eddie Leonard, and the song his latest creation, "Ida, Sweet as Apple Cider."[10] About to be fired, Leonard (and Jolson) sang it, although he had been ordered not to. Its reception was so strong that Leonard kept his job and the song sold one million copies during its first year.

Leonard had originally wanted to be a professional baseball player, but after seeing his batting average, John McGraw, the manager of the Baltimore Orioles, advised him to change his name from Lemuel Golden Toney and to try show business. Toney was the son of a landed Virginia family that had lost everything in the Civil War.

Eddie Cantor never had anything to lose. Born on the Lower East Side, Edward Israel Iskowitz was an orphan by the age of 2 and was raised by his grandmother, Esther Kantrowitz. A book-keeping error when she registered her grandson for school changed his name to Kantor. When he first met Ida Tobias in 1903, she urged him to change his first name to "Eddie" because she didn't think "Izzy" was a proper name for an actor. Cantor's first professional job in vaudeville involved his doing an imitation of Eddie Leonard singing "Ida, Sweet as Apple Cider." Once he married Ida, he continued to sing it as a sign of his lifelong affection.

## "You're the Flower of My Heart, Sweet Adeline" (1903)
Lyrics by Richard H. Gerard (1876–1948), music by Harry Armstrong (1879–1951)

In 1896, according to a newspaper report written twenty-five years after the fact, "a girl who worked at the music counter of a New York department store" inspired an 18-year-old prizefighter named Harry Armstrong to write a melody.[11] Another newspaper story says that he originally wrote a chorus without a verse, entitled it "Down Home in Old England," and submitted it to a New York publisher, who declined to publish it. Because he was especially fond of barbershop quartet singing, Armstrong wove an echo into the melody because he thought it would attract quartets during the heyday of barbershop singing. An "echo song" creates its effect by repeating a key word, phrase, or line. The song remained a tune without words until 1903, when Armstrong moved from Boston to New York City to work for Jerome Remick's music-publishing firm. There he met Richard H. Gerard, a staff lyricist, and asked him to add words. Gerard changed the title to "You're the Flower of My Heart, Sweet Rosalie." When publisher after publisher turned it down, Gerard suggested that they change the title. A short time later, the two men saw a poster advertising a farewell concert tour by the famous soprano, Adelina Patti. That was all the inspiration they needed, except that her name was difficult to rhyme. They changed the name of the girl just a little and shortened the title to "Sweet Adeline." Gerard wisely made use of Armstrong's echo in his lyric: "Sweet Adeline, / My Adeline."

Although M. Witmark & Sons published the song, its sales were slow until a vaudeville quartet called the Quaker City Four came looking for new material. They rejected song after song until they saw "Sweet Adeline." One of the quartet's members said, "That's what we've been looking for." Unfortunately, Gerard was unable to adapt to new song styles that reflected the coming of ragtime and jazz. He could write only the passé ballads that told a sentimental story. By 1927, he had left the music business and was working for the New York City Post Office. Yet he still carried a business card that identified him as the author of the "world famous song, 'Sweet Adeline.'"[12]

## "Give My Regards to Broadway" and "The Yankee Doodle Boy"
[*Little Johnny Jones*] (1904)
Lyrics and music by George M. Cohan (1878–1942)

George M. Cohan loved to wrap himself in an American flag as he ran around the stage, singing the patriotic songs he wrote. He was born into a family of second-generation Irish-American performers on July 3, 1878, even though one of his best-known songs asserts that this "real live nephew

**FIGURE 3.3**  George M. Cohan. Courtesy of Photofest.

of my Uncle Sam" was "born on the Fourth of July." He was a complete man of the theater—playwright, composer, lyricist, director, actor, singer, and dancer—although it was often impossible to distinguish between the man and the character he portrayed. In show after show, he played an Irish-American patriot and cock-o'-the-walk New Yorker who strutted back and forth across the stage and up and down Broadway as if he owned both of them. Oscar Hammerstein once said of him, "Never was a plant more indigenous to a particular part of earth than was George M. Cohan to the United States of his day."[13]

Cohan's first important show, *Little Johnny Jones*, was an unabashed flag-waver. It tells the story of a jockey who rides a horse named Yankee Doodle in the English Derby. He is accused of throwing the race but is cleared and eventually wins the heart of pretty Goldie Gates from San Francisco. Cohan's idea for the show and for the character of Jones came from a newspaper story about a famous American jockey, Tod Sloan, who had ridden King Edward VII's horse in the 1901 Derby. He was ideal for someone like Cohan to play—short of stature but very energetic—and that was all the motivation Cohan needed; a few weeks later, he had finished both book and score. Always a very fast worker, he insisted that he wrote only simple songs with simple harmonies and limited range. In other words, he wrote what would be easy for him—and everybody else—to sing.

Early in the show, when Cohan sang "Yankee Doodle Boy" in his characteristic nasal twang, the audience heard something irresistibly new. Cohan performed its slangy lyric with a panache rarely seen in the decorous world of the musical theater, known for Mittel-European operettas and languid musical comedies populated by upper-class stiffs. Johnny Jones was a regular American guy, always on the move. In an interview a few days after the opening, Cohan described the key to his shows: "Speed! Speed! And lots of it. That's the idea of the thing. Perpetual motion!"[14]

Toward the end of the second act, Jones remains behind in England to defend his name, but a trusted friend sets sail to uncover the evidence aboard ship that will clear him. When the friend finds it, he is to fire two flares. Stuck in England, his fate in the hands of others, Jones sings softly and sadly to himself, but, when the flares arch across the sky, Jones turns to the audience to celebrate in a stirring chorus of what would become one of Cohan's best-known songs:

> Give my regards to Broadway,
> Remember me to Herald Square,
> Tell all the gang at Forty-Second Street
> That I will soon be there.

**"Meet Me in St. Louis, Louis"** (1904)
Lyrics by Andrew B. Sterling (1874–1955), music by Kerry Mills
(1869–1948)

When the Louisiana Purchase Exposition, also called the St. Louis World's Fair, was on everybody's mind, many composers turned to it for inspiration. Songs during the first several decades of the new century were especially responsive to important people and events—"Hello Frisco" about the opening of transcontinental telephone service, "Dance and Grow Thin" about the first fad for dieting, and "Lucky Lindy" about the exploits of Charles Lindbergh, among many others. The Fair illuminated its visitors with the new incandescent light bulbs, and nourished them after a fashion by the still new hot dog and ice-cream cone. Scott Joplin wrote a new rag, "Cascades," in honor of the Fair's waterfalls, but the song that caught everyone's ear was about an independent-minded wife named Flossie, who leaves her husband a note to tell him she has gone to the Fair. It offers a tempting invitation: she promises him a good time at the Fair and afterwards—"We will dance the Hoochee Koochee, / I will be your tootsie wootsie"—if he will join her there. The promise borders on sexual abandon—first the dance and then the cuddling.

Kerry Mills and Andrew Sterling wrote "Meet Me in St. Louis, Louis" as a promotional song before the Fair opened. It had already become a hit by opening day and was popular enough to serve as the Fair's unofficial anthem. Although the song has survived for more than a century, singers often drop the verse, even though it changes the outlook of the song. Rather than a giddy evocation of the Fair's pleasures, it is really the story of Flossie's declaration of independence. Its appeal begins in the first line of the chorus: "Meet me in St. Louis, Louis." The amusing repetition anticipates "Hoochee Koochee" and "tootsie wootsie," and suggests the sexy playfulness of the lyric. The idea for the repetition came to Mills and Sterling when they ordered a mixed drink called a Louis served by a bartender named Louis. The song's lilting melody and tripping lyrics make it easy to overlook Flossie's small revolution. In an America that prized nothing more than domestic propriety and the work ethic, she kicks up her heels to pursue pleasure for its own sake and lets the household take care of itself. She is good spirited but also capable of just a little defiance: "Don't tell me the lights are shining anyplace but there."

**"How'd You Like to Spoon with Me?"** [*The Earl and the Girl*] (1905)
Lyrics by Edward Laska (1894–1959), music by Jerome Kern (1885–1945)

Everybody who wrote songs admired Jerome Kern for the innovative and intoxicating melodies that so enriched America's popular music for thirty years. Nobody remembers Edward Laska, one of his early lyricists, even though he was largely responsible for Kern's first hit. A producer of musicals had asked the lyricist for a song that exploited the rage for the new slang term, "spooning," a naughty early twentieth-century synonym for kissing or petting or making love. Laska asked Kern if he could do anything with it, Kern said yes, and promptly turned out a tune. They took it to the producer, who made them wait while he saw other people. Kern, who had a temper and a sharp tongue, grew so angry that he dragged Laska to the office of producer Charles Frohman to sing it for Alf Hayman, Frohman's close associate. Hayman liked the melody but asked if they would make some changes in the lyric. Laska agreed, but Kern balked, "The hell you will. We don't make changes for assistants." Again he charged off with Laska in tow, this time to the Shuberts. Kern brazenly demanded to see Lee, the more important of the brothers. He pretended to be a protégé of Reginald DeKoven, a star whose show for the Shuberts had just opened to raves. The bluff worked. Lee Shubert bought the song and assured them that it would appear in *The Earl and the Girl,* a new English musical being adapted for Broadway.[15]

Onstage in "How'd You Like to Spoon with Me," a boy and girl exchanged syncopated invitations to spoon while chorus girls swung out over the audience on flower-festooned swings. Audiences left the theater singing not something from the original score but Kern and Laska's jaunty little conversational duet:

> [She]
> How'd you like to hug and squeeze?
> [He]
> Indeed I would.
> [She]
> Dangle me upon your knees?
> [He]
> Oh, if I could.
> [She]
> How'd you like to be my lovey dovey?
> How'd you like to spoon with me?

Years after Kern died in 1945, a cousin claimed that he had not written the song in 1905, but had borrowed it from a tune the cousin had written in high school. Either way, the composer used the song again in 1909 when he was in England, trying to persuade his future wife to marry him. Rather than speaking, the shy composer would play the piano for her for hours. "I never heard such piano playing in my life," Eva Leale Kern said many years later. "As he played I would float off to another world." She was especially fond of "How'd You Like to Spoon with Me?" though she refused to believe that he had written it. When he showed her the sheet music cover with his name on it, her reserve began to melt.[16]

By the time he and Laska wrote their hit song, Kern had been struggling to break into the theater in both London and New York. Because most Broadway musical comedies were adaptations of West End hits with new songs by American songwriters, it was very difficult for young songwriters to place songs. Oscar Hammerstein explained how Kern would do it: "After rehearsing the stale old songs, Kern very cleverly could casually play one of his tunes. On hearing Kern's song, the director would say, 'Maybe we can find a place for that in the show.'"[17] In his first ten years in show business, Kern wrote nearly 200 interpolations designed to make British shows sound more American. He did not write complete scores until 1915.

## "In My Merry Oldsmobile" (1905)
Lyrics by Vincent Bryan (1878–1937), music by Gus Edwards (1879–1945)

More and more people were talking on the telephone, going to the movies, and driving automobiles as new inventions sparked major changes in American attitudes and behavior. The values of domesticity declined as young women cast off their corsets with the same nonchalant grace that delighted audiences when Vernon and Irene Castle one-stepped to "The Castle Walk" and "Alexander's Ragtime Band." Greater affluence meant that ordinary people had more time for leisure and play, and lovers could be alone together as they parked in Lover's Lanes and nuzzled in the balconies of movie houses, taking lessons in kissing from Clara Bow or John Gilbert.

No machine changed America more than the automobile. In 1905, there were 77,000 cars on the road. Thirty years later, there were 24 million. Initially, though, sales were slow. In 1905, to promote the Oldsmobile, Ransom E. Olds had two of his cars driven from Detroit to the Lewis & Clark Centennial Exposition in Portland, Oregon. Because the terrain was often hazardous, newspapers covered the trip for its entire forty-four days. The story directly inspired Gus Edwards and Vincent Bryan's "In My Merry Oldsmobile."

Sexual innuendo dominates Bryan's lyric as Johnnie Steele and his "dear little girl" fly down the road. They "spoon to the engine's tune," they "spark in the dark," and he lets her know that "you can go as far as you like with me." Ultimately, though, he anticipates marriage inseparable from the automobile and the freedom it gives them in the song's most memorable lines: "Down the road of life we'll fly, / Automobubbling you and I." Aside from its rollicking optimism, the song implicitly intertwines changing attitudes toward family values; the behavior of young people, especially unmarried girls; and sex.

### "In the Shade of the Old Apple Tree" (1905)
Lyrics by Harry H. Williams (1879–1922), music by Egbert Van Alstyne (1878–1951)

Composer Egbert Van Alstyne was content to write melodies that anyone could hum and remember. The first of several tales about the song's origin says that his inspiration came from an old apple tree that stood somewhere between Centenary School and a high hill to its south in his hometown of Marengo, Illinois. Another version says that when he was a youngster, Van Alstyne's family spent its summers in Gobles, Michigan, in a house surrounded by Michigan white pines. During one of those summer visits, Van Alstyne wrote some of his first melodies in their shade. Beyond the house and the pines, apple farms covered the area.

By 1896, when he turned 18, Van Alstyne had written and published a few instrumentals. Soon after, he met Harry Williams, his most frequent collaborator. They moved to New York City to make their fortunes as songwriters though they had only $10 between them when they arrived. Van Alstyne supported both of them on the little he earned, playing piano and plugging songs. On a hot Sunday afternoon in Central Park, the homesick young men complained that there wasn't a single apple tree in the entire park. One of them added that there also wasn't a decent piece of apple pie anywhere in the City. The next morning, back at Jerome Remick's music publishing company where Van Alstyne worked, they realized that they had the idea for a song about the Midwest they missed so much. Before they left, they had turned their day of yearning into what would soon become the most successful of their several hundred collaborations.

It's a pleasant enough story that resembles many others about the struggles of country boys in the big city, but the more likely story is that the two men wanted to write a ballad because, as Williams put it, "only the ballad touches them." They wrote the chorus, both music and words, almost immediately, but they could not complete the verse and set the song aside. A year later, a melody came to Williams as he rode the subway. When he got home, Van Alstyne was out so Williams sat down at the piano, picked out the notes with one finger, and wrote them down on a piece of paper. The publisher they approached turned it down because "you must put a death or something in it to make women cry. Cut out that poetry and get down to earth." Within a few days, they had written the tale of someone who returned to his home village with flowers for the new grave "in the shade of the old apple tree." Williams called it "the trashiest thing I ever wrote."[18]

**"Mary's a Grand Old Name"** [*Forty-Five Minutes from Broadway*] (1905)
Lyrics and music by George M. Cohan (1878–1942)

After the run of *Little Johnny Jones*, Broadway producer A.L. Ehrlanger asked George M. Cohan, "Do you think you could write a play without a flag?" Cohan answered, "I could write a play without anything but a pencil." Cohan once explained how he wrote:

> My plan is to collect a half a dozen characters, make them well acquainted with each other, and with me, put them down on paper and then just let them run along. Whenever they want to say something I let them say it. After I have finished one act I haven't any more idea than you have what the next one will be.

Erlanger wanted Cohan to construct a vehicle for Faye Templeton, an actress and singer of great warmth and good humor. Ehrlanger had also signed the young comedian, Victor Moore, who went on to a long career on the stage and in movies. As always, Cohan's new play combined sentiment, comedy, and music, along with locales that were exciting in themselves or that he made exciting. One day, a friend of Cohan's who lived in the nearby suburb of New Rochelle had boasted that he had all the pleasures of rural life only forty-five minutes away by train.

As a result, Cohan called his show *Forty-Five Minutes from Broadway*. The plot concerns Mary, a household maid who nurses a cranky millionaire with patience and skill. The townspeople expect her to be his beneficiary but, because his will has gone missing, his fortune goes to his heir. Eventually, the lost will appears and Mary gets both the money and the man she loves. The score's most important song, "Mary's a Grand Old Name," gives Mary, played by Templeton, an opportunity to explain why she appreciates her name:

> And there is something there
> That sounds so square,
> It's a grand old name.

The song was a great success for Templeton, but she began to worry that Moore's performance eclipsed her own. Because she sang "Mary" in the first act, she asked Cohan to write her a new song for Act Two. He replied, "Miss Templeton, you're a big hit and you're great—great. You have ten percent of the gross and you're going to make a lot of money. Now you get right up there in the saddle and ride along. Everything is going to be okay." Six weeks later, Templeton sent Cohan a message: "I'm saddle sore."[19]

**"Nobody"** [*Abyssinia*] (1905)
Lyrics by Alex Rogers (1876–1930), music by Bert Williams (1874–1922)

"Nobody" was the perfect song for the great comic performer Bert Williams, who wrote it, made it his theme song, and came to detest it. "Before I got through with 'Nobody,'" he said, "I could have wished that both the author of the words and the assembler of the tune had been strangled or drowned."[20] Two years after he introduced "Nobody" in *Abyssinia*, a musical with a score by several important African American songwriters, including Will Marion Cook and Jesse A. Shipp, he appeared in the first *Ziegfeld Follies* and remained with Ziegfeld off and on through 1919. In 1921, Eubie Blake and Noble Sissle's *Shuffle Along* broke Broadway's unofficial color line; never again would African Americans be systematically excluded, even though they were often limited to appearances in all-black shows. Between 1910 and 1921, there had been virtually no African Americans on the Broadway stage—except Bert Williams.

"Nobody" was so powerful as Williams' signature song because it was a *comic* song of racial protest. Part of the reason also lies in Williams, himself. One contemporary observer called the song "a doleful and ironic composition, replete with his dry observational wit, and is perfectly complemented by Williams' intimate, half-spoken singing style."[21] Williams' scratchy old recording depicts a man who grumbles as he absorbs the day-in-and-day-out trials and tribulations of a world he only half understands, yet he describes his misery and defiance only to himself. He has hurt no one, but he will help no one until others stop hurting him. He may be powerless and at times he sounds like a detached observer, but he has also drawn a sharp emotional line for himself. Williams' onstage performance began with his searching for a notebook in the pocket of his raggedy frock coat. Once he had it, he began to sing as he slowly turned the pages until he found the name he wanted: "Who soothes my thumpin', bumpin' brain? . . . Nobody." Williams would draw out the long o in "nobody" to create a combination of the comic and the tragic. W.C. Fields called him "the funniest man I ever saw—and the saddest man I ever knew."[22]

**"Wait Till the Sun Shines, Nellie"** (1905)
Lyrics by Andrew B. Sterling (1874–1955), music by Harry Von Tilzer (1872–1946)

On Christmas Eve and again on the last workday of the year, New York Stock Exchange traders gather on the floor to sing Harry Von Tilzer and Andrew Sterling's "Wait Till the Sun Shines, Nellie." No one knows how the tradition started or how far back it goes, but it is at least as old as 1934. It's as indeterminate as how the song came to be written in the first place. There is a story that says the composer got the idea from a newspaper report of a poor family in which a reporter wrote, "The sun would once again shine for them after the storm." The second explanation is the more likely, perhaps because Von Tilzer had a reputation for people-watching and then using everyday situations as the basis of his songs. Either he heard someone speak the title line in a hotel lobby or, more dramatically, when he ducked into a crowded doorway to escape a sudden shower. He noticed a young couple because the woman was crying. The rainstorm had spoiled their plans for a day at Coney Island, but the young man reassured her, "Wait till the sun shines, Nellie." When Von Tilzer got home, he went to work immediately to write the song. He told his friend, lyricist Andrew Sterling, about what had happened and Sterling was smart enough to write a love lyric in which sunshine soon replaces the rain.[23]

### "Will You Love Me in December as You Do in May?" (1905)
Lyrics by J.J. Walker (1881–1946), music by Ernest R. Ball (1878–1927)

Dapper Jimmy Walker became one of New York City's most famous, flamboyant, and corrupt mayors, but he was a state senator when he started to write song lyrics in his spare time. One day, he met Ernest Ball, who had already spent three years trying to break in as a composer. His few published songs were flops despite his gift for melody. He had moved to New York in 1899 in response to an ad for an accompanist. He didn't get the job because, despite his excellent piano playing, he had a number of ugly cuts on his face from a recent football game. By 1903, he was working as a song plugger when he met Walker. The young politician handed him a lyric on a sheet of wrinkled paper and asked if he could set it to music. Most of what Ball read didn't impress him, but two lines caught his attention:

> Will you love me in December as you do in May?
> Will you love me in the good old-fashioned way?

Ball carried the scrap of paper in his pocket for two months without being able to write a tune. Finally he tried a different approach to Walker's words. Instead of thinking musically and trying to construct a melody, he pictured a blonde girl and then a gray-haired man. As he wondered what it was like to grow old, a tune began to come to him. Years later, Walker described watching Ball work at the piano:

> I'll never forget the night when Ernie ran his magical fingers over the keyboard, plucking out the tune he was improvising, note by note. He finally swept both hands over the keys in the broad

chords of the finished melody, and I knew that a hit had been born. I clasped Ernie about the shoulders and kissed his cheek.[24]

Ball and Warner published the finished song later that year. It became Ball's first hit. More importantly, it got him thinking about his approach to writing. Rather than worrying about being clever or selling sheet music, he said, "Then and there I determined I would write honestly and sincerely of the things I knew about and that folks generally knew about and were interested in." It was, he believed, a matter of writing from his heart to theirs.[25]

# Chapter 4
## 1906–1910

### "Chinatown, My Chinatown" (1906)
Lyrics by William Jerome (1865–1932), music by Jean Schwartz
(1878–1956)

Soon after the turn of the century, in a show called *Hoity Toity*, a young
piano player named Jean Schwartz contributed musical atmosphere for a
scene in a music store. His eagerness impressed William Jerome, the show's
librettist, and they soon became friends, even though one was Jewish and
the other Irish—the two immigrant groups that dominated Tin Pan Alley.
In fact, they titled one of their songs "If It Wasn't for the Irish and the Jews."
The ever-practical Jerome, originally named William Jerome Flannery,
dropped his last name when he noticed that the population of the Alley was
becoming less Irish and more Jewish. Schwartz and Jerome wrote a lot of
songs together, always aiming at what the public was interested in.

An article in the *New York Times* for November 8, 1914 invited readers
to "let your memory wander backward for a score of years into Songland." It
imagines a movie, which shows two songwriters "digging" into their brains
for an idea:

> It may be William Jerome and Jean Schwartz—you see them work-
> ing to release an idea—and presently Jerome remarks:
> "I say, Jean, let's go sightseeing; it might turn over something."
> "Immense," replies Jean; "let's go down to Chinatown just for the
> fun and the old times of it."
> And off they go, and you see them all along the trip, for you are
> sightseeing on the film with them. It's Chinatown now, and you go
> with them in the roundup of celestial Chink-land until presently
> they stop—it's an inspiration. You follow them back home to the

**FIGURE 4.1**    Jean Schwartz, a Jewish composer who collaborated with Irish lyricist William Jerome. Courtesy of Photofest.

studio, or to anywhere there's a piano, and are with them while they work and with them you are on the scene of the making of the newest song, "Chinatown, My Chinatown."[1]

"Chinatown" went nowhere until Eddie Foy interpolated it into his revue, *Up and Down Broadway,* in 1910, but it did not become a hit, according to Schwartz, until Louis Armstrong "played it hot" twenty years later. He added, "I still wouldn't give you a nickel for that tune."[2] Orchestra leader Paul Whiteman's experience with the song was less satisfying than Armstrong's. On a live broadcast, as he was about to give the downbeat for "Chinatown," he had an impulse to change to "China Boy." People coast-to-coast heard paper rustling as the band members went looking for the right sheet music. When they finally began to play, the result was a discordant mess; the musicians in the rear hadn't heard the change. Whiteman whispered that they should switch back to "Chinatown," but by now the rear rows had found "China Boy." A second cacophonous mess went out over the air. At just that moment, a loose screw gave out and Whiteman's podium crashed to the floor.[3]

Despite all that noise, "Chinatown" is important because it began a fad for Chinese ethnic songs that lasted for most of the decade. Both the faux-Asian style of the music and the stereotypical references to "almond eyes" and a "dreamy," dimly lit setting (sometimes an indirect reference to opium use) became common. Before that, ethnic songs usually limited themselves to the Irish, Italians, and Jews.

### "I Wish I Had a Girl" (1907)
Lyrics by Gus Kahn (1896–1941), music by Grace LeBoy (1890–1983)

Gus Kahn was one of the most underrated American lyricists even though he wrote hit songs for thirty-four years. Maybe it's because he died when he was only 55, or because he usually wrote for Tin Pan Alley rather than Broadway, or because he preferred to live in Chicago rather than New York or Hollywood. However you explain it, Kahn never got the recognition he deserved, even though he wrote such standards as "Making Whoopee," "Love Me or Leave Me," "It Had to Be You," and "I'll See You in My Dreams." Peter Flynn put it succinctly: "His work expressed both the capricious energy of the Jazz Age and the forlorn escapism of the Depression."[4] His last important ballad, "You Stepped Out of a Dream," became a hit shortly before his fatal heart attack in 1941.

In the course of his career, Kahn worked with twenty-nine different collaborators, including Richard A. Whiting, Walter Donaldson, Vincent Youmans, Harry Warren, Sigmund Romberg, and Jerome Kern. He set words to naughty comic numbers and soaring romantic ballads. He especially admired Kern's music, but they had never met. Kahn said, "If one day I could write with Kern, I'd be the happiest man in the world."[5] When Kern moved to Hollywood in the 1930s, the two men finally were introduced. Kahn told him that his greatest ambition was to write a song with him. Kern replied, "You've been writing pop songs, and I've been writing show tunes, but I had hoped that one day I would write a song with you."[6] Shortly before his death, Kahn collaborated with Kern on his last published lyric, "Day Dreaming."

Kahn insisted on living in Chicago, but because so many composers were eager to work with him, they would either mail him a lead sheet or they would take the train to see him. His wife, Grace LeBoy, would play the tune over and over for him because "it would give Gus a chance to think it all the way through." He could not play piano and, his wife said, he had no singing voice, "but he sure had a great ear."[7] Kahn and LeBoy had met and begun to work together in 1907, when he was an unknown lyricist and she a young woman who was eager to write songs. She became his first collaborator and, in 1908, his wife and the co-writer of their first hit, "I Wish I Had a Girl."

LeBoy described her husband's working method: "In the morning he'd get up, put on his golf clothes, and then he'd have breakfast. Then we'd go to work. He'd work on the words and I'd play the piano . . . Sometimes he'd get it right away, while there were other times when it would take him months until he got it the way he wanted it."[8] In the afternoon, Kahn played golf, but even on the course, he would be thinking about a lyric. Later, when he was working with Walter Donaldson, the composer would take a new melody out to Kahn on the golf course and, by the end of the afternoon, Kahn would have completed his round of golf and his newest lyric.

### "School Days" (1907)
Lyrics by Will D. Cobb (1876–1930), music by Gus Edwards (1879–1945)

In 1907, Gus Edwards began his own touring vaudeville revue, *School Boys and Girls*. To keep it going successfully for the next twenty years, he spent a lot of time combing the country for young talent to hire—including

**FIGURE 4.2** Gus Edwards, songwriter and vaudevillian, and the young members of his "School Boys and Girls" troupe. Courtesy of Photofest.

Groucho Marx, Eddie Cantor, Walter Winchell, Sally Rand (whose fan dance titillated the customers at the 1933 Chicago World's Fair), Ray Bolger, and George Jessel. Several years earlier, during the Spanish-American War, the U.S. Army sent him to perform at an army camp to help take the soldiers' minds off the terrible food. While he was there, he met a lyric writer named Will Cobb. Cobb had developed a habit of scribbling lyrics on pieces of wrapping paper when he was working as a clerk in a department store before he became a full-time lyricist. He also appears to have had a superstitious streak: he claimed that he wrote all his hits that way, even using his shirt cuffs when there was no paper around. When he used regular paper and thought carefully about what he was writing, the result flopped.

Soon after Edwards and Cobb agreed to collaborate, Edwards convinced his new friend to join him for a vacation at Greenwood Lake, New Jersey, where the town constable guided them to the best fishing spots. More importantly, the police officer had a young daughter whose calico dress became the inspiration for Cobb's most important lyric. Despite the help from the child's father, the two men caught very few fish. Instead, they wandered through the woods until one afternoon Cobb pulled a large piece of wrapping paper from one of his pockets. Edwards smoothed out the crumpled page and read the words, "School days, school days, / Dear old golden rule days." Back at their hotel, sitting at an old piano, Edwards worked to find a tune. Just as he finished, Cobb entered the room. "That tune sounds all right," he said. "Here's the verse." A half hour later, Edwards had finished the song.

Edwards liked to say that his only method of composing was setting household words to music. Few songwriters wrote more frequently about domestic subjects and family life. He was also unusual in that he couldn't notate music. Instead, he used letters of the alphabet, which someone would later turn into notes. Through the years they worked together, friends knew Cobb and Edwards by the nicknames "Words" and "Music."[9]

**"Cuddle Up a Little Closer, Lovey Mine"** [*The Three Twins*] (1908)
Lyrics by Otto Harbach (1873–1963), music by Karl Hoschna (1876–1911)

Karl Hoschna was sure he was losing his mind. Raised in a musical family from Bohemia and a graduate of the Vienna Conservatory, he had been an oboe soloist with Victor Herbert's Orchestra in New York for two years when he came to believe that vibrations from the oboe's double reed were affecting his sanity. To save himself, he wrote to M. Witmark & Sons, explaining his ailment and asking for a job. He soon became one of the music publisher's best arrangers and orchestrators. Meanwhile, Otto Harbach had given up studying law when his eyesight began to fail, and was working as an advertising copywriter. One day, he was riding a streetcar when he passed a giant billboard for a show starring Faye Templeton. He thought to himself, "I wonder what it would be like to write a musical show."[10] Both their lives changed when Charles Dickson, a well-known Broadway leading man, approached Witmark with the idea of turning a contemporary farce into a musical to be called *The Three Twins*. On Witmark's recommendation, he paid Hoschna and Harbach a flat fee of $100 each to provide him with a score. For one of the songs, Hoschna dredged up a melody he had written for a vaudeville sketch; Harbach then added words for what became the score's most important song, "Cuddle Up a Little Closer." The success of the song and the show established Hoschna and Harbach as important theater songwriters. Harbach's career continued through the 1930s with such songs as "Indian Love Call" and "Smoke Gets in Your Eyes," but Hoschna died suddenly in 1911 at the age of 35, when everyone was still singing the collaborators' latest hit, "Every Little Movement."

The lyrics to "Cuddle Up" were purposely ambiguous, like many of the lighthearted love songs from the first years of the twentieth century. They teased and flirted behind double-entendres and sexual innuendo. Although Harbach's reputation rests largely on such lavish romantic operettas as *Rose Marie* and *The Desert Song*, he titillated audiences with suggestive show titles (*Tickle Me, Up in Mabel's Room*) and provocative lyrics.[11] The dramatic changes in attitudes about sex did not appear until the 1920s, but they began indirectly twenty and even thirty years earlier. Harbach's 1908 lyric places two lovers on the beach late at night. When the boy grows "more bold," the girl suggests that they leave, but he chooses to sidle closer and murmur, "Cuddle up a little closer, lovey mine," because he loves her from "head to toesie." The tone is playful, the language even childlike, but the young man is confident and his intent is clearly seductive. None of this means they don't love one another, but the purity that had been so important just a few years earlier has suddenly—and permanently—gone missing.

## "Harrigan" [*Fifty Miles from Boston*] (1907)
Lyrics and music by George M. Cohan (1878–1942)

George M. Cohan idolized Ned Harrigan. During the last thirty years of the nineteenth century, Harrigan was a comic performer who became a writer of lyrics and books for two dozen Broadway shows about the Irish in New York. He was a major figure in the development of the American musical. Cohan said of him, "Harrigan inspired me when I applauded him from a gallery seat. Harrigan encouraged me when I first met him in after years and told him of my ambitions. I live in hopes that some day my name may mean half as much to the coming generations of American playwrights as Harrigan's name has meant to me."[12] In 1907, when he was writing a sequel to *Forty-Five Minutes from Broadway* entitled *Fifty Miles from Boston*, Cohan wanted to pay musical tribute to his idol. He set the show in the small Massachusetts town where his family used to vacation when The Four Cohans took a break from touring during the summers of George's boyhood, and named one of the main characters Harrigan. Then Cohan invited the elderly songwriter to the opening night performance. In Act Three, James C. Marlowe, the actor playing the character of Harrigan, faced the audience and began to sing:

> Who is the man who will spend or will even lend?
> Harrigan, that's me![13]

"Harrigan" was the last of Cohan's songs to become a standard.

**"Take Me Out to the Ballgame"** (1908)
Lyrics by Jack Norworth (1879–1959), music by Albert Von Tilzer (1878–1956)

**"Shine on, Harvest Moon"** [*Follies of 1908*] (1908)
Music and lyrics by Jack Norworth (1879–1959) and Nora Bayes (1880–1928)

**FIGURE 4.3**   Jack Norworth. Courtesy of Photofest.

Jack Norworth was a successful vaudevillian and songwriter, and the second of Nora Bayes' five husbands. She was one of the highest paid women in show business and a first-class diva. In summer, when Broadway shows often closed because of the heat, she took her vaudeville act on the road, traveling in a private railroad car and reserving an entire floor at the finest hotel in every town.

A disputed but persistent anecdote says that Bayes heard Norworth singing "Harvest Moon" backstage during rehearsals for the 1908 *Ziegfeld Follies*. Later, she wandered into his dressing room to say, "I like that song. Can I have it?" He supposedly answered, "As long as you take me with it."[14] They married soon after—maybe. Some believe that they were already married and working together before Norworth wrote the song. Either way, when Bayes caught him dallying with a chorus girl, she threatened to leave him. He pleaded with her to stay and she agreed, but from then on their onstage placard read:

Nora Bayes
Assisted and Admired By
Jack Norworth

Norworth probably wrote "Harvest Moon" by himself and then Bayes did enough fiddling with the lyric to have her name added to the sheet music. The result was the greatest of the many "moon" songs popular at the time. Some believe that Gus Edwards and Edward Madden wrote "Harvest Moon," and Dave Stamper, Bayes' piano player, said he wrote it but gave it to Norworth and Bayes for a flat fee. It was common for songwriters to sell songs outright for quick cash, so we cannot know for sure. What is certain is that Norworth sang it in variety before Bayes reintroduced it in the 1908 *Ziegfeld Follies*. The other big song in the *Follies* that year was "Over on the Jersey Side," a salute to the newly completed Holland Tunnel that featured showgirls dressed as automobiles who, when the stage lights dimmed, turned on their headlights.

1908 was the *Follies'* second year. Then, in 1911, Florenz Ziegfeld added his own name to the title. The idea was to mount a revue with a French flavor, thanks to the urgings of his wife, the European soubrette Anna Held. The use of *Follies* as the title was supposed to suggest the *Folies Bergère*, something elegant, Gallic, and risqué. Harry Smith, who wrote the dialogue and lyrics for the first (and five of the first six) *Follies*, explained the choice of the name differently. Formerly, he had been a newspaper reporter with his own column, "Follies of the Day." He adapted the title when he wrote his first libretto, *Follies of the Year*, and Ziegfeld further adapted it to *Follies of 1907*.[15]

Riding the 9th Avenue El, also in 1908, Jack Norworth saw an ad that read, "Baseball Today—Polo Grounds." Before he left the train, he had penciled an idea for a lyric on a scrap of paper: When a beau invites "baseball mad" Katie Casey to a show, she agrees to go only if he will take her to a ballgame instead. It sounds ordinary enough, but a female baseball fan was unusual in 1908. Photographs of ballparks from the time show an almost solid mass of men in white shirts and straw hats. The verse also suggests that the gap between being Irish and being accepted as American had virtually disappeared. In the rarely sung second verse, Norworth describes Katie's all-American (and distinctively female) passion for the game:

> Katie Casey saw all the games,
> Knew the players by their first names.

Neither Norworth nor composer Albert Von Tilzer had ever seen a baseball game when they wrote "Take Me Out to the Ballgame." Von Tilzer finally saw a game in 1928, but Norworth not until 1940, when the Brooklyn Dodgers honored him at Ebbetts Field. Although Chicago Cubs broadcaster Harry Carey began the practice of singing the song during the seventh-inning stretch at Wrigley Field, it had first been played in a major league park in 1934. Another Harry, a successful songwriter whose last name was Ruby ("Three Little Words," "Who's Sorry Now") said, "I wrote a letter to God the other day and I said, 'Dear God, why did you let somebody else write 'Take Me Out to the Ballgame?' "[16] As for Norworth, he did not write another hit, but he lived off the two songs for the rest of his life. He explained that "as soon as spring training begins, the bands start playing, 'Take Me Out to the Ballgame,' and that lasts right through the World Series. And then they start playing 'Harvest Moon,' and that carries me through until spring again."[17]

**"By the Light of the Silvery Moon"** (1909)
Lyrics by Edward Madden (1878–1952), music by Gus Edwards (1879–1945)

**"Moonlight Bay"** (1912)
Lyrics by Edward Madden (1878–1952), music by Percy Wenrich (1880–1952)

In the first years of the twentieth century, a large number of new songs were beguiling waltzes that couples could sway to romantically, but they were also intimate in startling new ways. Their lyrics were indirectly suggestive and often humorous, but there could be no doubt about the intentions in such songs as "By the Light of the Silvery Moon," "How'd You Like to Spoon with Me," and "If You Talk in Your Sleep, Don't Mention My Name." Propriety had required respectable women to be passive and demure for many years, but now they were ready to loosen their corsets and find their pleasures in the world. Through Charles Dana Gibson's idealized Gibson Girl, the public embraced the idea of a young woman who was attractive and well mannered, but who was also attending a ball, riding a bike, and even daring a dip in the briny in the company of other young men and women. You could count on her good sense even when she had no chaperone—up to a point. She offered a mixed message at a time when attitudes and behavior were changing.

In "By the Light of the Silvery Moon," Edward Madden's lyric tells a love story characterized by sweet sentiment as a young man pursues a young woman for a kiss. But Madden, most of whose songs were for Broadway musicals, wrote a verse that makes the good behavior a matter of artifice. The song is a one-act play, complete with setting, cast, and dialogue:

> Place park, scene dark,
> Silv'ry moon is shining thro' the trees;
> Cast two, me, you,
> Summer kisses floating on the breeze.

The behavior soon moves well beyond the deeply felt emotions and proper behavior of Victorian song. Lyrics about cuddling and embracing were almost as common as the extremely popular "moon songs" of the day. The young man pleads for the moon's help as he anticipates the result. Cuddling is ambiguous enough to suggest something unthreatening, but also bordering on more abandoned sexual behavior:

> Your silv'ry beams
> Will bring love's dreams,
> We'll be cuddling soon
> By the silvery moon.

During these early years of the new century, songs about the moon and moonlight kept coming. Asked about the song some years after he wrote it, composer Percy Wenrich remembered sitting at the Old Vienna Café in Atlantic City: "It was a swell night, with the moon streaming over the ocean. Just as I ordered another beer I thought I heard some guy ask the orchestra to play a piece called 'Moonlight Bay.' I was mistaken; they hadn't requested it, for the reason there was no such song, but I got to thinking what a swell title it would make and went home to work it. I also made dough on that piece."[18]

**"I Wonder Who's Kissing Her Now"** [*The Prince of Tonight*] (1909)
Lyrics by Will M. Hough (1882–1962) and Frank R. Adams
(1883–1963), music by Joseph E. Howard (1878–1961) and
Harold Orlob (1885–1982)

Joe Howard got the idea for "I Wonder Who's Kissing Her Now" when he heard a college student utter the line to a friend. They were at a party, but the young man was grumbling because a particular woman had not arrived.[19] Howard, a famous vaudevillian and songwriter at the turn of the century, wrote the melody and got Will M. Hough and Frank R. Adams to write the lyric. But Howard was known as a "lifter." He had a reputation for taking credit for songs he did not write, and this may well have been his most egregious example. Harold Orlob, an arranger who was working for Howard, had written the melody for the score to a new musical, *The Prince of Tonight*. It was common at the time for publishers to own the copyright for new songs, but Howard claimed for years that he wrote "I Wonder Who's Kissing Her Now" and used it as his theme song; he also got all the royalties. In 1947, when 20th Century Fox released a screen biography of Howard, also entitled *I Wonder Who's Kissing Her Now*, Orlob sued. He asked for no monetary damages but wanted to have his name listed as the composer. The out-of-court settlement credited both men as co-composers.

The words by Will Hough and Frank Adams are a classic example of the simple conversational lyric of the time, designed to sound familiar. A series of questions, it repeats sentence structure—"I wonder who's kissing," "I wonder who's teaching," and "I wonder who's looking"—as well as the title line. It also uses internal rhyme ("eyes," "sighs," and "lies"), as well as assonance that carries the listener through most of the lines ("I," "buying," "wine," "I" again, and "mine" in a single line). Hear the lyric twice and you virtually have it memorized.

**"Put on Your Old Gray Bonnet"** (1909)
Lyrics by Stanley Murphy (1875–1919), music by Percy Wenrich
(1880–1952)

In a Tin Pan Alley world devoted mainly to young love, moonlit strolls, and spooning, along with automobile rides and lovers' lanes, what are the chances of success for a song about a couple celebrating its fiftieth wedding anniversary by taking a buggy ride? Not good, unless you're a couple of struggling songwriters so desperate to write a hit that you can't take no for an answer.

When an unsuccessful lyricist named Stanley Murphy approached composer Percy Wenrich with a lyric he called "Put on Your Old Sunbonnet," Wenrich liked it well enough to go looking for a piano. Everyone brushed him off. One publisher told him, "This is a publishing house, not a studio." Finally, a manager at Jerome H. Remick Company agreed to let him work for half an hour. When his time was up, the young writer asked for another half-hour. The manager refused. When the conversation grew heated. Remick came out of his office to see what the problem was. He listened to both sides and gave Wenrich the time he needed. He finished the tune and showed it to Remick, who was about to leave for a weekend in Atlantic City. He agreed to consider it and decide by Monday. When Wenrich returned, Remick, known in the music business for having no musical talent, agreed to publish it because "here's a song even I can sing. Any song that even I can't forget must become a hit." At that point, he sang the song back to Wenrich several times, each time making the same mistake in the lyric. He kept changing "sunbonnet" in the title line to "gray bonnet." When Wenrich tried to correct him, the publisher said, "Let it stay that way. It sounds better."[20]

## "A Perfect Day" (1910) and "I Love You Truly" (1901)
Lyrics and music by Carrie Jacobs Bond (1862–1946)

Carrie Jacobs Bond wrote in her autobiography, "The only thing that seems to me at all remarkable about my life is that I was nearly thirty-two before I ever even thought of having a career . . . It was the necessity of supporting myself and my little son that made me a writer of songs."[21]

The first American women to establish a music-publishing firm and earn a living as a professional songwriter, Bond made a virtue of necessity and a career of determination and good fortune. She also made a lot of money. Though it sounds unlikely, "A Perfect Day" sold eight million copies of sheet music in its first year. During World War I, when she toured army camps in Europe, doughboys asked her to sing it so often that she confessed years later that she had grown "tired" of hearing it.[22]

The story of its composition resembles other stories of songs from the nineteenth and early twentieth centuries. A number of Sentimental Ballads rely on similar explanations of their origins, including perfect first drafts that never needed revising. Bond was watching the sun set over Mt. Rubidoux from her fourth-floor room at the Mission Inn in Riverside, California, when she wrote the lyric that begins, "When you come to the end of a perfect day." She explained years later, "While dressing for dinner I thought how I wished I could express my thanks to my friends in some little way, just out of the ordinary; and almost at once came the words for 'A Perfect Day.' I wrote them very hurriedly; I did not have time to change a word or a sentence. I took them down and read them at the dinner that evening, then put them in my purse and thereupon forgot them." Three months later, touring the Mojave Desert, she began to sing the words to a spontaneous tune. One of her friends observed, "Carrie, you have another song, haven't you?" and she replied, "Well, maybe I have."[23]

"A Perfect Day" is skillfully written, despite its sentimentality. First, it raises a question to be considered in joyful but quiet solitude, a reflection on the meaning of a perfect day "to a tired heart" when "dear friends have to part." Its answer in the second stanza provides a memory that will never fade and the discovery of "the soul of a friend we've made." Its comparison of the end of a day with the end of a longer journey also suggests the possibility that the day represents the passing of a lifetime.

Although she had never imagined that she would have a career as a songwriter, Bond loved to make up songs when she was a child. Her second husband, Dr. Frank Bond, whom she married in 1880, encouraged her to write down the melodies that came to her even though he refused to let her publish them. His sudden death after only seven years of marriage changed her life dramatically. In her early thirties; she found herself living in genteel poverty, partially disabled by rheumatism, with a 9-year-old son to support. She earned a meager living by taking in lodgers. She also hand-painted ceramics to sell and, as she worked, hummed tunes to herself as she had as a girl. These tunes became the basis for her first collection of self-published songs, *Seven Songs as Unpretentious as the Wild Rose.*

Serendipity appeared at just this moment: Jessie Bartlett Davis, a professional singer who lived next door, was called away while she waited for her manager and another man to call. She asked Bond to entertain them until she returned. When they arrived, Bond invited them into her apartment. The manager noticed her manuscripts and asked her to perform them, probably nothing more than a polite way to pass an awkward moment. The song she chose was "I Love You Truly." Ironically, she declined his offer to have the song performed professionally, because she had not copyrighted it or any of her songs.

She soon had second thoughts. The more dramatic version of the story says that she called Davis from a drug store. The soprano, who had made "Oh, Promise Me" into a hit, agreed to perform the songs and loaned Bond the $500 it would take to publish *Seven Songs*, with delicate floral illustrations by Bond, herself. She sold them for only $1 a copy—and still made all that money.

## "Come, Josephine in My Flying Machine (Up She Goes!)" (1910)
Lyrics by Alfred Bryan (1871–1958), music by Fred Fischer (1875–1942)

A ride in an automobile was a possibility, but going for a spin in an airplane was nothing but fantasy. Back when cars and planes were new, songs about them offered opportunities for young lovers to be alone—a combination of freedom, privacy, and independence for a combination of adventure, love, and sex. Within a song lyric, the two seductive invitations were pretty much the same: "Come away with me, Lucille, / In my merry Oldsmobile" and "Come, Josephine in my flying machine/ Going up we go, up we go." Alfred Bryan's lyric combined a predictable invitation with a fantastical dream: "Whoa! dear, don't hit the moon, / No, dear, not yet but soon." Topical yet lilting, easy to sing and easy to remember, these were the kinds of songs that Tin Pan Alley songwriters hoped vaudeville singers would introduce in their acts.

"Come, Josephine" was the most popular of the airplane songs, but it was not the first. Within a year of the Wright Brothers' success, Renn Shields and George Evans had written "Come Take a Trip in My Airship." Between the first flight and the end of World War I, airplane song titles included "Papa, Please Buy Me an Airship," "Since Katy the Waitress Became an Aviatress," "I Was Married Up in the Air (I've Been Up in the Air Ever Since)," and "Wait Till You Get Her Up in the Air, Boys." They all made the same assumption—when an attractive young woman climbs into the cockpit, she leaves her inhibitions behind. In 1909, six years after the Wright Brothers' flight, Ziegfeld's featured star, the beautiful Lillian Lorraine, circled up and over the audience in a miniature airplane hanging from the ceiling of the New Amsterdam Theater, scattering roses while she sang Gus Edwards and Matt C. Woodward's long-forgotten trifle, "Up, Up, Up in My Aeroplane."

Fred Fischer, born in Germany, soon dropped the "c" from the spelling of his name so it would look more American.

## "Down by the Old Mill Stream" (1910)
Lyrics and music by Tell Taylor (1876–1937)

William "Tell" Taylor had been a traveling salesman who sang in stores to convince managers to buy the tunes he was peddling. Eventually, he began to act professionally in Chicago and to write and publish his own songs. On a 1908 visit to Findlay, in Northwest Ohio, where he had studied music at Findlay College, he spent an afternoon fishing along the Blanchard River, which would soon become the "old mill stream" of his most important song. He daydreamed about his childhood, a girl he had once loved, and an old working mill that used to stand along the river. He wrote the song that afternoon: a nostalgic recollection of the time when the lovers were young and their love was new. Although they are old now, they have not forgotten the "old mill stream" where they first met. Although he kept his publishing business in Chicago, he later bought a farm in Findley and divided his time between the two places.

Friends convinced Taylor not to publish the song because they did not believe it would sell, perhaps because it sounded more like an old-fashioned Sentimental Ballad than the syncopated ragtime songs that dominated Tin Pan Alley. Two years later, he published it himself. Soon afterwards, a vaudeville quartet called The Orpheus Comedy Four sought him out because they were looking for a song that was new and different. They introduced it successfully in Saginaw, Michigan, and wired Taylor to say the song was a great success but needed a second verse. When he sent it to them, they wired back, "Rotten," but it remained part of the song. Taylor decided to try selling the sheet music himself. Playing and singing new songs in five- and ten-cent stores was common at the time, so a Woolworth's in Kansas City gave him permission to try his luck. In two days, he sold the thousand copies he brought with him.

## "Grizzly Bear" (1910)
Lyrics by Irving Berlin (1888–1989), music by George Botsford (1874–1949)

## "The Castle Walk" (1912)
Music by James Reese Europe (1881–1919) and Ford T. Dabney (1883–1958)

The Dance Craze was everywhere. Between the rambunctiousness of the new animal dances set to ragtime songs and the elegance of Vernon and Irene Castle, syncopation was helping America throw off Victorian behavior as fast as it could, manners and morals be damned. It was also making ragtime acceptable and respectable. Once Irene discarded her corsets and bobbed her hair (and millions of women followed suit), she taught the estimable Mrs. John D. Rockefeller how to shake her shoulders, though in a suitably decorous manner. By toning things down, Irene was making this kind of movement appealing to proper whites, even though the younger generation was practicing the real thing—the turkey trot, the camel walk, the lame duck, the monkey glide, the kangaroo hop, the bunny hug, and more. More than once, ragtime dancers found themselves in court.

As ragtime danced its way from disrepute to respectability—from whorehouses to vaudeville stages to hotel supper clubs—the "Grizzly Bear" was the animal dance that escalated the mania into the Dance Craze that lasted through the decade. Richard D. Barnet, Bruce Nemerov, and Mayo R. Taylor described it as "a swooping, swaying walk that ended with a tight bear hug."[24] The tune had first appeared in 1910 as a piano rag by George Botsford, but it took off only after Irving Berlin added a lyric that began with a bit of invented history about how the eponymous dance had started in San Francisco, and then followed with a quick lesson in rhyme. He wrote a conventional ragtime lyric—"Throw your shoulders t'ward the ceiling, / Lawdy, Lawdy, what a feelin'"—but also managed a triple rhyme whose syllables cascaded over the music without pausing to breathe:

> Talk about yo' bears that Teddy Roosevelt shot,
> They couldn't class with what
> Old San Francisco's got.

In addition to Berlin's lyric, the song got some essential help from Fanny Brice, then a young singer in burlesque. When the company manager required her to do a "specialty number" for a benefit, she turned in a panic to Irving Berlin to beg him for a song. He went backstage to sing two songs for her: "Sadie Salome, Go Home," which he demonstrated in a Yiddish accent, and "Grizzly Bear." She used both songs, including her own Yiddish-inflected version of "Sadie." "I had never had any idea of doing a song with a Jewish accent," she said many years later. "I didn't even understand Jewish, couldn't speak a word of it. But, I thought, if that's the way Irving sings it, that's the way I'll sing it." For the performance, she wore a starched dress that began to itch: "I'm trying to squirm it away, and singing and smiling." Thus began the career of Fanny Brice as a comedienne who did Yiddish accent songs.[25]

To meet the demand for dancing, restaurants were hiring orchestras and installing dance floors as people did the one-step and the foxtrot anywhere and everywhere—during their lunch breaks in factories and at tea dances on their way home. Officials as far afield as New Haven, Chicago, Boston, and Dallas announced bans on the scandalous dances. The Dallas police chief insisted, "You must be able to see daylight between the dancers." New York's mayor drew up a bill for the State Legislature barring the dances, because the young people "were exceeding the speed limit." When some young people went on trial in Boston for taking Berlin's lyric literally— "Snug up close to your lady"—their lawyer asked if he might sing the words for the judge. Within a few bars, everybody on the jury had joined in and the judge threw the case out of court.

In 1914, Berlin worked with the Castles when they starred in *Watch Your Step*, the first musical for which he wrote a complete score. It was the first score to consist largely of ragtime songs. Together, they were at the center of the Dance Craze. In addition to their appearance on Broadway, the Castles toured, wrote books, opened nightclubs, and started dance studios. In a controversial move, these avatars of elegance and modernity hired an African American music director, the first time such a thing had happened. They chose well. James Reese Europe led his orchestra for dancing at San Souci, their extravagant nightclub that featured marble mirrors, a cover charge, and a $100-per-hour fee for a private dance lesson with Vernon. In the spring of 1914, Europe and Ford T. Dabney wrote eight instrumental dance pieces for the Castles, including "Castle Walk," a rollicking one-step, which took its name from the Castles' signature dance. When they performed, Europe's orchestra was on the bandstand behind them. David Jasen writes, "The sight of the golden couple whirling to the music of nineteen black men lingered in the minds of their audiences long after . . . If they had never seen anything like the Castles, they had never seen anything like the dignified and sophisticated society orchestra either."[26]

# Chapter 5
## 1911–1915

**"I Want a Girl (Just Like the Girl That Married Dear Old Dad)"** (1911)
Lyrics by Will Dillon (1877–1966), music by Harry Von Tilzer (1872–1946)

One wag wrote that the chorus to "I Want a Girl (Just Like the Girl That Married Dear Old Dad)" is "an eternal ode to the Oedipus complex."[1] Composer Harry Von Tilzer, born Adam Gummbinsky in 1872, ran away from home at the age of 14, and lyricist Will Dillon, born in 1877, hooked up with a vaudeville act rather than go to college. They had probably never heard of Sigmund Freud, let alone Oedipus, but they did know how to craft songs that fit the fads and fancies of the day. In February 1911, Von Tilzer got an idea for a song title that sent him looking for Dillon. Songs that mentioned girls in the titles were very popular, but three years earlier Dillon had started a fad by mentioning a girl in an unusually long title: "I'd Rather Have a Girlie Than an Automobile or Anything Else I Know." Dillon liked Von Tilzer's idea, but immediately changed the title's opening words from "I'd Like a Girl" to "I Want a Girl." It took them about an hour to finish the chorus that begins:

I want a girl, just like the girl that married dear old Dad,
She was a pearl and the only girl that Daddy ever had.

This is one of those songs whose verses are largely overlooked. In the first verse, a boy's mother tells him to marry when he's grown if he wants to find happiness. Now that he's an adult, he learns that he can find no one to match her. In the second, a son watches his aged parents, still happily married.

## "The Sweetheart of Sigma Chi" (1911)
Lyrics by Byron D. Stokes (1887?–1974), music by F. Dudleigh Vernor
(1893?–1974)

Like Yale's "The Whiffenpoof Song," "The Sweetheart of Sigma Chi" is
one of the few college songs to cross over as a popular hit and a standard.
Notre Dame's "Fight Song" and Michigan's "Hail to the Conquering Hero"
may be more muscular, "Dartmouth Undying" more elegiacally melodic,
and "Far Above Cayuga's Waters" (Cornell) more sonorous, but "The Sweetheart of Sigma Chi" became a popular love song typical of its time—sweet,
sentimental, and innocent. Stokes wrote the words between classes one afternoon on the Albion College (Michigan) campus in June 1911 soon after
his initiation in the fraternity. He said some years later, "The magic of our
Ritual . . . was the source of my inspiration." His reading of his own words
slips easily into the purple. "Sweetheart," he said, "does not refer to any actual sweetheart in the earthly sense . . . All earthly love fades into nothing-
ness in the light of true brotherhood." Later that day, he found Dudleigh
Vernon practicing the organ in the College chapel. The less "poetic" Vernon
remembered, "I placed the words 'By' had given me on the music rack and
improvised some melodies to go with the verses. After about an hour I had
written what finally seemed to click."[2] The song was part of the celebration of the twenty-fifth anniversary of Albion's Sigma Chi chapter. Neither
young man expected the song to survive beyond the occasion, but it became an immediate hit when they published it themselves. Regardless of
Stokes' intentions, the song quickly evolved into a love ballad about the
"sweet coed."

## "Ragtime Cowboy Joe" (1912)
Lyrics by Grant Clarke (1891–1931), music by Maurice Abrahams
(1883–1931) and Lewis F. Muir (1884–1915)

Songwriters were always on the lookout for a hook. Joe Abrahams turned
up one day at his Uncle Maurice's house in Brooklyn wearing full cowboy
regalia. His uncle was so tickled by the sight of little Joe's outfit that he used
it as the basis for his next hit, "Ragtime Cowboy Joe." Composer Lewis F.
Muir put the finishing touches on the tune and Grant Clarke added the lyrics based on Uncle Maurice's idea.

A music promoter named Harry Cohn helped the song become a Number One hit when he took a particular interest in it. He said, "I would sometimes sing it fifty, sixty times a night, all over New York."[3] Actually, Cohn
was a trolley car conductor who moonlighted as a plugger until he got a job

with Universal Pictures and moved to Southern California, where he eventually became president of Columbia Pictures and one of the most heartily detested people in Hollywood. When thousands turned out for his funeral, someone remarked to comedian Red Skelton that he was surprised by the size of the crowd. Skelton replied, "It proves what Harry always said: 'Give the public what they want and they'll come out for it.' "[4]

**"When Irish Eyes Are Smiling"** [*Isle o' Dreams*] (1913)
Lyrics by Chauncey Olcott (1858–1932) and George Graff, Jr. (1886–1973), music by Ernest R. Ball (1878–1927)

**"My Wild Irish Rose"** [*A Romance of Athlone*] (1899)
Lyrics and music by Chauncey Olcott

Chauncey Olcott was born in Buffalo, New York, and studied in England before he became a star of vaudeville and Broadway musicals, usually about the Irish. He wrote only the words, often with composer Ernest R. Ball and a co-lyricist, usually George Graff. In 1898, he and his wife visited Ireland. As they walked together in Glengaris, County Cork, a young boy gave Olcott's wife a flower. She asked what its name was. He answered, "Sure, it's a wild Irish Rose." She put the rose in an album, and, some time later, when Olcott was working on the score for a new show, *A Romance of Athlone*, he asked his wife for title ideas for a song. She opened the album and pointed to the flower. "There's the title for your new song," she said serendipitously. He wrote "My Wild Irish Rose" without any collaborator; it was one of his few solo efforts.[5]

A decade later, after he, Ball, and Graff had finished the score for their new show, *Isle o' Dreams*, Olcott asked his collaborators to work with him on an additional Irish song. There were already three in the production— "Mother Machree," "Kathleen Aroon," and the title song—but Olcott wanted a fourth. The result, "When Irish Eyes Are Smiling," was the most popular song of the decade and probably Olcott's most important song. Unfortunately, the show was a dud. Although it ran only thirty-two performances, the song has remained popular for a century. Ball's waltz feels like an Irish folk song but has the standard structure of a Tin Pan Alley tune, while Olcott and Graff's lyric has what Thomas Hischak calls, affectionately, "such lyrical blarney" as "the lilt of Irish laughter" and "sure they steal your heart away." The irony in all this writing of sentimental Irish songs is that Ball and Graff were among Tin Pan Alley's most skilled and prolific professionals, but neither of them was Irish.[6]

## "Peg o' My Heart" (1913)
Lyrics by Alfred Bryan (1871–1958), music by Fred Fisher (1875–1942)

Catchy tunes about feisty Irish-Americans appealed to American audiences as far back as the 1880s. Even though Fred Fisher had emigrated from Germany, he composed more Irish songs than almost any other Alleyman. Alfred Bryan was equally prolific because, he explained, "there are a million ways of saying 'I love you'"[7] Fisher was so enthusiastic after seeing Laurette Taylor's starring performance as the spunky title character in the long-running 1912 play, *Peg o' My Heart*, that he wrote the song as a tribute to her and invited Bryan to add a suitable lyric. They also entered it in a contest for a song to call attention to the play, even though "Peg" had nothing to do with it beyond its title. Fisher intended it as a tribute to Taylor and used the connection to capitalize on the play's popularity. Fisher and Bryan won the $1,000 first prize. Then, with Taylor's picture on the sheet music, the song promptly became a hit even though she never sang it in public. It was published on March 15, 1913, just before St. Patrick's Day, and first sung by early recording star Irving Kaufman after he stumbled across the sheet music on a shelf in the publisher's office.

## "By the Beautiful Sea" (1914)
Lyrics by Harold Atteridge (1886–1938), music by Harry Carroll (1892–1962)

Harry Carroll and Harold Atteridge's "By the Beautiful Sea" was an important song during the Dance Craze, even though it had nothing to do with dancing. The song was perfect for the quickstep, one of the lightest and fastest of the ballroom dances that were all the rage between 1910 and World War I. It was also the most popular of a large batch of "seashore" songs that had a lot of appeal during the 1910s and 1920s, among them Lucien Denni and Roger Lewis' "Oceana Roll," Vincent Youmans and Irving Caesar's "Peach on a Beach," and Sigmund Romberg and Ballard MacDonald's "I Love To Go Swimmin' with Women."

Carroll and Atteridge worked for J.J. Shubert although Carroll eventually left for California while Atteridge remained in New York to write books and lyrics for musical comedies and revues. His description of his work made it sound more mechanical than creative. He said that he wrote between midnight and 5 a.m., "in long hand under an electric lamp, and always alone."[8] He also said that, because he was a close observer of human behavior, it usually "takes me from thirty minutes to an hour to write the finished lyrics for a song." Riding the subway downtown one evening, he scribbled the lyric to "By the Beautiful Sea" on the back of an envelope and handed it to Carroll that night. Carroll wrote the melody immediately.[9] When Atteridge was working on a revue ("By the Beautiful Sea" was first performed in vaudeville), he and Shubert would "map out" the show before searching for a composer, while Atteridge began to write the lyrics for the score. He normally wrote thirty-five songs for a show, although only two dozen remained by opening night. When Atteridge died at 51, he had already written the books for more than forty musicals.

### "Keep the Home Fires Burning" (1914)
Lyrics by Lena Guilbert Ford (1870–1918), music by Ivor Novello (1893–1951)

"Keep the Home Fires Burning" was an English hit during World War I, but it is actually half American and was equally popular on both sides of the Atlantic. Originally called "Till the Boys Come Home," it is the most important English patriotic song of the war, even though it is the result of collaboration between a Welsh composer and an American lyricist. Novello, who would become a successful writer of English operettas characterized by lavish spectacle and soaring romantic melodies, was only 21 when the

FIGURE 5.1   A scene from Irving Berlin's *Stop! Look! Listen!*, one of his earliest musical comedies. Courtesy of Photofest.

war started. His mother begged him to write a patriotic song but, dismayed by how second-rate most of these songs were, he refused. When she tried to pressure him by writing one of her own entitled, "Keep the Flag A-Flying," he changed his mind, perhaps to get her to stop. Once he finished the melody, he contacted Lena Ford, a family friend and a divorcee with a young son. She had been living in London for a number of years and had dabbled in lyric writing.

As he was trying to explain to Ford what kind of lyric he wanted, a maid came in to put some logs on the fire. "That's the theme I want!" Novello said, "The fireside burning brightly." Within half an hour, Ford polished off the lyric, while Novello revised the melody. He was so pleased by the result that he asked singer Sybil Vane to introduce it and offered to accompany her. When they came to the refrain, Novello realized that the audience had begun to pick up the tune and was joining in. They sang it over and over again.

Novello earned £15,000 from this one song, a very large sum at the time. Ford failed to share in the success because she and her son were killed in a Zeppelin raid in March 1918. There was initially some dispute over the source of the title, though it now seems clear that Novello coined the memorable phrase.[10]

### "The Girl on the Magazine" [*Stop! Look! Listen!*] (1915)
Lyrics and music by Irving Berlin (1888–1989)

One day in 1914, as actress Eileen Ruby was posing for the famous illustrator Harrison Fisher, Irving Berlin dropped by for a visit and a chat. He and Eileen knew each other because she was the wife of Harry Ruby, Berlin's musical secretary, who would soon become an important songwriter in his own right. Several weeks later, Berlin dropped by again. He said that last time, watching her sit for a portrait, he had gotten an idea for a song. He had entitled it "The Girl on the Magazine" and placed it in the score he was writing for a new show called *Stop! Look! Listen!*

During the previous few years, advances in technology had lowered the cost of color printing and made magazines widely available and extremely popular. During the years before the United States entered World War I, such magazines as *Ladies' Home Journal, Ladies' Home Companion*, and *Redbook* had more than a million subscribers each. In articles and short stories, they guided their readers on idealized relationships before and within marriage. Their full-color covers usually featured striking but serene women dressed in elegant dresses and gowns. Berlin translated that idea into a lavish Broadway production number that focused on beautiful women.

**FIGURE 5.2**  Gilda Gray dancing the Shimmy in *The Ziegfeld Follies.* Courtesy of Photofest.

Although the score consisted largely of ragtime songs, this number was Berlin's first try at what showbiz parlance called a "girlie song"—a ballad for a tenor and a parade of chorus girls whose costumes link them to the song. The character in the song is a young man who is smitten by the beautiful young woman he sees on the cover of a magazine. He knows he will never meet her, but he dreams of finding "a girl as sweet," because he knows that "if she ever came, / I would love her the same / As I love her on the cover of a magazine." The staging posed four showgirls as if they were a single painting on the cover of *Vogue.* As tenor Joseph Santley sang, they came to life and walked out of the cover onto the larger stage.

### "I Wish I Could Shimmy Like My Sister Kate" (1915)
Lyrics and music by Armand J. Piron (1888–1943)

The only reason Armand J. Piron's name appears on the sheet music to "I Wish I Could Shimmy Like My Sister Kate" is that publisher, songwriter, and all-around scoundrel Clarence Williams stole the song from Louis Armstrong. In those days, Clarence was the man to go see if you were black and you had written a song. He would transcribe it for you, arrange for a copyright, and cut himself in on the royalties. One commentator observed, "As fast as you could do the number, he could write it down." Many of the songs list Williams' name with the real writers listed beneath: "After he got through, he had more of your number than you did." He never did pay Armstrong the $25 he had promised him. Bass player Pops Foster put it best: "Louis never did get nothin' for it. Clarence was a real horse thief."[11]

Williams had also been writing and publishing songs with a popular New Orleans violinist named Armand J. Piron. Where Williams was pushy, Piron was a soft-spoken gentleman. Eventually, Piron wanted to get out of publishing. He sold Williams all of his copyrights, including songs they had written together and some he had written on his own. Williams found one of Piron's tunes that he thought had the potential to be a hit. Instead of disbanding the publishing company, he changed the song's name to "I Wish I Could Shimmy . . .," and, in 1924, published it himself. But Piron had copyrighted it in 1919 and his orchestra had been performing it even though he had never published it.

So who really wrote it? Armstrong always claimed that he was the composer, but in those days, in New Orleans, tunes floated around for years before somebody wrote them down and filed for copyright. In 1939, Piron told an interviewer, "That's not Louis' tune or mine . . . That tune is older than all of us. People always put different words to it. Some of them were too dirty to say in polite company. The way Louis did it didn't have anything to do with his sister Kate."[12] In fact, Armstrong's version was a bawdy tale about the dancing prowess of a highly regarded Storyville madam named Kate Townsend. Her sister says that if she could learn to imitate Kate, she would get the attention of "all the boys in the neighborhood."

The Shimmy was a sexy dance in which the shoulders, and thus everything attached to them, shake back and forth rapidly in time to driving music. Gilda Gray, a dancing star of the *Ziegfeld Follies* in the 1920s, claims to have started the dance, but denied that its name came from her answer to a question about her dancing, 'I'm shaking my chemise." Mae West disputed Gray's claim, saying she saw a dance called the Shimmy-Shawobble in black nightclubs and renamed it the Shimmy.

## "Paper Doll" (1915)
Lyrics and music by Johnny S. Black (1891–1936)

The story of "Paper Doll" isn't very long, even though the song took twenty-seven years to become a success. Johnny S. Black wrote it in 1915, but it wasn't published until 1930 and didn't become a hit until 1943. Music publisher Edward B. Marks turned it down but finally took it in desperation when Black insisted on playing it on a violin with a trained canary sitting on his shoulder and chirping as he played. Black didn't live long enough to see the song's success; he died in 1936. Seven years later, in the middle of World War II, *Time* announced its success in its own peculiar style, known then as "Timese": "This musical tickler was mooning out of every radio and juke box in the U.S."[13]

Black had been making a hand-to-mouth living playing piano and boxing while he tried to write songs. Just before he entered the ring for a bout, the young women he loved told him that she was leaving because she was in love with a songwriter, not a boxer. Black lost the fight but recorded his feelings in the lyric to "Paper Doll." Another story—entirely different—claims that he adapted a song called "My Girl," written by a showgirl who became his first wife. The woman sued when the song became popular and the court awarded her a share of the royalties.

# Chapter 6
## 1916–1920

**"Darktown Strutters' Ball"** (1917)
Lyrics and music by Shelton Brooks (1886–1975)

Shelton Brooks' vaudeville act included an imitation of the black comedian Bert Williams. It was so good that Williams remarked, "If I'm as funny as he is, I got nothin' to worry about."[1] Brooks also tried his hand at songwriting. In 1910, he came up with a random melody that he couldn't get out of his head. One day, sitting in a restaurant, he overheard a heated quarrel between a man and woman. She was warning him not to leave her: "Some of these days, you're gonna miss me, honey."[2] Brooks could not believe his ears; the words fit his melody perfectly. He finished the song and took it to Sophie Tucker, who was often helpful to young African Americans who aspired to write songs. Suddenly, Shelton Brooks was a songwriter.

Late in his life, Irving Berlin said that the secret of the success of "Alexander's Ragtime Band" was "the idea of inviting every receptive auditor within shouting distance" to become part of what he called "the happy ruction."[3] What was modern about the song was its call to join in the revelry. It anticipated such songs as Berlin's "Pack Up Your Sins" and "Puttin' on the Ritz," the Gershwins' "Sweet and Low Down," and Brooks' "Darktown Strutters' Ball." Berlin's call, "Come on and hear," became for Brooks the more smoothly assured "I'll be down to get you in a taxi, honey."

There was such a ball every year in Chicago. The prostitutes would wear elegant gowns and the pimps turned out in white tie, spats, and top hats. The police agreed to look the other way as long as there was no trouble. When Ian Whitcomb tracked Brooks down in 1969, the 83-year-old songwriter told him where the song came from and how he transformed a story he heard into the song: "Now I heard about this working man . . . He gets an invitation to an affair to be given by the local pimps. A Big Ball. All a mistake and he should never have been asked." The song turns the pimps into the vaguer "strutters" to make the evening more universal in its appeal. For anyone with lingering doubts about whether Brooks knew what he was writing, he called his song "a jolly romp . . . with words that have internal combustion. It must have been sung a trillion times."[4]

## "Smiles" [*The Passing Show of 1918*] (1917)
Lyrics by J. Will Callahan (1874–1946), music by Lee S. Roberts (1884–1949)

Irving Berlin said that every song written in wartime is a war song. Most of the great war songs of World War II had nothing to do with war directly; they were about the longing and loneliness of the women who remained behind. "Smiles" was a war song from World War I, but it too had nothing to do with war—except perhaps for the relief and optimism it offered a weary public.

Lee S. Roberts, an aspiring songwriter, attended a meeting of the Music Merchants Association in Chicago, where he heard an inspirational speaker begin his remarks with a story about traveling to a prison to speak. As he entered accompanied by guards, he noticed a young man in the front row and smiled at him. The young man smiled back and then turned to smile at the man behind him. That man turned to the man next to him and smiled. The speaker continued, "There were smiles everywhere. The faces of the entire audience seemed to be wreathed in smiles—even before I had said a word."

Listening to the speaker recall the incident, Roberts noticed a word on the back of a Murad cigarette box, "Smiles." He said to the person next to him, "Smiles. That's a good word for a song."[5] The next morning, Roberts put the cigarette box on the piano and went to work. When a musician friend thought it had potential, he sent to it a partially blind lyricist named J. Will Callahan along with a suggestion for a title. No publisher would take the completed song, so Roberts published and promoted it himself. Within six months, it had become a hit and eventually earned the two songwriters an estimated $500,000.

## "Rock-a-Bye Your Baby with a Dixie Melody" [*A Plantation Act*] (1918)
Lyrics by Joe Young (1889–1939), music by Jean Schwartz (1878–1956)

## "My Mammy" [*Sinbad*] (1920)
Lyrics by Sam M. Lewis (1885–1959) and Joe Young (1889–1939), music by Walter Donaldson (1893–1947)

The lyrics to "Rock-a-Bye Your Baby with a Dixie Melody" and "My Mammy" have what they needed if Al Jolson was going to sing them—the South and Mammy. There he was, smeared in blackface, down on one knee, crooning and belting with a sob in his voice. "My Mammy," combined with Jolson's performance style, was so indelible that "coon songs" about African American mothers soon became known euphemistically as "mammy songs." Despite its jazzy syncopation, it was also reminiscent of nineteenth-century songs in its desire to return home to mother. In fact, it identifies two of Stephen Foster's compositions, "Old Black Joe" and "Swanee River," as songs the singer longs to hear once more. Although Jolson was one of the most important singers of the twentieth century, his insistence on perform-ing in blackface throughout his career diminished his standing as racial attitudes and singing styles changed, beginning in the 1920s.

Jolson introduced "Rock-a-Bye" in a movie rather than onstage. It was one of three songs in *A Plantation Act*, a synchronized sound film that pre-ceded *The Jazz Singer* by nearly a year. Although he was touring the country in *Sinbad* in 1919–1920, he returned to New York for a recording date and had dinner with Saul Bornstein, general manager for Irving Berlin Music. Bornstein, who loved "mother songs," showed Jolson one he was about to publish. Even though its "coon song" sentiments were outdated by the early 1920s, and even though it was nowhere near as good as "Rock-a-Bye," Jolson immediately agreed to sing it during the rest of the tour. He was already sing-ing "Rock-a-Bye" as well as George Gershwin and Irving Caesar's "Swanee."[6]

Although "My Mammy" is indelibly associated with Jolson, William Frawley—the same William Frawley who played Fred Mertz on *I Love Lucy*—first introduced it in vaudeville. Lyricists Sam Lewis and Joe Young had re-peated the words "Mammy, Mammy" to cover sixteen bars in the second chorus, but Jolson soon changed the words to "Mammy, look at me. Don't you know me? I'm your little baby." The reference supposedly refers to his memory of his mother's dying in childbirth when he was 8. He rushed into her room only to find that she did not recognize him. The story underscores the suggestion by numerous scholars that blackface provided an emotional outlet for Jewish performers as well as a performance style that enabled them to escape the poverty and repressed behavior of the Lower East Side.[7]

**"Dardanella"** (1919)
Lyrics by Fred Fisher (1875–1942), music by Johnny S. Black (1891–1936)

**"Hindustan"** (1918)
Lyrics and music by Oliver Wallace (1887–1963) and Harold Weeks (1893–1967)

**"Palesteena"** (1920)
Lyrics and music by J. Russel Robinson (1892–1963)

The exotic strain in popular music was especially popular around the time of World War I. Perhaps it offered a romantic distraction from difficult and dangerous times. But the history of one of the most successful of these songs provided anything but reassurance for the people involved. In 1919, Johnny Black wrote "Totem Tom-Tom," an instrumental whose history was as exotic and eccentric as its melody. One version says that Black moved to New York from Cincinnati after he'd written a number of songs without any success. One reporter said that his songs "lacked something because he had never been really in love." Soon after, he fell in love with an Oriental dancer. He sat "in his kitchenette over a ballroom, with the photograph of the girl he loved in front of him," and wrote the song in an hour.[8]

When a successful composer and sometime lyricist named Fred Fisher first heard it, its unusual bass line intrigued him. He asked Black to add a chorus, and he added a lyric about a lonesome maid trapped in a Turkish harem. He also changed its name to "Dardanella," derived from The Dardanelles, and his publishing firm released it. Black was only 28 when he wrote it, but later called it his "gift to the musical world."[9]

Fisher was something of a character with the kind of background typical of Tin Pan Alley during those years. Born Albert von Breitenback in Cologne in 1875, he emigrated when he was 25 and changed his name to Fred Fischer—"Fred" from "Friedrich," a Germanic name he associated with strength, and "Fischer" from a sign he saw on a passing truck. During World War I, he changed the spelling to "Fisher" to make it less German. He soon established a reputation for writing successful popular tunes and for eccentric behavior. When he felt anxious, he would pull bills from his pocket and tear them into pieces, and sometimes he'd have a garbage truck pull up to his door so he could throw away all the left-over copies of his songs that had flopped.

Many of these songs about faraway places—what James Bloom called the "manufactured exotic"[10]—earned their composers and lyricists a great deal of money. Fisher told vaudevillian Felix Bernard that he made such a bundle on the song that he gave Black a year's contract and handed out bonuses to the members of his staff. Three of them immediately quit and used the money to open a rival publishing company.[11]

"Hindustan" and "Palesteena" also capitalized on the fad that evolved from the craze for Hawaiian songs that began in 1916. Most songs set in Honolulu or along Waikiki Beach—with such titles as "When I'm Down in Honolulu Looking Them Over" and "They're Wearing Them Higher in

Hawaii"—were comic and more interested in sex than lifelong love. Exoticism soon found a more romantic setting in Asia and the Middle East, and the resulting songs emphasized tropical settings, languid lovelies, and overheated eroticism in either a desert tent or under gently swaying palms. Yet they were, at bottom, Tin Pan Alley exercises in writing songs for the market. Their lyrics rely on stereotypical images, while the music recreates what Americans would recognize as the common musical sounds of these cultures.

Composer George Gershwin, aged 19, and lyricist Irving Caesar came up with the idea for "Swanee" as a sequel—and a takeoff—after "Hindustan." They wanted to be ready with their new song when Oliver Wallace and Harold Weeks' enormously popular hit began to fade.

J. Russel Robinson was a white songwriter who often collaborated with such black composers and lyricists as Noble Sissle, Fats Waller, and James P. Johnson. He also cut countless numbers of piano rolls and joined the Original Dixieland Jazz Band in 1919 when their piano player died of influenza just as the band was about to leave on a tour of Europe. He remained until the band split up in 1923; one of their 1920 recordings included his composition "Palesteena," along with two other songs he wrote, "Margie" and "Singin' the Blues."[12] Despite its exotic sound, it was also known as "Lena from Palesteena" and had a comic lyric by Con Conrad. Comic performer Eddie Cantor had the hit recording.

In 1922, just as the fad seemed ready to decline, Howard Carter and George Herbert discovered Tutankhamen's tomb. The resulting furor took many forms, including an Egyptian influence on women's clothes and furniture design, and a number of popular songs that, once again, merged the exotic, the erotic, and the comic. The most important of these songs was "Old King Tut" by Harry Von Tilzer and William Jerome, given a suitably bawdy reading by Sophie Tucker. Even President Herbert Hoover named his pet German shepherd "King Tut."

### "Let the Rest of the World Go By" (1919)
Lyrics by J. Keirn Brennan (1873–1948), music by Ernest R. Ball (1878–1927)

At first the West was there for the taking. As settlers began to establish farms and towns, Americans began to speak of it as a cornucopia, a second Eden, and nineteenth-century songs envisioned it as a utopian garden. Although it remained grist for the dime novel's mill in the early twentieth century, it was also becoming domesticated. It had become a place for a family, living in peace and harmony, at its center a deeply felt love between a man and a woman. In such a place a family could thrive. As early as 1844, Henry Russell and George Pope Morris wrote:

> Where once frown'd a forest a garden is smiling,
> The meadows and moorlands are marshes no more;
> And there curls the smoke of my cottage, beguiling
> The children who cluster like grapes at the door.[13]

By 1919, the vision of a still-idealized West had become part of a gentle love story, in which a young man and women set out to make their own lives together. Once they find "a spot to call our own," the remainder of their dream will follow:

> We'll build a sweet little nest,
> Somewhere in the West
> And let the rest of the world go by.

The original sheet music illustration portrays a young couple, sitting on top of a high hill, their backs to the viewer, their arms wrapped tightly but easily around one another, as they look toward the undefined far horizon. In the immediate aftermath of World War I, the image, like the point of view within the song, promised a respite from struggle, a peaceful future, and the quiet contentment of love that lasts.

Written less than a year after the Armistice, it does not feel like a war song, but, unlike songs that viewed the return home satirically—"How Ya Gonna Keep 'Em Down on the Farm" and "I've Got My Captain Working for Me Now"—"Let the Rest of the World Go By" longs for a return to a serene settled time before the War. The West is the place where Americans can still escape from the horrors of Europe and the complexities of life in the more settled East.

### "Mandy" [*Yip, Yip Yaphank, Ziegfeld Follies of 1919*] (1919)
Lyrics and music by Irving Berlin (1888–1989)

Although Irving Berlin wrote "Mandy" in 1917, for his World War I revue, *Yip, Yip Yaphank*, it did not become a hit until he revised the lyric for the *Ziegfeld Follies of 1919*. Berlin had previously written a cakewalk called "The Sterling Silver Moon," with references to a woman named "Mandy" in the lyric. One day, in a music store, he learned that people were asking for a song called "Mandy," but were told there was no song by that name. Berlin immediately recalled "Sterling Silver Moon" and had its cover replaced with a new title, "Mandy." For the *Follies*, he revised the lyric but kept the name.

That's what became a hit. It certainly wasn't the last time that Berlin would respond to public taste. "The mob is always right," he said in a 1940 interview. "It seems to be able to sense instinctively what is good, and I believe that there are darned few good songs which have not been whistled or sung by the crowd."[14]

A draftee in World War I, Berlin was not especially fond of military life. He was an insomniac who did most of his writing after everyone else had gone to bed. He was also a patriot who believed he could make his greatest contribution with his songs. Once he had convinced his reluctant superiors to let him develop an all-soldier show to benefit Army Relief, he sent for Harry Ruby, his musical secretary. Ruby moved out to Long Island and lived in the barracks with Berlin. The future songwriter ("Three Little Words," "Never theless") described Berlin's method of working:

> He'd come up to me in the morning while I was out there at Yaphank with him and he'd say, "Harry, got a pencil and some music paper?" and I'd say sure, and he'd say, "Take this down," and sing me a melody . . . I'd ask him, "When the hell did you write *that*?" And he'd say, "Oh, I was up all night. Do you like it?" And I'd say it was great, and I'd play it back for him to hear what he'd dictated—and he'd listen, and he'd say, "You got one chord wrong in there." And he'd be right—He couldn't *play* the chord, but he could *hear* it all right![15]

## "You'd Be Surprised" [*Ziegfeld Follies of 1919*] (1919)
Lyrics and music by Irving Berlin (1888–1989)

Songwriting isn't as easy as it looks. Here's something that Irving Berlin scribbled under the title, "You'd Be Surprised":

> You'd be surprised! You'd be surprised!
> I realize you'd be surprised!
> I must say that I recognized
> Surprised you'd be—you'd be surprised!

He knew exactly how bad it was because he had written it to demonstrate "how the mentally lazy or the uninitiated would go about the work of building the title line into a song. They would write a lyric concerning one or several of the innumerable surprising things of life. They would possibly—No, *probably!*—jumble up their song with *all* the surprising things they could think of, thereby losing simplicity, and the chorus would be just a noisy blah."[16]

Maybe Berlin's most important word was "simplicity." He had to have known just how simple his best lyrics were, how the emotionalism registered with the listener in such a direct, uncluttered way. Like every songwriter, Berlin used catchphrases for titles and key lines in his songs. Cousins to clichés, they were familiar and immediately accessible, but they ran the risk of feeling flat or, in Berlin's own words, "commonplace or bromidic."[17] The trick lay in what you did with them. In this case, Berlin's lyric told the story of a nebbish who becomes an assertive, skillful, impassioned lover when he and a woman are alone. The sudden change and the unlikely places where it occurs are what make the song so funny. That Eddie Cantor, the quintessential schnook, recorded it after introducing it in the *Ziegfeld Follies* also helps to explain its popularity.

## "The Japanese Sandman" (1920)
Lyrics by Raymond B. Egan (1890–1952), music by Richard A. Whiting (1891–1938)

Composer Richard A. Whiting was only 47 when he died, but he was a top songwriter in Hollywood through the first decade of sound pictures. Like Irving Berlin, he was noted for the simplicity of his melodies. They were easy to remember because they were engaging, catchy, and singable, with enough variety and unpredictability to keep them interesting. Because he was writing for the movies in the 1930s, he often had to tailor his songs to storylines or stars. He wrote everything from the swinging, foot-stomping march, "Hooray for Hollywood" to the Shirley Temple signature song, "On the Good Ship Lollipop." He wrote the tender waltz "Till We Meet Again," the aria-like "Beyond the Blue Horizon," and the seductive "Sleepy Time Gal."

Years earlier, Whiting had written, "It's Tulip Time in Holland," which sold a million and a half copies of sheet music. Then he met a bank teller named Raymond Egan, who shook his hand and said, "I write lyrics."[18] They wrote "Till We Meet Again" during World War I, and "The Japanese Sandman" after it. Once the War ended, two familiar kinds of songs became popular in new ways: songs about returning (the comic "How Ya' Gonna Keep 'Em Down on the Farm?") and songs set in exotic faraway places, the most successful being "The Japanese Sandman." The melody borrows the sound of what to Westerners sounded like Asian music, and the lyric portrays a mysterious "sandman" from "over the western sea" who appears as a peddler buying and selling used goods, "an old second hand man trading new days for old." The melody trips along in brief staccato snatches, helped by Egan's easy way with rhyming: "Then you'll be a bit older / In the dawn when you wake / And you'll be a bit bolder / With the new day you make."

Jerome Remick, owner of a major music publishing company, sent Whiting to see the great star Nora Bayes to sell her a song. Bayes greeted the composer cordially after a matinee and asked him to play the song that "Jerome had told me you had written for me." Bayes soon started to sing along and said, "It's a great song, Richard, and we'll put it in the act tonight. I'll introduce it and you can play for me." Whiting was very nervous about going onstage but he knew that what Bayes wanted, Bayes got. When the time came, she stepped to the front of the stage: "Ladies and gentlemen, tonight you are going to have the extraordinary privilege of hearing for the first time the most glorious song in the world—with the added attraction of hearing its composer at the piano." Whiting played, Bayes sang, and the audience cheered until they performed it again.

Back in her dressing room, she told Whiting, "Have Jerome print up the sheet music. I'll record it as soon as I can."[19]

## "Rose of Washington Square" [*Ziegfeld's Midnight Frolic*] (1920)
Lyrics by Ballard MacDonald (1882–1935), music by James F. Hanley (1892–1942)

Lyricists chose their words to ensure that male and female singers alike could sing them, but Ballard MacDonald did something unusual with "Rose of Washington Square." He wrote it as a song for a woman and gave her two different sets of lyrics, one labeled "ballad," the other "comedic." For the first, he wrote such cliché-laden lines as "A garden that never knew sunshine, / Once sheltered a beautiful rose," but then changed them for the comic narrative, "She's Rosie, the queen of the models, / She used to live up in the Bronx." Ethnic songs were coming to an end by the early 1920s, but MacDonald and James Hanley wrote the comic version for Fanny Brice to introduce in *Ziegfeld's Midnight Frolic*. It was not the only song Hanley wrote for the comedienne. A year later, he and lyricist Grant Clarke wrote "Second Hand Rose," one of her most important signature songs.

"Rose of Washington Square" is also unusual because so much of it is based on fact. Rose Cecil O'Neill was an important illustrator at the time, most famous for creating a popular cartoon character named "Kewpie." Known as the "Queen of Bohemian Society" because she had an apartment in Greenwich Village, she was the inspiration for MacDonald's lyric. The song is also a popular song version of a *roman à clef*—a fictional tale in which real people appear. The Rose in the song is an immigrant girl who, unlike her "Second Hand" namesake, escapes the Lower East Side to live a life of relative comfort as "Rosie the queen of the models." She frequents "Bohemian Honky Tonks" and poses in the nude for illustrator Harrison Fisher, because she has no other talents. Best known for his drawings of women, Fisher is usually recognized as a successor to Charles Dana Gibson, creator of the Gibson Girl two decades earlier.

### "When My Baby Smiles at Me" (1920)
Lyrics by Andrew B. Sterling (1874–1955) and Ted Lewis (1890–1971), music by Bill Munro

At the end of each chorus of "When My Baby Smiles at Me," entertainer Ted Lewis would cry out, "Is everybody happy?" The song and the catch-phrase became Lewis' signatures for the rest of his show-business career. He played clarinet and hired such top jazz musicians as Benny Goodman, Jimmy Dorsey, and Muggsy Spanier for his band, but his highly stylized way of combining corny jokes, schmaltz, and showbiz pizzazz made him a major star. He wore a battered top hat and accompanied himself with elaborate gestures as he half talked, half sang the lachrymose ballads he preferred. A Lewis performance might have sounded something like this:

> When ma' baby,
> I say, when my baby smiles at me,
> Gee, what a wonderful light that comes to her eyes . . .
> Look at that light, ladies and gentlemen.[20]

His theme song eventually ensnared him in a controversy that began when Harry Von Tilzer identified a problem caused by two songs with al-most identical titles: "When My Baby Smiles" and "When My Baby Smiles at Me." Von Tilzer claimed that the second song had been written and pub-lished first. He said that he had heard it at Rector's, a famous New York res-taurant, early in September 1919. When he learned that it was not protected by copyright, he suggested the title to piano player Bill Munro, who wrote a melody and improvised lyrics for the chorus.

After he had paid for orchestrations and advertising, Von Tilzer learned that Irving Berlin had written a song with a similar title. The involved par-ties agreed that the songs were entirely different except for the titles. When Harry Akst, Berlin's pianist, suggested that they toss a coin to see who would keep the original title, Berlin refused. The following week, an ad in *Variety* printed a copy of a letter from the Music Publishers' Protective Association saying that Berlin's song had been registered a month earlier than Von Til-zer's. At the bottom of the ad, Saul Bornstein, Berlin's professional manager, dismissed a statement attributed to Von Tilzer. "My imprint on a song," Von Tilzer allegedly said, "means a great deal more to the music buying public than his ever will."[21] This one time Von Tilzer was right: Berlin was the greater songwriter but Von Tilzer's song became the hit. Ironically, even though sheet music editions credit Bill Munro, Andrew G. Sterling, and Ted Lewis (and later Von Tilzer as well), Munro wrote the song by himself and copyrighted it in January 1920.

# Chapter 7
## 1921–1925

**"All By Myself"** (1921)
Lyrics and music by Irving Berlin (1888–1989)

One of the great sources of Irving Berlin's longevity as a songwriter involved a contradiction: on one hand, his ability to figure out what was permanent; and on the other, his quick adaptation to changing attitudes, styles, and standards. He also had the rare ability to express the emotionalism beneath the public mood with unequaled lucidity. As Jerome Kern wrote about him in 1925, "He honestly absorbs the vibrations emanating from the people, manners, and life of his time, and in turn, gives these impressions back to the world—simplified—clarified—glorified."[1] No song before "All By Myself" so completely captures its writer's credo: that a song should be "easy to sing, easy to say, easy to remember, and applicable to every-day events."[2] Its success in 1921 confirmed his recognition that tastes were changing. It was his first stab at a new kind of song—what he called a "sob song"—though this time he combined it with something else he wrote with great success—the rhythmic ballad. It was a love song, no matter how sad, with a beat.

Berlin wrote "All By Myself" at an especially busy time. He had just finished the score for *The Music Box Revue*, his first undertaking with his producing partner, Sam Harris. It was a great hit. As one reviewer put it, "The sumptuous and bespangled revue cannot possibly earn them anything more substantial than the heartwarming satisfaction of having produced it at all."[3] Yet Berlin continued to write songs without pausing and, almost as soon as the show opened, he began to plan for the next edition. You could hear the confidence in his voice when he told an interviewer, "In the next two years, American syncopation will so influence the classical music of the world, that New York will be getting operas from Vienna filled to the brim with our own native jazz."[4]

75

Even though the content of "All By Myself" is melancholy, its tempo and beat give it something like the drive found in ragtime songs from the 1910s and uptempo jump tunes still to come in the 1930s and 1940s. Yet the origin for this particular song was bleaker than its beguiling tempo suggests. Echoes of the loneliness which he carried with him for many years after his first wife died in 1912, only six months after they married, had to have been part of it, even though they had already inspired one song, his first important ballad, "When I Lost You." It is also important that Berlin wrote "All By Myself" the year before his mother died. One of his biographers calls it "a meditation on solitude and the misery of growing old alone."[5] Even if Berlin's lyric was not a direct response to his mother's weakening condition, it certainly reflected his own state of mind. Part of his gift lay in how he could redefine aspects of his life within the conventions of commercial popular songs that reflected the experiences of millions of people. At his best, he could capture the mood of the nation in thirty-two bars.

In this case, instead of writing for a Dance Craze, he was writing about the loss of someone he loved. After the carnage of World War I, America wanted to party, but it was not immune to the melancholy of the "sob song" and, later in the decade, the "torch ballad." Berlin said, "When I see we're shy on sentimental ballads, I sit down and write one,"[6] but he usually had the ability to recognize what was coming before most of his competitors and then dart in a new direction. His images here are both familiar and evocative as he links them to the language of loneliness, from sitting "alone with a table and a chair" to getting "lonely / Watching the clock on the shelf." Finally, the lyric links the word "hate" to the terrible fear of growing old alone.

Although Berlin had been writing such boisterous dance tunes as "Alexander's Ragtime Band" and "Everybody's Doing It Now," the success of "All By Myself" soon led him to write such mournful ballads as "What'll I Do," "Remember," and "All Alone." "All By Myself' was a major transition between what he usually wrote and the great songs that he would go on to write in the decade ahead.

**"Do It Again"** [*The French Doll*] (1921)
Lyrics by Buddy DeSylva (1895–1950), music by George Gershwin (1898–1937)

**"Do, Do, Do"** [*Oh, Kay!*] (1926)
Lyrics by Ira Gershwin (1896–1983), music by George Gershwin (1898–1937)

By the time he and Ira wrote *Lady Be Good*, their first Broadway collaboration, George Gershwin had written at least 125 songs with both his brother and other lyricists. In 1919, he and Irving Caesar wrote "Swanee," his first hit. By 1922, he had placed interpolations in more than a dozen shows. He also wrote six numbers with Ira for *A Dangerous Maid*, a show that never reached Broadway, even though it included "Boy Wanted," with Ira's clever lyric in the form of a newspaper classified: "He must be able to dance. / He must make life a romance." By the time he was in his mid-20s, George was known around town for his talent, ambition, and egotism. He once ran into producer-director Jed Harris, also something of a prodigy, and introduced himself:

> "I'm George Gershwin."
> "Yes, I know," Harris replied, "I've seen you in theater lobbies, Mr. Gershwin. I think you're a wonderful songwriter."
> "I am," Gershwin said, "Aren't I?"
> "The best."
> "There's a question I've been wanting to ask you. How old are you, Mr. Harris?"
> "I'll be twenty-seven in February."
> "Shit!" Gershwin said. "I'm twenty-eight."[7]

Back in the early 1920s, George and lyricist Buddy DeSylva were hanging around in the offices of music publisher Max Dreyfus when DeSylva prodded the composer to write another hit. Gershwin improvised a melody; DeSylva listened for a few minutes and then began chanting, "Do it again, do it again." He probably wrote the lyric very quickly, at least if Ira Gershwin was a reliable witness. He once watched DeSylva set a lyric to an unidentified early melody by his brother. Michael Feinstein tells the story: "[DeSylva] wrote one line and then another. He left several blank lines and wrote another, supplied one a little farther down, and then went back and put in the second line and then the fourth line and in an hour, he had a finished, polished lyric."[8] Gershwin began to play the tune at parties until Gallic star Irene Bordoni heard it. She swept across the room and declared, "I mus' have that song! It's for me!" DeSylva's risqué lyric helped her make the song a hit in her new vehicle, *The French Doll*.[9] The song was always one of George's favorites, perhaps because he recognized in it the beginnings of his distinctive style. He once said of his musical apprenticeship, "As I had a searching mind, ordinary harmonies, rhythms, sequences, intervals and so on failed to satisfy my ear. I would spend hour upon hour trying to change them around so that they would satisfy me. After a patient apprenticeship at this I began developing along more original lines."[10]

Four years later, for the score to *Oh, Kay!*, George and Ira collaborated on another "Do" number called "Do, Do, Do," in which two attractive young people pretend to be newlyweds. It was all part of an elaborate musical comedy plot involving bootlegging on Long Island. An hour before dinner one night, Ira told George that he would like to do something with the sounds of "do do" and "done done." They climbed up to their studio on the third floor and, in half an hour, finished the refrain even though Ira often labored for days over a single line. He was sure it took no longer than that, because his fiancée had just called to say she could come for dinner. When she arrived a half-hour later, "we played her the complete refrain."[11]

Songs from the 1920s through the 1940s are often much sexier, even more erotic, than their surfaces suggest. "Do It Again" and "Do, Do, Do" are classic examples, but Ira insisted that "Do, Do, Do," even though its refrain begins, "Do, do, do / What you've done, done, done / Before, Baby," is "a catchy song about a kiss and nothing else . . . Whatever may have been hinted at or outspokenly stated in other songs of mine, 'Do, Do, Do' was written for its face, not body, value."[12] Maybe so, but "Do It Again" is also ostensibly about a kiss, even though a hug and a kiss in a popular song often suggests a lot more than a hug and a kiss.

### "Carolina in the Morning" (1922)
Lyrics by Gus Kahn (1886–1941), music by Walter Donaldson (1893–1947)

Walter Donaldson wrote for Broadway and Hollywood, but mainly he was an Alleyman, a quintessential professional who wrote the music, the words, and sometimes both. He landed his first Tin Pan Alley job in 1910, demonstrating songs for a publisher, but the boss fired the 17-year-old kid for writing his own songs on company time. By 1922, he was a well-established professional with a number of hits to his credit, including "The Daughter of Rosie O'Grady," "How Ya' Gonna Keep 'Em Down on the Farm," and "My Mammy." So it was no surprise that he had never lived on a farm when he wrote "How Ya Gonna Keep 'Em Down on the Farm." He was a bachelor when he wrote that tribute to married love, "My Blue Heaven," and had never been to either of the Carolinas when he wrote "Carolina in the Morning." The songs succeeded because Donaldson and his collaborator, lyricist Gus Kahn, knew how to write hits. One year, their publisher's firm sold five million pieces of sheet music, four million of them songs by Kahn. Sometimes, an idea would come to them while they were eating in a restaurant. They would jot it down on the tablecloth and take it home, and the waiter would charge them for the linen. They also understood the relationships that songwriters had to the South. Kahn said, "Our song boys are of

FIGURE 7.1    Gus Kahn, one of the most underrated of the major lyricists. Courtesy of Photofest.

the North. Paradise is never where we are. The South has become our never, never land, the symbol of the land where the lotus blossoms, and dreams come true."[13]

"Carolina" was one of the best and most successful songs about returning. When large numbers of single men and women left the farms and villages of the Midwest and South for New York City, music publishers realized they had a new audience. Instead of writing about the excitement of city life, songwriters turned to nostalgic recollections of what the newcomers had left behind, or high-spirited ragtime songs about the anticipated return to a better place left behind. Irving Berlin wrote some of the best of these songs ("Settle Down in a One-Horse Town," "When the Midnight Choo-Choo Leaves for Alabam','" "I Want to Go Back to Michigan"), but Donaldson and Kahn ran him a close second.

Kahn and Donaldson eventually developed their own way of working together. Donaldson would strike one chord and then another, both at random, and develop a melody from how they sounded, one after the other. Then he would play the result over and over again, revising and refining. Kahn would be in the room listening, and would eventually begin to make requests: "That's it, try that last again." As Donaldson repeated a portion of the melody, Kahn would jot down some words—the last two lines of the chorus. Then he would work backwards and end by writing the verse.[14]

In this case, Kahn built the lyric from what he knew about farms, marriage and the South—a set of widely recognized associations, conventions, and images that provided the atmosphere the lyric needed. "Carolina in the Morning," was also a tour de force that demonstrated Kahn's mastery of both internal and triple rhymes: "Strolling with my girlie / Where the dew is pearly early / In the morning." In the 1920s, when they were so popular with lyricists, these techniques gave songs a lift that made them feel lighthearted and deliciously frivolous during the most deliciously frivolous decade of the century. The song is a gleaming example of how verbal byplay makes the familiar feel fresh.

### "I'll Build a Stairway to Paradise" [*George White's Scandals*] (1922)
Lyrics by Ira Gershwin (1896–1983) and Buddy DeSylva (1895–1950), music by George Gershwin (1898–1937)

By 1922, George and Ira Gershwin were working together more frequently and were beginning to adapt to one another's abilities. For the first act finale of *George White's Scandals of 1922*, they wrote "I'll Build a Stairway to Paradise," one of their best early songs, perfectly suited to White's latest extravagant revue, mainly a dance show with interspersed comedy numbers. George Gershwin described the staging: "Two circular staircases surrounded the [Paul Whiteman] orchestra on the stage, leading high up into theatrical paradise or the flies . . . Mr. White had draped fifty of his most beautiful girls in black patent-leather material which brilliantly reflected the spotlights."[15] When the curtain rose for an encore, the girls stripped off their gowns to reveal skimpy lingerie. Gershwin also admired Whiteman's arrangement of his syncopated march: "Paul made my song live with a vigor that almost floored me."[16] The composer was convinced that his "association with Mr. Whiteman in this show I am sure had something to do with Paul's asking me to write a composition for his first jazz concert. As you may know, I wrote the *Rhapsody in Blue* for the occasion."[17]

The Gershwins had originally written a song called "New Step Every Day." The singer in Ira's lyric boasts about learning many new dance steps. Both men thought the song was inadequate but lyricist Buddy DeSylva thought they could make it work by expanding the song's ending, "I'll build a stairway to Paradise, with a new step every day." They went to work after dinner one night and by 1 a.m. had a new version in which only that single phrase remained from the original.

**"Pack Up Your Sins (and Go to the Devil)"** [*Music Box Revue of 1922*] (1922)
Lyrics and music by Irving Berlin (1888–1989)

In retrospect, Irving Berlin wrote so many "plain-spoken ballads" like "What'll I Do" and "Say It Isn't So" that it is easy to overlook his extraordinary range and variety. Philip Furia describes the Gershwins' "Fascinating Rhythm" as Ira's "choosing the precise verbal shard to fit into each jagged musical space his brother provided,"[18] but earlier in the 1920s, Berlin had begun to experiment with the same kinds of irregular rhythms that define the Gershwins' song—in "Everybody Step" in 1921 and, more significantly, in "Pack Up Your Sins (and Go to the Devil)" in 1922.

When Ethel Merman sang "Pack Up Your Sins" in the 1938 movie *Alexander's Ragtime Band*, Joseph Breen, the chief administrator for the Motion Picture Production Code, took exception to the song and its performance. Dating back to 1930, the Code defined what was acceptable behavior in a Hollywood movie. Mainly it clamped down on profanity, excessive violence, and especially sex. "Pack Up Your Sins" never mentions anything sexual, but its invitation to stay up late to dance to a Hades jazz band led by Mr. Devil provides all the suggestive encouragement anyone needs. Its unique herky-jerky rhythms provide a percussive setting for an irreverent view of the afterlife in which Hell is a much more desirable "winter resort" than a Heaven where reformers send everyone to bed by 11 p.m. Much better to end up "down below," because "you'll never have to go to bed at all." Other 1920s songs that relished bad behavior—"I Want to Be Bad," "I Wanna Be Loved by You," and "I Have to Have You," among many others—involved one man and one woman, almost always young; they're Flapper songs. But Berlin's lyric is a naughty "good advice" song that lays out an irresistible path to the desired bad end.

The Breen Office, alert to any attempts to sneak past the limits it had established, had a long exchange of letters with 20th Century Fox, the studio that made *Alexander's Ragtime Band*. The Office wrote, "The lyric to 'Pack Up Your Sins (and Go to the Devil)' may be offensive to religiously inclined people. It contains one code violation, the phrase 'No one gives a damn,' and also the line, 'H-E-Double-L is a wonderful spot' may be deleted by censor boards." After the lyrics were modified, Breen once again recommended dropping the song from the movie because "it seems to burlesque one of the fundamental tenets of the Christian religion."[19] Once again, Berlin tweaked the lyrics and the Breen Office reluctantly went along. When Merman finally performed the song, she wore a tuxedo with a top hat and cane, but she barely moved. As the number ended, she lifted her arms over her head. Nothing more.

When the McCarthy Sisters had introduced "Pack Up Your Sins" in the *Music Box Revue of 1922*, an obscure songwriter sued Berlin for plagiarism. That sort of thing happened to successful composers all the time. Songs were brief and usually simple, and could earn a great deal of money. But going after "Pack Up Your Sins" was not a very smart idea. It was one of Berlin's characteristic double songs, involving the merging of two different melodies that fit together perfectly (Among the others are "A Simple Melody" from 1914 and "You're Just in Love" from 1950). His friends from the Algonquin Round Table testified in his defense, as did violinist Jascha Heifetz, who said that he had seen Berlin working on the song nine months before the show opened. Not surprisingly, Berlin was acquitted.

### "That Old Gang of Mine" (1923)
Lyrics by Billy Rose (1899–1966) and Mort Dixon (1892–1956), music by Ray Henderson (1896–1970)

### "(The Gang That Sang) Heart of My Heart" (1926)
Lyrics and music by Ben Ryan (1892–1968)

### "Wedding Bells (Are Breaking Up That Old Gang of Mine)" (1929)
Lyrics by Irving Kahal (1903–1942) and Willie Raskin (1896–1942), music by Sammy Fain (1902–1989)

Ray Henderson had not had much of a career when lyricists Billy Rose and Mort Dixon squeezed into his tiny office at Shapiro, Bernstein, the music-publishing house where he worked. A composer for a different company had written a melody for a lyric of Rose's but Billy disliked it. Rose invited Henderson to give his words a new tune. The composer finished it in a single afternoon and called it "That Old Gang of Mine." The next day, the three men met to polish the song and soon sold it to a third publisher. Henderson later said that he had the impression that Dixon had written nearly the entire lyric, but, typically, it was Rose who put the song over. Billy not only talked the top vaudeville team of Van and Schenck into performing it in the *Ziegfeld Follies*, he had the chutzpah to tell them to put a lamppost on stage and lean against it as they sang. The song was a hit but Ziegfeld told them to get rid of the lamppost.

When great numbers of people migrated from the Midwest and South to Chicago and especially New York in the half-century after the Civil War, music publishers greeted them with nostalgic songs about the farms and small towns they had left behind. By the 1920s, their children, old enough to marry and settle down, were forsaking the city for the new suburbs growing up on Long Island and in Westchester County to the north. Bachelors rented apartments in Manhattan; young married couples drove their automobiles or took the new commuter trains to Valley Stream and Scarsdale. Those who remained in the City found that old friends had disappeared, and songwriters took note of the change. Three of the best known of these songs are "That Old Gang of Mine," "(The Gang That Sang) Heart of My Heart," and "Wedding Bells (Are Breaking Up That Old Gang of Mine)." They portray the separation of neighborhood pals, perhaps because time has passed, perhaps because they married and moved away. The songs offer tender memories of male camaraderie expressed through their gathering "down on the corner" to sing barbershop harmonies, especially "Heart of My Heart," written in 1899 by a little-known actor and singer named Andrew Mack. "We were rough and ready guys," the singer remembers, "But oh, how we could harmonize." The song he remembers is a sentimental ballad of formal rhetoric but little charm: "Heart of my heart, I love you, / Life would be naught without you."

### "Yes! We Have No Bananas" [*Make It Snappy*] (1923)
Lyrics and music by Frank Silver (1896–1960) and Irving Cohn (1898–1961)

A jazz drummer and sometime songwriter named Frank Silver overheard a Greek fruit peddler answer a customer's question, "Yes, we have no bananas."[20] He knew at once that he had the catchphrase for what would turn out to be the most successful novelty song ever written. It's a good story, but is it true? Maybe a newspaper report about a banana blight in Brazil provided the inspiration, but it was easy enough for Silver and his collaborator, Irving Cohn, to assign it to a Greek fruit store owner, a stereotypical stock character on the vaudeville stage. The town of Lynbrook, Long Island, insists that the songwriters wrote it there and that a local merchant named Jimmy Costas coined the phrase. Others have said that a cartoonist named Tom Dorgan invented it and first used it in his comic strip, but before that, U.S. Marines returning from the Philippines after the Spanish-American War were telling stories about a Manila fruit vendor whose fractured English included the line.

Whatever its source, Silver and Cohn took the finished song to Waterson, Berlin & Snyder, who turned down their request for $1,000. Louis Bernstein at Shapiro, Bernstein offered to pay them and publish it if they rewrote it, beginning with the opening line that he said was "no good." They went to work right there, and nearly every songwriter in the office pitched in. James

Hanley wrote the line "There's a fruit store on our street." Somebody else added "It's run by a Greek," and lyricist Lew Brown finished the verse before Ballard MacDonald touched up the second verse. Sigmund Spaeth, who called himself the Tune Detective, said that if you sang the original words to the borrowed melodies, it would read, "Hallelujah, Bananas! Oh, bring back my bonnie to me. I was seeing Nellie home to an old-fashioned garden; but Hallelujah! Bananas! Oh, bring back my bonnie to me."[21] Spaeth was also concerned about infringing on the copyright to Cole Porter's 1919 song "In an Old-Fashioned Garden." When Silver and Cohn showed the song to Porter's publisher Max Dreyfus, he refused permission. Then he took the music sheet, scribbled a small change, and said, "But if you do it this way, it's okay." By the time everyone had joined in, the result was what music historian Douglas Gilbert called "as lovely a bit of bastardy as was ever seminated in the Alley."[22]

The song was so successful that it soon gave rise to imitators. Later that same year, James Hanley, Robert King, and Lew Brown—two of whom had contributed changes to the revised original—wrote "The 'Yes We Have No Bananas' Blues," and in 1930, for the movie *Mammy*, Irving Berlin wrote "The 'Yes We Have No Bananas' Variations."

### "Hard Hearted Hannah" (1924)
Lyrics by Jack Yellen (1892–1991), Bob Bigelow, (?) and Charles Bates (?), music by Milt Ager (1892–1979)

It would be hard to total up all the songs about the South, dating back at least as far as Stephen Foster's "Old Folks at Home" from 1851. They became doubly popular in the years after the Civil War through the 1920s, as large numbers of Southerners moved to New York, and songwriters and publishers began to trade in nostalgia. Returning became one of popular music's central themes for more than half a century. Songwriter Gerald Marks ("All of Me," "Is It True What They Say About Dixie?") said, "There are probably in the neighborhood of 200 songs written about Southern belles in crinolines and plantation-like dresses and none of the composers had ever been further South than 14th Street in Manhattan."[23] Nobody was better at turning out these songs in the 1910s and 1920s than composer Milt Ager and lyricist Jack Yellen. Between 1915 and 1930, working both together and apart, they wrote "Are You from Dixie?" "Lovin' Sam," "Alabama Jubilee," and "That's Where the South Begins." Ager had his first hit in 1918 when lyricist Grant Clarke gave him the title of a song called "Everything Is Peaches Down in Georgia." Even though he was a composer, Ager said many years later that "Clarke had given me the tune and I quickly got the lyric. I brought the song into the Feist Publishing House and there it languished on the shelf for a couple of weeks. One afternoon the man himself—Jolson!—walked into the office and asked Clarke, 'Ya got anything for me?' "[24]

Six years later, Ager and Yellen, who wrote a lot of songs together in the 1920s, including "Ain't She Sweet" and "Happy Days Are Here Again," were sitting in their office when a couple of lyricists named Bob Bigelow and Charley Bates dropped by to say that they had written, in Ager's words, "a germ of a gem" called "Hard-Hearted Hannah." Ager said it was a " 'Southern song,' but they just hadn't got it right. Well, Jack and I worked it up, got it published (with all four names on the sheet music) and it did all right. Maybe a hundred thousand copies."[25] The song tells the bluesy but humorous story of a "vamp of Savannah," who "loves to see men suffer." Its setting in Savannah rather than in the countryside, its rollicking blues beat, and its delight in a woman who punishes men for the sheer joy of it makes this a "blues song" derived from the "urban blues" in which women characters (and the singers who portray them) developed attributes of independence, defiance, and sexual hunger.

## "Lazy" (1924)
Lyrics and music by Irving Berlin (1888–1989)

Irving Berlin was bushed. After the demanding work of preparing the third (and final) *Music Box Revue*, the songwriter took a week's vacation in Florida. Lying on the beach, he realized how much he enjoyed being away from the pressures of his work—he loved being lazy. But he was still Irving Berlin, and it wasn't long before he turned his pleasure into a song he called "Lazy." Although few of his songs reflect the facts of his life directly, this one is immediately recognizable to anyone who hears it but also reflects the songwriter's personal outlook at the time he wrote it. It is also an example of what fellow songwriter Irving Caesar observed: Berlin's ability to write songs in which love was not the subject. It did not happen often, but the variety of these songs is striking, from "Shakin' the Blues Away" to "A Couple of Swells" to "Pack Up Your Sins." Although "Lazy" is also one of the songs that has nothing to say about love, its quiet reflectiveness, its clarity about its character's mood, and its deepening sense of time passing in the second verse that begins, "Life is short / And getting shorter," make it just melancholy enough to link it to the great Berlin "sob ballads" of the 1920s— "What'll I Do," "Remember," "How About Me?" and "All Alone."

The lyric's most evocative line has its own history. In 1923, George S. Kaufman and Marc Connelly collaborated on a play they called *The Deep Tangled Wildwood*. Its run of only sixteen performances led Connelly to remark, "Our play quickly faded from the public memory, but the title stayed alive in the words of Irving Berlin's popular 'Lazy.' "[26] Critic Richard Corliss notes with approval that Berlin's lyric was paying a "cheeky tribute" to his playwriting friends by concocting an elaborate rhyme from the title of their flop.[27] As the grown man in the song stretches and yawns, he longs for a child's innocent slumber. He wants "to peep / Through the deep / Tangled wildwood" until he falls asleep.

The original reference, which many listeners in the 1920s would have recognized, is to Samuel Woodworth's 1818 poem "The Old Oaken Bucket," long known for its sentimental remembrance of the joys of childhood:

> How dear to this heart are the scenes of my childhood.
> When fond recollection presents them to view!
> The orchard, the meadow, the deep-tangled wildwood,
> And every loved spot which my infancy knew.

### "When My Sugar Walks Down the Street" (1924)
Lyrics by Irving Mills (1894–1985) and Gene Austin (1900–1972), music by Jimmy McHugh (1894–1969)

### "I Can't Believe That You're in Love with Me" (1926)
Lyrics by Clarence Gaskill (1892–1947), music by Jimmy McHugh (1894–1969)

Rather than a collaboration between Irving Mills and Gene Austin, the lyric to "When My Sugar Walks Down the Street" is probably the work of Mills, who then gave Austin a cut-in as co-lyricist. Why would he do that? Austin had not yet become the big-time crooner who would eventually go on to sell 86 million records during his career. He was an unknown singer hired by Mills Music to demonstrate the song for a recording at Victor. Nathaniel Shilkret, who supervised Victor's recordings, liked his voice and paired him with one of the recording company's top singers, Aileen Stanley. Even so, Austin complained that Shilkret wanted Stanley to do most of the singing while he was limited to chirping "Tweet-tweet-tweet" in the background. The dispute faded once the song became popular.[28] Its success propelled Austin's career as maybe the most important American crooner before Bing Crosby. Decades later, when he was living in retirement in Las Vegas, Austin owned a parrot who greeted visitors by whistling the refrain of Austin's greatest hit, "My Blue Heaven," and then, believe it or not, croaking the words, "When whippoorwills call . . ." Once it finished, it asked a final question: "Why don't we sell this damn bird!"[29]

"When My Sugar Walks Down the Street" also made a lot of money for composer Jimmy McHugh, who used his royalties to move his parents into a new house. But he recognized that, while he would probably keep working with Mills because of his association with Mills Music, he needed a lyricist of his own. He needed someone he could rely on to provide song ideas and titles he could develop into melodies. He would continue to write with Dorothy Fields for several more years, but he also began to write with Al Dubin and Ted Koehler in the late 1920s and into the 1930s, and with Harold Adamson in the late 1930s and the years of World War II. The long association with Fields ended when she decided that she wanted to return to New York to write for Broadway.

Two years after "When My Sugar Walks Down the Street," McHugh collaborated briefly with Clarence Gaskill. The result was the lightly swinging "I Can't Believe That You're in Love with Me" for a Cotton Club revue. McHugh's biographer admired the song's "neat musical phrasing, which caught the nuance of the lyrics." McHugh was learning a great deal about songwriting during these years. He said, "I had learned a good deal about the demands which the popular song imposes upon the writer . . . It is the very limitation of the popular song that is the key to its greatness. The simple tune is the great tune. In the construction of commercial ballads, you try to limit the range to eight, or at most nine, notes, and to maintain an overall simplicity of theme so it will be easy to sing."[30]

## "A Cup of Coffee, A Sandwich, and You" [*Charlot's Revue of 1926*] (1925)
Lyrics by Al Dubin (1891–1945) and Billy Rose (1899–1966), music by Joseph Meyer (1894–1987)

Al Dubin did most of his best-known work with composer Harry Warren for the Warner Brothers' musicals of the 1930s, but he had begun to write and publish songs shortly before America's entry into World War I. By the mid-1920s, he was placing songs in revues and musical comedies. Even though Noël Coward had written much of the score for the original London production of *Charlot's Revue* in 1926, impresario André Charlot wanted another showstopper when the show moved to New York. "A Cup of Coffee, A Sandwich, and You" became Dubin's first important hit when Charlot bought it and had Gertrude Lawrence sing it just before the final curtain. Dubin was already in his mid-thirties, but co-lyricist Billy Rose was almost ten years younger.

Rose used to hang out at a deli where songwriters gathered. One night he asked composer Harry Ruby, "Has anybody ever thought of rhyming 'June' with 'macaroon'?" When everybody in the room applauded, a waiter handed him "a pencil and a clean menu and said, 'Mr. Rose, you're in business.'" That night Rose wrote what he says was his first song, "Does the Spearmint Lose Its Flavor on the Bedpost Overnight?"[31]

At the opening night party for *Charlot's Revue,* waiting for the newspaper reviews to arrive, Rose met Noël Coward for the first time. The songwriter-playwright-performer gave the diminutive Rose a long look, smiled, and shook his head as he said softly, "Naughty boy."[32] Who knows what Coward had in mind. Maybe he knew Rose's reputation as a finagler who could muscle his way into a collaboration with nothing more than an idea or a title, but would then lead the way by selling the song to a top publisher and convincing a star to perform it, thereby earning a lot of money for everyone, including himself. The composer of "A Cup of Coffee," Joe Meyer, said, "He was a co-writer on songs, a contributor. He had good abilities. He was a particularly good editor. He was a coordinator and he could bring things together. He knew how to throw away a line."[33]

Earlier in the decade, when Rose first decided to become a songwriter, he spent months in the New York Public Library studying the origin and history of songs, and then studying the songs themselves. He concluded that there were two kinds of songs, love songs and novelty songs. He chose novelty songs, and soon wrote two hits, "You Tell Her, I Stutter" and "Barney Google," based on the popular comic strip. He once told an interviewer in his distinctively staccato way, "Now get this—I had no particular desire to write music, but I saw no reason why I, with a little preparation and work, could not join the gold rush."[34]

Although Rose's name appears as co-lyricist on "Cup of Coffee," composer Joseph Meyer said that the title and most of the lyrics were Dubin's. Rose's biographer wrote, "Nobody clearly knew what he wrote or didn't write . . . Publishers tend to credit him with writing the songs known to bear his name as a lyricist. . . . But tales rumble on . . . that Billy could feed and toss in a remark and monkey around, but that others did most of the writing." Dubin found his inspiration in the most famous line from one of his favorite poems, "The Rubaiyat of Omar Khayyam." He turned "A loaf of bread, a jug of wine, and thou" into the song's colloquial title,[35] and followed it with a lyric defined by easy charm and youthful intimacy.

# Chapter 8
## 1926–1930

**"The Birth of the Blues"** [*George White's Scandals of 1926*] (1926)
Lyrics by B.G. DeSylva (1895–1950) and Lew Brown (1893–1958), music
by Ray Henderson (1896–1970)

   Although the blues began as an indigenous African American folk music
in the Mississippi Delta, they became a national American music when they
also became a performance music in the 1920s. In the previous decades, as
African Americans had begun to move to cities in large numbers, the blues
also became an urban music. They soon became so popular that the term
appeared in mainstream popular songs, and "blues songs," popular songs
that borrowed the feel and viewpoint of authentic blues, proliferated in Tin
Pan Alley and on Broadway. At the heart of both blues and blues songs
was a feeling of melancholy and longing, usually brought on by the loss of
love, but the urban blues were also more directly sexual with a strong note
of defiance, especially when the character in the song (or the singer) was a
woman.

   The most important blues song of the 1920s was Ray Henderson, Buddy
DeSylva, and Lew Brown's "The Birth of the Blues." The three men were
white, Henderson a Protestant from Western New York, De Sylva of Portu-
guese descent, and Brown a Jewish immigrant from Odessa. Although the
song lacks the blues' deeply felt sadness, it uses a bluesy feel to spin a fanciful story of how the blues began. Fortescue Deepelum wrote in the online
magazine *The Journal of Provincial Thought*:

> This Tin Pan Alley mythologizing was a necessary step in assimilat-
> ing the folk blues, smoothing them out, fitting them into the genre
> of popular song. The blues, according to this text, were straight
> from nature—the breeze and whippoorwill—but also born of the

**FIGURE 8.1**   B.G. DeSylva (left), Lew Brown, and Ray Henderson were instrumental in creating the sound of the 1920s. Courtesy of Photofest.

raffish underworld (the downhearted frail in the jail) and through musical invention, the "new note." It makes the blues instantly familiar and acceptable, like an instructional cartoon.[1]

To the degree that the song's lyric suggests something believable, its introductory performance beggars description. In *George White's Scandals of 1926*, the oleaginous song-and-dance man Harry Richman stood at the center of a circular staircase, while chorus girls dressed as angels fought over which was superior, classical music or modern blues. The solution was an excerpt from George Gershwin's still new *Rhapsody in Blue*. It sounds laughable, but sophisticated audiences of the day ate it up.

**"Black Bottom"** [*George White's Scandals of 1926*] (1926)
Lyrics by B.G. DeSylva (1895–1950) and Lew Brown (1893–1958), music by Ray Henderson (1896–1970)

Henry "Rubberlegs" Williams of the famous black vaudeville team, Butterbeans and Susie, said, "That dance is as old as the hills. Done all over the

South—why, I remember doing it myself."[2] No matter who gets the credit for writing "Black Bottom," it was a popular dance that probably originated in New Orleans years before it first appeared as sheet music.

Perry Bradford's "The Original Black Bottom Dance" was a 1919 revision of his earlier "Jacksonville Rounders' Dance" from 1907. He explained, "It was a dance they were doing in Jacksonville way back, but people didn't like the title because 'rounder' meant pimp, so I wrote some new lyrics . . . and renamed it."[3] Blues singer Alberta Hunter may have introduced it, but even though she copyrighted it, there are so many variations and borrowings that it is hard to know for sure if she added to the writing. At first, people thought its name came from one of its characteristic movements— a slapping of the backside—but it really comes from the Swanee River's black bottom mud. Blues singer Gertrude "Ma" Rainey took another approach when her 1927 double-entendre blues song, "Ma Rainey's Black Bottom," emphasized the title's bawdiness. Her lyric explains that the boys in the neighborhood want to learn the dance because they want Rainey to show them "her black bottom."

In 1924, Broadway producer George White saw a dance to Bradford's music in a Harlem show called *Dinah*. He bought the rights to the number and hired Ray Henderson, Lew Brown, and Buddy DeSylva to turn it into a new song. Danced by Ann Pennington in *George White's Scandals of 1926*, their version is the one that became a national craze, almost as popular as James P. Johnson and Cecil Mack's "Charleston," performed on Broadway in *Runnin' Wild* the year before. In 1927, New York's Roseland Ballroom sponsored a Black Bottom marathon contest, and dance teacher Arthur Murray acknowledged the dance's crudeness but said that he was trying to revise it so it could become the leading dance of the coming social season. In that same year, a woman identified only as Miss Bradhurst Black Bottomed for 19 miles before she collapsed.

## "The Blue Room" [*The Girl Friend*] (1926)
Lyrics by Lorenz Hart (1895–1943), music by Richard Rodgers (1902–1979)

Even though composer Richard Rodgers, lyricist Lorenz Hart, and librettist Herbert Fields had set their 1925 hit, "Dearest Enemy," during the American Revolution, it was as tuneful and suggestive as mid-1920s musical comedy audiences wanted. Helen Ford starred as the seductive New York hostess who detained British troops by entertaining their officers while Washington re-formed his army in Washington Heights. Ford said she took the part because of a scene in which she had to sneak

**FIGURE 8.2**  Composer Richard Rodgers (center) with book writer Herbert Fields and lyricist Lorenz Hart (with omnipresent cigar). Courtesy of Photofest.

onstage with the chorus to avoid being seen: "I made the entrance in a barrel. At the time, this was shocking, you know? It was a wonderful entrance, and it was cute and it was funny, with the English redcoat soldier chasing me with one of my slippers in his hand, and obviously I had no clothes."[4]

Before the show finished its run of 301 performances, the threesome was back at work on something set in the present—about an amateur who enters a six-day bike race and his successful pursuit of both the victory cup and the daughter of a professional cyclist. Fields pasted together the plot that Rodgers said was inconsequential but perfect to hang songs on—none better than "Blue Room," the song that Stanley Green called "that classic of city-life contentment"[5] and Alec Wilder said was the "first wholly distinctive Rodgers song."[6] Hart appears to have written the lyric in Atlantic City just before tryouts began. During the writing, cleverness begat cleverness. Rodgers explained that he began the second, third, and fourth bars of the melody on the same note and followed it with a note that rose a half-tone in each successive bar. That pattern gave Hart the idea of using triple rhymes on the repeated notes. Then, for emphasis, he repeated the word "room" on the rising half-tones—"blue room," "new room," and "for two room." He did the same thing in the second chorus—"ball room," "small room," and "hall room."[7]

Hart often wrote with amazing speed, especially during rehearsals. When he needed to add a stanza to one of the songs in the *The Girl Friend*'s score, a reporter wrote that he "seemed to be disappearing behind pieces of the set; while dancers in rehearsal pounded the floor, furniture was being moved, lights were adjusted, and cast and crew were calling out to one another, he would finish the thing in minutes."[8] More important than his speed was his understanding of what a lyric required. He once told a reporter to find the "essential phrase" in a hit song's first line and then choose words to put to it—not "the most trite word" but "something living, a word everybody uses. People don't go around talking about 'love' and 'dove.' They do talk about 'blue rooms,' so I wrote a song of that name."[9]

**FIGURE 8.3**   In 1921, Vincent Youmans (left) collaborated with a young songwriter who called himself Arthur Francis but eventually began to write under his real name, Ira Gershwin. Courtesy of Photofest.

### "I Know That You Know" [*Oh, Please*] (1926)
Lyrics by Anne Caldwell (1867–1936), music by Vincent Youmans (1898–1946)

Vincent Youmans used to whistle his new melodies through his teeth. These were the 1920s, and he was writing the buoyant tunes that solidified his reputation. He was a terrific songwriter, but he was never satisfied with what he wrote or how others treated it. His insistence on being both a producer and director as well, plus his heavy drinking, brought him down much too soon. He died of tuberculosis at 48. After the great success of *No, No, Nanette* in 1925, the composer was more dissatisfied than ever because he saw how much more money the show's producer made than he did. He told friends, "Nobody is going to make any money off my music but me."[10] Otto Harbach, who wrote the book and a few of the lyrics to *No, No, Nanette*, called him "a nice kid who wanted to do everything. He wanted to be manager. He wanted to be dressmaker. He wanted to raise the money. He wanted to hire the theater. If he had just stayed as a composer, he would have been the greatest of them all."[11]

Despite his dissatisfaction, Youmans was in great demand after *Nanette*. Eventually, he signed to write a show to be called *Oh, Please* with a book by Harbach, lyrics by Anne Caldwell, and starring Beatrice Lillie. Lillie had gotten her start when she auditioned a tearjerker called "After All That I've Been to You" for British producer André Charlot in the hope that she would be invited to sing it for the Royal Family and have them promptly dissolve into tears. She ended her performance by collapsing onstage in what one writer called "a melancholy heap." Charlot decided that she had a great future as a comedienne.[12]

Because *Oh, Please* was geared to her, its thin plot led to a series of comic confusions through which the elegantly addled Lillie would stumble. At the first rehearsal, however, she announced with Youmans present that the songs were "hopeless" and only her comedy would save the show. Although the songs were not up to Youmans' standards, it's also true that Lillie could not sing romantic ballads believably. Youmans felt that her comedy clashed with his songs. After watching her rehearse several times, he began to refer to her as "that turkey."

Not surprisingly, there came a last straw. As the show traveled from Philadelphia to Hartford to New Haven to Atlantic City before opening in New York, it began to improve. Youmans agreed to write an additional song for Lillie, but he became furious when she persuaded producer Charles Dillingham to cut one of Youmans' songs and replace it with an interpolation. When the show opened in New York, the critics loved her but made virtually no mention of the score, even though it included the lively rhythm number "I Know That You Know," in which a lover expresses loyalty before a good-night kiss.[13]

## "Mountain Greenery" [*Garrick Gaieties of 1926*] (1926)
Lyrics by Lorenz Hart (1895–1943), music by Richard Rodgers (1902–1979)

The first edition of *Garrick Gaieties* in 1925 was so successful that it ran much longer than it was supposed to. When the Theater Guild called to ask composer Richard Rodgers and lyricist Lorenz Hart to write another score for a second edition, the two songwriters hesitated. They knew that the dazzle of being discovered could happen only once, and they knew everyone would be watching to see how they did this time. But they liked the idea of working with the same people again.

Once they agreed, they set to work against a tight deadline. Both men liked that kind of pressure. Hart said that they wrote most of the score at rehearsals; the trick was to stay a day ahead of what the director and performers needed. They wrote one number in no more than half an hour. "I scribbled off the lyrics," Hart said, "while Herb [librettist Herbert Fields] wrote the lines and Dick didn't even sit down at the piano—he just wrote off the notes." They wrote another song on a Thursday, rehearsed it on Friday, and performed it on Saturday. They called their songs for the show "happy travesties."[14]

The big song from the second edition of *Garrick Gaieties* is a sequel of sorts to the big song from the first edition. Without "Manhattan," there would have been no "Mountain Greenery." Without a youthful tour of Manhattan, in which two lovers spend a weekend together, there almost certainly would not have been a song in the same style about a couple of newlyweds—just as youthful, just as smart, just as romantic, just as much in love as the pair in "Manhattan"—who decide to leave the city for a cottage in the woods. With Hart once again playing with sly, tricky rhymes between and within lines, "Mountain Greenery" is less a song about the country than what happens when urban sophistication collides with rural life. The cocky but loving city showoff has moved to the woods. No rube could ever have pulled off the triple rhyme, "Beans could get to keener re- / Ception in a beanery, / Bless our mountain greenery home."

## "Among My Souvenirs" (1927)
Lyrics by Edgar Leslie (1885–1976), music by Horatio Nicholls (1888–1964)

Mediocre songwriters, even bad songwriters, sometimes come up with a fine song. Not often, but it happens. Herman Hupfeld, who wrote the great "As Time Goes By" and the very good "Let's Put Out the Lights and Go to

Sleep," was more likely to write something like "Yuba Played the Rhumba on His Tuba." Similarly, Horatio Nicholls, a prolific English composer, wrote such instantly forgettable songs as "Queen of the Sea" and "Here's Health Unto Our New King" (including the line, "British labour gave its skill and it's giving me a thrill"). Lawrence Wright Music Co., Ltd. published the songs because Wright and Nicholls were the same person.

In 1927, lyricist Edgar Leslie sailed for England, where he collaborated with Nicholls on several songs. Nicholls was thrilled, because he considered Leslie to be America's finest lyricist. Their collaboration led to "Among My Souvenirs," a gentle ballad in which a sorrowful lover transforms souvenirs into touchstones of his equally sorrowful memories. It was, without question, Nicholls' best song and one of Leslie's most durable ballads.

Another story says that Al Dubin, who collaborated with Harry Warren on such standards as "Forty-Second Street" and "Lullaby of Broadway" in the 1930s, actually wrote the lyrics to "Among My Souvenirs" because he needed some quick cash to get into a small-stakes poker game. He scrawled them on an envelope from an old gas bill and sold them to Leslie for $25. The story is believable because Dubin, like a lot of other songwriters, did this sort of thing at the start of his career, and more established songwriters were known to buy a lyric and pass it off as their own. When composer Fred Ahlert, Jr. asked Leslie, "It it true that Al Dubin wrote the lyric for 'Among My Souvenirs?'" Leslie exploded, "I paid for it!"[15]

**"Funny Face"** and **"The Babbitt and the Bromide"** [*Funny Face*] (1927)
Lyrics by Ira Gershwin (1896–1983), music by George Gershwin (1898–1937)

**FIGURE 8.4** Adele Astaire, Leslie Henson, and Fred Astaire in a scene from the Gershwins' *Funny Face*. Courtesy of Photofest.

The score to *Funny Face* gives a pretty good idea of what went into making a 1920s musical comedy work, especially when it started so badly. Originally called *Smarty*, the show nearly closed during its pre-Broadway run in Philadelphia. Richard Rodgers, who was in town for the tryouts for *A Connecticut Yankee*, wrote to his wife about the Gershwins' new show, "God will have to do miracles if it is to be fixed."[16] It starred Fred and Adele Astaire, and it may have looked great on paper, but the score was weak, the book was worse, and Robert Benchley, one of the librettists, had pulled out. But the other writers came up with a more upbeat book, the producers hired comedian Victor Moore to provide essential laughs, and George and Ira wrote new songs. The title song, about being loved despite being ordinary-looking, is cheerful rather than resigned, and "He Loves and She Loves" is happier than the fine song it replaced, "How Long Has This Been Going on?"

The other song that flipped the show was "The Babbitt and the Bromide." The idea for the lyric came to Ira when he heard Billy Kent, one of the show's comics, say, "Heigh ho, That's life!"[17] The bromide inspired Ira to write a lyric about two sophisticates who can think of nothing to say when they meet except to exchange banalities. Once he finished it, Fred Astaire took him aside to ask, "I know what a Babbitt is, but what's a bromide?" A few minutes later, producer Vincent Freedley also took him aside, "I know what a bromide is, but what's a Babbitt?"[18] Ira's immediate sources for the title language came from Sinclair Lewis' satiric novel, *Babbitt*, about George F. Babbitt, the title character who embodies the conformist mediocrity of life in a small Midwestern city, and from a 1906 essay by humorist Gelett Burgess, "Are You a Bromide? Or, The Sulphitic Theory Expounded and Exemplified According to the Most Recent Researches into the Psychology of Boredom." The lyric recreates the meaningless clichés exchanged by the B and the B when they meet by chance once in each of several decades.[19]

The song was the last written during the show's out-of-town run. On a Thursday night in Wilmington, the audience consisted "of no more than two hundred mostly pretty and young and pregnant DuPont matrons,"[20] but the number stopped the show. *Funny Face* opened on Broadway a week later to begin a successful run of 244 performances.

**"How Long Has This Been Going on?"** [*Rosalie*] (1927)
Lyrics by Ira Gershwin (1896–1983), music by George Gershwin (1898–1937)

A surprising number of love songs do better the second or third time around. One of the main problems George and Ira Gershwin were facing during the Philadelphia run of their new musical, *Funny Face*, was the lukewarm reception for "How Long Has This Been Going on?" George and Ira originally wrote it for Adele Astaire and Jack Buchanan when their characters kiss for the first time. The problem seemed to lie with Adele, who, despite her great charm, "lacked the depth to sustain a serious ballad."[21]

One day, Ira got a call about the song from Shapiro-Bernstein, a major music publisher. The company had bought a different song with the same title and was about to publish it: "Yours is getting you nowhere, so how about taking it out of the show." Ira found their suggestion gratuitous: "I told him it wasn't a one man decision . . . I told him I couldn't help him at that moment." But when *Funny Face* moved on to Atlantic City, everyone agreed to replace the song with "He Loves and She Loves." Ira said that it was "not as good a song but . . . one that managed to get over" with audiences.[22] Philip Furia says that they dropped the song because a new leading man, Alex Kearns, could not reach the high notes.[23] The second irony: Two months later, producer Florenz Ziegfeld heard the song and liked it, and added it to the Gershwins' score to *Rosalie*, which opened on Broadway three months after *Funny Face*. That gave Ira a new but easily solved problem: "There being no spot in the show for it as a duet, it became—with a few line changes—a solo." As for the other "How Long Has This Been Going on?" that prompted the initial phone call to Ira in Philadelphia, Ira said he never heard of it again and did not know if it had ever been published.[24]

### "Sometimes I'm Happy" [*Hit the Deck*] (1926)
Lyrics by Irving Caesar (1895–1996), music by Vincent Youmans (1898–1946)

Vincent Youmans and Irving Caesar agreed to collaborate with English lyricist Clifford Grey on a score for an American version of a five-year-old English musical, *A Night Out*. During the heyday of the musical comedy, with Kern, the Gershwins, and Rodgers and Hart writing hit scores that were made in America, the idea of adapting an English show for American audiences was a return to a time when transplanted English musicals had dominated Broadway.

Youmans and Caesar often worked in Youmans' apartment, but their few efforts at one particular new song went nowhere. They and Youmans' ex-mistress, opera star Grace Moore, were spending more time chatting and drinking than working. Then Caesar remembered "Come on and Pet Me," cut from *Mary Jane McKane*, a musical the two men had worked on in 1923. Caesar asked Youmans to play it but the composer insisted he couldn't remember the melody. Maybe that's because Oscar Hammerstein had originally written a second-rate lyric for it. Moore pitched in; she told Vincent that she'd never heard it and asked him to play it as a favor to her. With each bar of music, Caesar seemed to find new words. In a half-hour, the old lyric that began with a quadruple rhyme and the repetition characteristic of Hammerstein, "Come on and pet me, / Why don't you pet me? / Why don't you get me / To let you pet me?" had become the evocative "Sometimes I'm happy, / Sometimes I'm blue, / My disposition / Depends on you." Ironically, Hammerstein, the purveyor of romantic innocence, had written something sexy, and it took Caesar to add something romantic.

Songwriters frequently recycled material when a song was cut or a show flopped. *A Night Out* closed after its two-week tryout in New York; it never had an official Broadway opening. Two years later, though, Youmans newest show, *Hit the Deck*, opened to rave reviews, with particular critical praise for the rhythm ballad "Sometimes I'm Happy." Youmans had added it to the score he wrote with lyricists Clifford Grey and Leo Robin. Shortly after the show opened, Caesar returned to New York from a long European trip. As he strolled along Fifth Avenue, he met a friend, who congratulated him on the success of his song. Caesar couldn't believe what he was hearing, especially when Youmans had refused to give him and producer Harry Frazee permission to use it for a show called *Yes, Yes, Yvette*, an unsuccessful attempt to capitalize on the success of Youmans and Caesar's *No, No, Nanette*. Caesar tracked down Youmans to give him two choices: get a new lyric or pay a stiff weekly royalty for every company of the hit show. Youmans chose to pay.[25]

### "Strike Up the Band" [*Strike Up the Band*] (1927)
Lyrics by Ira Gershwin (1896–1983), music by George Gershwin (1898–1937)

*Strike Up the Band* was one of George and Ira Gershwin's few failures, their first since *A Dangerous Maid* in 1921. During the year of Babe Ruth's sixty home runs and Charles Lindbergh's flight across the Atlantic, its story was too cynical to capture the public's mood. George S. Kaufman's book was a satire of pro-war patriotism that followed the adventures of magnate Horace J. Fletcher, who tries to control the American cheese market by persuading the U.S. Government to declare war on Switzerland. The show closed in Philadelphia. Three years later, a new librettist, Morrie Ryskind, softened the political satire, made the love story more romantic, and gave the lovers a happy ending. The show ran for 191 performances, a respectable run in the 1920s. The Gershwins had initially agreed to write the score for Kaufman's satire before he had written the book. George was not political but Ira's views were Leftist, and he probably looked forward to working with Kaufman. Nonetheless, after the failure of the original version, the Gershwins replaced many of the original songs and revised the ones that remained. The first score resembled Gilbert and Sullivan; the new one was driven mainly by Swing and included such well-known songs as "I've Got a Crush on You" and "Soon."

Stories proliferate about how a melody or lyric comes to a songwriter who then needs no more than fifteen or thirty or sixty minutes to finish the song. But it wasn't always that easy. During preparations for the original *Strike Up the Band*, the Gershwins were staying at a hotel in Atlantic City. Late one night, Ira went up to his room but first looked to see if there was any light under George's door. It was dark. He had just started to read the Sunday papers when George walked in. Ira said, "I thought you were asleep." 'No,' George explained, "I've been lying in bed thinking, and I think I've got it." He was referring to the show's title song, what he had taken to calling "the march." The hotel had set up a piano in one of their rooms. George played the refrain almost exactly as it was in its finished form and asked Ira if he liked it, but Ira replied, "Are you sure you won't change your mind again?" When George said, "Yes, I'm pretty sure this time," Ira said, "That's good. Don't forget it."

George had already written four different marches. Ira said, "Each time I had said that's fine, just right, I'll write it up . . . and each time, George said, 'Not bad, but not yet. Don't worry, I'll remember it; but it's for an important spot, and maybe I'll get something better.'" The first four he wrote at the piano; this one he wrote lying in bed.[26]

The infectious march that George finally settled on took some of the sting out of Kaufman's sour view of patriotism. Like Kaufman's book, Ira's verse mocks jingoism, but in the refrain, he sets aside the satire for a rouser that feels as if he was writing for a marching band.

### "Doin' the New Low Down" [*Blackbirds of 1928*] (1928)
Lyrics by Dorothy Fields (1905–1974), music by Jimmy McHugh (1894–1969)

After Jimmy McHugh and Dorothy Fields wrote the songs for several of the exuberant all-black revues at Harlem's Cotton Club, producer Lew Leslie hired them to do the score for *Blackbirds of 1928*, a new all-black revue on Broadway. Three weeks before it opened, Leslie added dancer Bill "Bojangles" Robinson to the cast. At virtually the last minute, McHugh and Fields had to turn out a specialty number for him—his only appearance in the show. Robinson sang "Doin' the New Low Down" as he tap-danced up and down a flight of five steps. It was his Broadway debut, but he had first done his famous "stair dance" when he was a headliner at the Palace Theater in 1921. He knew about crowds up in Harlem or in a vaudeville house.

This was Broadway's "carriage trade," but it, too, responded to his infectious singing and dancing.

Even though a dance called the Low Down was entirely fictional, numerous songs used the term because it suggests something just disreputable and sexy enough to be a little bit dangerous. Its meanings range from mean and underhanded to something soulful, as in Eubie Blake and Noble Sissle's "Lowdown Blues" and George and Ira Gershwin's oxymoronic "Sweet and Lowdown." And, in the 1920s and 1930s, something black. It was often treated as if it was a dance done in Harlem. The titles written between 1926 and 1931, when the great black performers of the Harlem Renaissance were drawing whites uptown, include Fred Rose's "When Jenny Does Her Low Down Dance," Irving Berlin's "When the Folks High Up to the New Low Down," and Harry Revel and Mack Gordon's "Doin' the Uptown Lowdown."

Robinson eventually moved on to dancing in movies, most notably in *The Little Colonel*, where he repeated his "stair dance" with Shirley Temple, aged 7. Audiences were so taken by their performances together that they appeared together in three more Temple vehicles. Between 1935 and 1938, the deepest years of the Great Depression, she was the movies' biggest box-office draw. Robinson and Temple's joint performances marked the first time that a black and white danced together on the screen, although the black portrayed a servant and the white was a child.

Robinson eventually returned to Broadway, where he starred in *Hot Mikado* in 1939. At the end of the curtain call each night, he would grab one of the chorus girls onstage and lead her into a Lindy Hop. As he left the stage to the audience's ovation, he would lean out toward the house and say, "Thank you all. Thank you all. I've never had such a good time since I've been colored!"[27]

## "Hooray for Captain Spaulding" [*Animal Crackers*] (1928)
Lyrics by Bert Kalmar (1884–1947), music by Harry Ruby (1895–1974)

Harry Ruby said that he and lyricist Bert Kalmar had no set rule for working together, "but we have found it more profitable . . . to build songs together, instead of completing the lyric or the tune first . . . Sometimes we write simply to the lyric; sometimes to the tune. Sometimes we start with a line and build together to the finish."[28]

The song and dance that Groucho Marx did to Kalmar and Ruby's "Hooray for Captain Spaulding" in *Animal Crackers* demonstrate his inspired madness as much as anything he ever did. It is so interwoven with another song, "Hello, I Must Be Going," that they are often assumed to be two parts of the same song. They are certainly alike in their disruption of conventional reality. Spaulding, a famous (but probably fraudulent) African explorer, returns to the United States, where the wealthy Mrs. Rittenhouse throws a party for him. Every time he starts to talk about his accomplishments and to greet the guests improbably, "Hello, I must be going," they interrupt by singing the song's title line—"Hooray for Captain Spaulding / The African explorer"—until the celebration spins wildly out of control.

The original version of the song had to be edited to comply with Hayes Code directives. After Mrs. Rittenhouse sings, "He was the only white man to cover every acre," Groucho was to sing, "I think I'll try to make her." It also included a word from Yiddish, an uncommon habit in the 1920s. Groucho sings, "Did someone call me schnorrer?" A schnorrer is a sponger; thus the implication that Spaulding is a con artist.

The real Spaulding, whose name Groucho borrowed, might have been a cocaine dealer who had avoided arrest for a long time because he threatened to name names and destroy the reputations of his famous customers. A number of studio moguls paid him hush money to keep him quiet, although he was eventually arrested and sent to prison.

**"I'd Rather Be Blue"** [*My Man*] (1928)
Lyrics by Billy Rose (1899–1966), music by Fred Fisher (1875–1942)

Fred Fisher and Billy Rose were a couple of guys on the move and the make. Rose was eager to make something of himself and make a bundle in the process. Fisher was a shrewd eccentric. Although Rose wrote some good lyrics on his own, he was usually what can generously be called an "idea man." He would approach a lyricist with an idea or an especially evocative word, he would cajole and push and provoke the other lyricist to finish the resulting lyric, and then he'd claim a full share of the royalties as co-lyricist—and get it. He and Edward Eliscu collaborated on the lyric for "Without a Song" in 1929; he and Ira Gershwin were co-lyricists for "Cheerful Little Earful" in 1930. But he was the only lyricist for "I'd Rather Be Blue."

Fisher was one of the first songwriters to work in Hollywood. By the time he got there, he had already written "Come, Josephine in My Flying Machine (Up She Goes!)," "Peg o' My Heart," "Dardanella," "Chicago," and "Ireland Must Be Heaven for My Mother Came from There"—even though he was a Jewish immigrant from Germany. One day, when he and Irving Thalberg, MGM's head of production, passed in the hall, Thalberg asked who that was. A flack answered, "Fred Fisher, the symphony writer." Thalberg later called Fisher into his office to ask if he could write a symphony. Fisher replied, "Get me a pencil, boy. When you get me, you get Beethoven, Mozart, and Chopin." On the spot, Thalberg commissioned him to write a symphony. For the next four months, Fisher walked around the movie lot wearing a slouch hat and carrying a portfolio under his arm. When anyone spoke to him, he replied with a Weber and Fields accent. He worked the con so well that MGM paid him $500 a week for sixteen weeks and never asked where the music was.

"I'd Rather Be Blue," one of several songs Fisher and Rose wrote together, had nothing in it that resembled the blues—except for the word "blue" in the title and the lyric's torchy outlook set to a melody that was more uptempo than most torch songs; the singer would rather be "blue over you" than "happy with somebody new." The "oo" sounds Rose relies on can suggest a melancholy wail but also a jazzy bounce. The finished song has a little bit of both.

### "I've Got a Crush on You" [*Treasure Girl*] (1928)
Lyrics by Ira Gershwin (1896–1983), music by George Gershwin (1898–1937)

George Gershwin was always the bon vivant and lady's man. Friends said that he "reserved one unpublished little waltz for affairs of the heart." According to publisher and raconteur Bennett Cerf, he would tell the young lady of the moment, "You're the kind of girl that makes me feel like composing a song," and then he would lead her off to his suite. He would sit at the piano and say, "It will be dedicated to you," and then he would recompose the familiar song.[29]

The song was probably the childlike and deceptively innocent, "I've Got a Crush on You," which George and Ira eventually used in *Treasure Girl* (1928) and then, after that show flopped, again in the second version of *Strike Up the Band* (1930). It was the only time they used a song in two shows. When Ira thought back on the decision many years later, he expressed surprise because the brothers had so much new material on hand for the revised version. For many years, Ira thought of the song as uptempo and "exceedingly hot" until he heard singer Lee Wiley's recording. Her approach was "slow, sentimental, and ballady," and the more Ira listened, the more he liked it. Since then, it has been performed almost exclusively as a tender ballad.[30]

### "Nagasaki" (1928)
Lyrics by Mort Dixon (1892–1956), music by Harry Warren (1893–1981)

Through the late 1910s and most of the 1920s, an exotic strain balanced the slaphappy nonsense of such songs as "Barney Google" (1923) and "Does the Spearmint Lose Its Flavor on the Bedpost Over Night?" (1924). From "Under the Yellow Arabian Moon" (1915) to "Hindustan" (1918) to "Dardanella" (1920), music and words suggested the strangeness of their settings.

Another batch used the exoticism to create a setting for sexual humor,[31] as in "Please Don't Take My Harem Away" (1919) and Jerome Kern and P.G. Wodehouse's "Cleopatterer" (1917). The wackiest of all, Harry Warren and Mort Dixon's "Nagasaki," combined the two strains—the exotic and the nonsensical—in an unfathomable but irresistible lyric. The words have nothing to do with Nagasaki, Japan, or even Asia. They combine Dixon's sometimes-bawdy nonsense with what *Time Magazine's* Richard Corliss called "Warren's effervescent syncopation dragging folks onto the dance floor."[32] The songwriters create a world as long-lasting as a bubble, a place where men chew "tobaccy" and women "wicky-wacky-woo."

Publisher Jerome Remick had not wanted to publish it when Warren and Dubin first showed it to him because, Warren said, "He thought it had too many notes and was too complicated." Even so, it remained a jazz favorite for decades. Ironically, that meant that listeners almost never heard the lyrics and, Warren continued, "the whole idea of the song was Dixon's. He was one of those romantics who drooled about faraway places with strange-sounding names. I don't think he had any idea what Nagasaki looked like, which was probably all to the good."[33]

## "Sonny Boy" [*The Singing Fool*] (1928)
Lyrics by B.G. DeSylva (1895–1950) and Lew Brown (1893–1958), music by Ray Henderson (1896–1970)

*The Jazz Singer* was such a success for Warner Bros. and Al Jolson that the studio immediately began a second sound picture, *The Singing Fool,* starring their larger-than-life star. The movie's seven songs came from a number of different sources. Most, like "There's a Rainbow 'Round My Shoulder" and "The Spaniard That Blighted My Life," were already associated with Jolson. The score also included Ray Henderson, Lew Brown, and Buddy DeSylva's "It All Depends on You," which Jolie had sung on Broadway three years earlier. The new songs were "I'm Sitting on Top of the World" and "Little Fella," but Jolson disliked the juvenile ballad.

Henderson, Brown, and DeSylva were working on a new show in Atlantic City when they received a surprise phone call from Jolson late one night. He needed a new song as fast as they could write it. They tried to beg off, but he reminded them how much their careers owed to him. DeSylva asked him how old the child was supposed to be. Jolson answered, "He is about three, and standing at my knee." "Fine," said DeSylva, "I have two lines ready. 'Climb upon my knee, sonny boy; although you're only three, sonny boy.'"[34] The threesome stayed up all night to write "Sonny Boy" and then called Jolson back the next morning to sing it to him. He loved it. But the team had written it as a joke. Aware that Jolson loved mawkish ballads that would let him emote and roll his 'r's, they wrote the worst possible song they could, confident that he would go for it. They were right. Jolson's subsequent recording became the biggest-selling record of his career.

**"Sweet Lorraine"** (1928)
Lyrics by Mitchell Parish (1900–1993), music by Cliff Burwell (1898–1977)

Mitchell Parish earned a reputation for writing lyrics for songs that had been around as instrumentals, even though he wrote new songs, too. Aside from occasional collaborations with Hoagy Carmichael, he usually worked with such lesser-known composers as J. Fred Coots, Peter DeRose, Maceo Pinkard, and Cliff Burwell. When he wrote the lyric to Burwell's only important song, "Sweet Lorraine," Parish had recently escaped from the Mills Publishing Company to go out on his own. "Sweet Lorraine" was his first hit. He said his inspiration was a girl he had known on the Lower East Side named Sadie Moscovitz.

"Sweet Lorraine" became a standard because Nat "King" Cole needed to get out of a difficult situation. Ten years after Rudy Vallee's initial recording had had modest success, Cole was playing with his trio in a Los Angeles club. He was a 20-year-old jazz musician who had never sung in public, but a loud drunk insisted that he sing. Nat refused, but the customer persisted until the club owner told Cole he had to do it. The crowd responded so enthusiastically to Cole's performance of "Sweet Lorraine" that he began to sing—reluctantly at first, but more and more often. Later that same night, after Cole's vocal, the owner put a tinsel crown on his head and said, "I crown you Nat "King" Cole."[35]

**"You're the Cream in My Coffee"** [*Hold Everything*] (1928)
Lyrics by B.G. DeSylva (1895–1950) and Lew Brown (1893–1958), music by Ray Henderson (1896–1970)

In 1922, composer Ray Henderson and lyricist Lew Brown—one born in Buffalo, New York, the other in Odessa, Russia—met and began writing songs together. Brown had spent so much time in high school writing parodies of popular songs that his Latin teacher in the Bronx bluntly told him to "abandon Caesar and concentrate on song writing."[36] Buddy DeSylva, who had already written the words for "California, Here I Come," "If You Knew Susie," and "Somebody Loves Me," made it a threesome in 1925. Together, says John Lahr, they "charted the romantic exuberance of the 1920s."[37] They worked together off and on until 1931.

Henderson's son Horace said that Tin Pan Alley "was a huge, tangled plate of spaghetti with everybody having worked with everybody else . . . The publishers had little rooms with pianos in them and they would work in these rooms. It's like it was a big club. They could wander from one of these publisher's offices where they were writing a song to the next office and write another song with another writer at the same time."[38] Yet DeSylva, Brown, and Henderson worked together seamlessly for the most part, so "intimately and harmoniously that it was not always clear where the work of one ended and that of the other two began."[39] Some days, Henderson worked on the lyrics, and at other times Brown and De-Sylva fed musical ideas to Henderson. Although Brown supplied the gags and DeSylva the sophistication, David Ewen wrote that "they functioned with a unanimity of thought, feeling, and style, as if they were a single person."[40] One observer described them as "they pass scrawled pieces of paper back and forth. They talk over the chorus completely before they write it. Sometimes they use a rhyming dictionary and a thesaurus, but mainly they rely on what happens when they toss a piece of paper back and forth."[41]

When they began work on *Hold Everything* in 1928, they had already collaborated on songs for three editions of *George White's Scandals*, as well as a successful score for *Good News* ("Best Things in Life Are Free," "Varsity Drag," "Button Up Your Overcoat"). Their method of writing was set by then. Once they laid out a show in New York, off they went to Atlantic City, where they took three adjoining suites in the same hotel. Ray Henderson said that before they left:

> We might have a couple of titles, a couple of lines; we might even have a couple of tunes. And when we thought we had enough, we *always* went to Atlantic City to The Ritz. It got to be a habit. De-Sylva and Brown would go into the bedroom and knock out a lyric, and then they'd bring it into the living room with me, and we'd set it. We'd work on a song that we might have started in New York or conceived in Atlantic City. We'd stick at it. We'd stay in the suite all day. If we got enough done, we might go out for a little fresh air, and then come back and work some more. That was the same routine, day in and day out. And to show you how meticulous DeSylva was . . . We'd finally get the verse knocked out, and Buddy would write the song neatly on a piece of foolscap and fold it in half. He put it on the right side of the table near the piano. He got the biggest kick out of that. He'd go over and pick it up and feel it and say, "Well, we're coming along."[42]

Despite all the work—and a cast that included Bert Lahr—the show's out-of-town runs in Newark and Philadelphia flopped. The producers changed some cast members and, in Philadelphia, Brown and DeSylva handed them two new songs, including "You're the Cream in My Coffee." Producer Vincent Freedley said, "Those two songs plus the change in the cast made the difference. We went to Boston and practically sold out. And then we came to the Broadhurst Theatre and ran nearly two years."[43]

**"Broadway Melody"** [*Broadway Melody*] (1929)
Lyrics by Arthur Freed (1894–1973), music by Nacio Herb Brown (1896–1964)

When Nacio Herb Brown first gained a reputation as a songwriter on the West Coast, Irving T. Thalberg, the chief of production at MGM, suggested that he write for the movies. He declined because he was making a lot of money in real estate, but when the market crashed, he changed his mind.

**FIGURE 8.5**  Composer Nacio Herb Brown and lyricist Arthur Freed pose with Bing Crosby and Marion Davies. Courtesy of Photofest.

By then he had met a lyricist named Arthur Freed in a music store and they had begun to collaborate, usually sitting together at the piano with a title in mind, and then fitting melody and lyric to one another.

In 1929, when Thalberg decided to make the first MGM movie that would be "All Talking! All Singing! All Dancing!" he considered a number of song-writers, including Billy Rose and Fred Fisher. Even though Billy Rose hired a full orchestra to demonstrate his songs, in the end Thalberg hired Brown and Freed, who auditioned with Brown at the piano and Freed singing. When Freed admitted that he wasn't much a singer, Thalberg said, "I like your songs better."[44] He liked them so much that one of them—"Broadway Melody"—became the movie's title. Thalberg paid each man $250 but they eventually earned a half-million in royalties, primarily from the title number, "The Wedding of the Painted Doll," and "You Were Meant for Me."

Because the studios had little experience with book shows, most of the early musicals were revues and few used top stars in case they flopped. "We don't know whether the audience will accept a musical on film," Thalberg told his staff, "So we'll have to shoot it as fast and as cheaply as we can."[45] *Broadway Melody* was an exception, even though its story was weepy and cliché-ridden. It became the top grossing film in 1929, and won the Academy Award for Best Picture. It was so successful that it created a vogue for musicals over the next few years: "It set the entire attitude toward filmmaking in that year, and in 1929 alone no fewer than seventy-five musicals were released."[46]

Brown and Freed's career of writing for early movie musicals for nearly a decade was so successful that their songs became the score for arguably the greatest of all movie musicals, *Singin' in the Rain*. Yet, despite his hits, Brown never thought much of the melodies he wrote. He remained partial to classical music and thought more highly of his one serious composition, *American Bolero*, than of all his pop tunes—all those melodies on which his reputation so "largely and deservedly" rested.[47]

**"Love for Sale"** [*The New Yorkers*] (1930)
Lyrics and music by Cole Porter (1891–1964)

**"I Cover the Waterfront"** (1933)
Lyrics by Edward Heyman (1907–1981), music by John Green (1908–1989)

After a series of failures at the beginning of his career, Cole Porter fled to France early in the 1920s to lick his wounds by living high on the financial and sexual hog. He wrote a few songs for French revues but returned near the end of the decade to try Broadway again, this time with great success. Of his first four shows, three had scores whose songs reflected his experience as an irreverent expatriate who loved France but wanted to come home: *Paris, Fifty Million Frenchmen,* and *The New Yorkers.* Reviewer Richard Watts, Jr., writing in the *New York Herald Tribune,* observed tongue-in-cheek that "Mr. Cole Porter continued his studies in natural history."[48] Among the songs were "You Don't Know Paree," "The Boyfriend Back Home," "I'm a Gigolo," "Take Me Back to Manhattan," and "I Happen To Like New York."

The major exception to Porter's genial approach was "Love for Sale," a torchy ballad from *The New Yorkers* about a city's seamier side. First written by Porter as he walked the streets of London one night, it was originally performed by Kathryn Crawford as a streetwalker, who sang it in front of a smart nightspot with a nearby street sign reading "Madison Avenue." The song drew strong criticism and was eventually banned from the airwaves. Percy Hammond's original review in the *New York Herald Tribune* called Crawford "a lily of the gutters," but added, "When and if we get censorship, I will give odds it will frown upon such an honest thing."[49] Despite the outcry, not everyone disapproved. Peggy Hopkins Joyce suggested that black singer Elisabeth Welch include it in her nightclub act. One night, Irving Berlin, actor Monty Woolley, and songwriter-producer E. Ray Goetz came to hear Welch and recommended her to Porter. To ease the strong disapproval of the song among all-white audiences, Welch replaced Crawford a month after the opening and the setting was moved to the Cotton Club in Harlem. In the 1930s, it was less controversial for a prostitute to be black. Porter responded to the controversy, "I can't understand it. You can write a novel about a harlot, paint a picture of a harlot, but you can't write a song about a harlot."[50] David Grafton wrote that it was Porter's "all-time favorite."[51]

Despite the frivolity of the rest of the score, "Love for Sale" remains a forceful portrait more than eighty years later. It is a straightforward statement of a point of view, in which the young woman feels neither self-pity nor regret. She refers to herself as "unsoiled" but also "spoiled." She speaks of the "appetizing young love" she offers, but also admits, "I've been through the mill of love." If anything in the song is euphemistic, it is the use of the word "love."

Just as melancholy as "Love for Sale," and just as typical of the shadowy ballads of the Great Depression, "I Cover the Waterfront" was initially the title of a 1932 best-selling novel by Max Miller. It then lent its name to both a movie and a song a year later. Because the song became a hit so quickly despite its darkness, the movie was changed at the last minute to make room for it. The sheet music incorrectly claimed that the song was "inspired by the United Artist Picture of the same name." According to Poynter Institute

Senior Scholar Roy Peter Clark, Miller's book is "a series of loosely connected nonfiction yarns, a vivid account of oceanside life . . . fishermen, con
artists, publicists, celebrities, smugglers, and spies, a world that Miller ex-
plores with an improbable combination of sentimentality and cynicism."[52]
Heyman's much simpler lyric is about lost love, a lonely wail sung along a
waterfront "in the still and the chill of the night."

### "Mood Indigo" (1930)
Lyrics by Irving Mills (1894–1985), music by Duke Ellington
(1899–1974) and Barney Bigard (1906–1980)

The story of "Mood Indigo" says something about the business side of
popular music in the 1920s and continuing into the 1930s, as well as the relationship between white publishers and black songwriters and performers.
From such giants as Duke Ellington and Thomas "Fats" Waller, to such lesser-
known figures as Shelton Brooks and Maceo Pinkard, many gifted black
composers and lyricists were turning out songs despite the constraints they
faced. It is also revealing about Ellington's unusual approach to composing.

By 1927, Irving Mills was a "powerbroker in the business,"[53] a hugely successful publisher and promoter of songwriters and their songs. When he offered to become Ellington's manager in exchange for approximately half the
composer-bandleader's income, Ellington leaped at the opportunity. As a result, the Ellington Orchestra began to appear at the Cotton Club in Harlem
and his recordings were soon being distributed and publicized nationally. By
1929, he had already appeared in motion pictures. Some have accused Mills
of exploiting a black man's talent, but without Mills, Ellington would never
have become as famous or as wealthy so quickly. Many of the other great
bandleaders of the 1920s and 1930s, black and white alike, died penniless.

When Ellington first wrote "Mood Indigo," he called it "Dreamy Blues."
As with many of his early compositions, he built it from bits and pieces of
older jazz numbers. He remembered that it was the first piece he wrote to
be played on the radio. "The next day," he recalled, "wads of mail came in
raving about the new tune, so Irving Mills put a lyric on it."[54] Although the
publisher sometimes wrote words for songs, he would also assign the job
to someone on his staff but give himself a cut-in. Lyricist Mitchell Parish,
who worked for Mills Music, said many years later that he wrote the "Mood
Indigo" lyric.

As for the music, jazz saxophonist Barney Bigard had apparently learned
the main theme in New Orleans from his teacher Lorenzo Tio, who called
it a "Mexican Blues." Then what was Bigard's role and what was Ellington's?
One commentator suggests that classical music would have called "Mood

Indigo" an example of "Variations on a Theme."[55] Trumpeter Clark Terry said years later:

> This thing that Barney Bigard used to play, [Ellington] made a tune of that, "Mood Indigo," that Barney used to warm up [his instrument] . . . Ellington took these things and made tunes out of them. A lot of guys get the wrong idea. They say, "Well, he stole from these guys." But these guys, that's as far as it would have ever gotten . . . It was a great facility [on Ellington's part] to make something out of what would possibly have been nothing.[56]

When the musicians arrived at the studio at 4 a.m. after an eight-hour session, no one knew exactly what they would record. Sitting shirtless but, as always, wearing his porkpie hat, Ellington doodled at the piano, looking for something promising. One story says that the screech of a bad microphone interrupted him. He began to use the jarring sound in his head and to improvise from it. The musicians began to improvise on their own until he quieted them and began the rehearsal. Before they finished, together they had formed a new, distinctive composition. "Out of the chaos," Maurice Zolotow wrote, "there has miraculously developed an intricate, smoothly blended unity . . . Suddenly, the piece arrives at the finish—and it is a rounded performance, with its beginning, middle and conclusion,"[57] and Ellington is ready to record "Mood Indigo."[58]

Billy Strayhorn also explained Ellington's method: "His first, last and only formal instruction for me was embodied in one word: observe . . . Ellington plays the piano, but his real instrument is his band. Each member of his band is to him a distinctive tone color and set of emotions, which he mixes with others equally distinctive to produce a third thing, which I like to call the Ellington Effect."[59]

Ellington told an interviewer:

> When we're all working together, a guy may have an idea and he plays it on his horn. Another guy may add to it and make something out of it. Someone may play a riff and ask, "How do you like this?" The trumpets may try something together and say, "Listen to this." There may be a difference of opinion on what kind of mute to use. Someone may advocate extending a note or cutting it off. The sax section may want to put an additional smear on it.[60]

Ellington said that the mood of "Mood Indigo" is simple: "Just a story about a little boy and girl. They are about eight and the girl loves the boy. They never speak of it, of course, but she just likes the way he wears his hat. Every day he comes to her house at a certain time and she sits in her window and waits. Then one day he doesn't come. 'Mood Indigo' just tells how she feels."[61]

## "Rockin' Chair" (1930)
Lyrics and music by Hoagy Carmichael (1899–1981)

One of Hoagy Carmichael's favorite songs portrays an old black lady in the rural South rocking on her porch. Reflecting on her lifetime while she waits for Judgment Day, she asks someone to fetch her a gin. Once Carmichael had finished it, the great jazz singer Mildred Bailey made it her signature song. So completely was she associated with it that she soon became known as "The Rockin' Chair Lady." Bailey was a large woman, and one version of the song's origin says that Carmichael got the idea for it when the two of them were talking one day. Bailey was sitting in a child's chair and, when she stood up, the chair came with her. She said, "This old rockin' chair's got me, I guess."[62]

It's a funny line, but a more believable story tells about Granny Campbell, an old black woman who lived on the outskirts of Bloomington, Indiana, Carmichael's hometown, where she made high quality corn-mash liquor. There was also another Bloomington character who made home-brewed beer. Carmichael said that it didn't matter which story was true, because his lyric picks up where his 1927 song, "Washboard Blues," leaves off. Both have a sense of quiet resignation, both are set along a river, and both portray an infirm old woman waiting to die. As Richard Sudhalter explains, "Like 'Washboard,' it is a song about the realities of life far from city sophistication or Broadway artifice."[63] Both songs also reflect one of Carmichael's persistent attitudes: "Change always upsets me. My music is often about things lost to me. Simple things like rocking chairs, the weather of my childhood, moods and memories, and landmarks."[64]

"Rockin' Chair" began as a song called "When Baby Sleeps," and evolved into its final form as Carmichael revised and rewrote over a period of sixteen months. At first, he said, it "didn't seem terribly important." He wrote the lyric with his mother in the room "and tried it out on her first. She, too, was not overly impressed."[65]

## "Something to Remember You By" [*Three's a Crowd*] (1930)
Lyrics by Howard Dietz (1896–1983), music by Arthur Schwartz (1900–1984)

Between 1929 and 1935, Arthur Schwartz and Howard Dietz wrote the scores for six Broadway revues. Although both men eventually wrote book shows for Broadway and songs for the movies, and Dietz became a major publicist for MGM, they owed their reputations to the flourishing of stylish, satiric revues in the 1930s. Unlike the lavish revues produced by Florenz Ziegfeld and Earl Carroll earlier in the century, they were done on a relative shoestring. Instead of extravagance, they relied on sophistication and irreverence. They were, in Thomas S. Hischak's words, "a more cerebral kind of variety entertainment."[66] Even so, Schwartz was known for the lush romanticism of his music and Dietz for lyrics that bordered on the purple. James Gavin described them as "breathless, soaring displays of bygone Broadway and Hollywood glamour. They sound like outpourings of the most romantic heart."[67] Yet Dietz believed that Schwartz also was "a great judge of lyrics. He had an editorial mind and an ear for the fitness of sound."[68]

Schwartz in turn insisted that Dietz was a very funny man. For example, when he was a young journalism student, the future lyricist entered a contest to see who could invent the shortest and most provocative newspaper headline. Dietz won in a walk with, "Pope elopes."[69] Schwartz was impressed by how fast his partner could write. Schwartz once dared him to set a lyric to a melody he would play. He chose a well-known tango named "Jalousie." In ten seconds, Dietz had it: "Cyd Charisse, Get off that mantelpiece. You are a shock there. We need a clock there."[70] Even so, Dietz thought of himself as a movie executive: "Anything else is just a sideline. Some people crochet afghans for an outside interest. I write lyrics."[71]

In 1924, when Schwartz was still an unknown, he decided that he wanted to work with the already established Dietz. Figuring he had nothing to lose, he wrote, telephoned, and wired: "I'd love to work with you . . . I think you are the only man in town to be compared to Larry Hart, and from me that's quite a tribute, because I know almost every line Larry has written."[72] Dietz declined the offer but, in 1928, a theater director asked if Schwartz would be willing to collaborate with Dietz for what would become the songs for their first revue together, *The Little Show*. Working together convinced both of them that they made a good match.

While he and Dietz were working on the score for their third revue, *Three's a Crowd*, Schwartz played a melody that he had written in England with the English lyricist Desmond Carter. Because he didn't think much of the song they had called "I Have No Words," Schwartz insisted on playing it fast. Dietz tried to get him to slow down but Schwartz insisted, "You can't make a ballad out of that. It's a tinkly chorus number." Fortunately, Howard was just as stubborn as Arthur. "No," he shot back, "It's just right. Play it again as slowly as you possibly can, you'll see." By the time Schwartz got what Dietz called "the tinkly rhythm" out of his system and Dietz had added a lyric, they had completed "Something to Remember You By" for Libby Holman to sing to a sailor played by a bandleader named Fred MacMurray.[73]

**"Would You Like to Take a Walk"** [*Sweet and Low*] (1930)
Lyrics by Billy Rose (1899–1966) and Mort Dixon (1892–1956), music
by Harry Warren (1893–1981)

**"Cheerful Little Earful"** (1930) [*Sweet and Low*]
Lyrics by Billy Rose (1899–1966) and Ira Gershwin (1896–1983), music
by Harry Warren (1893–1981)

**"I Found a Million Dollar Baby (In a Five and Ten Cent Store)"**
(1931) [*Crazy Quilt*]
Lyrics by Billy Rose (1899–1966) and Mort Dixon (1892–1956), music
by Harry Warren (1893–1981)

Lyricists Al Dubin and Mort Dixon were good friends and drinking
buddies who frequented saloons and whorehouses at any and all hours.
As a result they were almost always broke. Billy Rose spotted them during the mid-1920s because they were turning out hits. However, they did
their best work when they were drunk. According to composer Abner Silver, Rose "kept them in liquor, gave them a few bucks." When they would

**FIGURE 8.6** Billy Rose. Courtesy of Photofest.

arrive at his office, the drinks and cigarettes were on the table. They would talk and tell jokes until Rose thought they were ready. He would say something like, "I've got three titles. Which shall we work on?" As they worked, he watched the way they constructed each line, how they used rhyme, and how they struggled to find the catchy phrase for the start of a chorus. He learned the craft by watching two lyricists who had already done it. As soon as they finished a song, Rose was out the door on the way to a publisher.[74]

Often, the composer for their lyrics was Harry Warren. He described how the three-sided songwriting collaboration worked, "Billy was a catalyst, and very ambitious. He had some good ideas of his own, but he bought ideas from other writers and possibly appropriated others. He had a compulsion to be rich and famous. That might not be admirable in some people, but you need that kind in show business. They get things going when the rest of us can't." Warren described the way each man worked with his collaborators. Of Rose he said:

> Billy could be cruel, but he was a great feeder. He'd sit with the boys and say, "Now come on, you can do better than that." He'd ask for another line, or he'd come up with a clause himself. He'd make a thrust at a phrase; but he stimulated the real lyricists to produce. Somehow, a song would get done, but he couldn't easily work without another lyricist.[75]

With Dixon, Warren saw a similarity to Johnny Mercer. Dixon, he said, would:

> sit in a room and just look at you; never said a word, never batted an eye. Mort would just sit at the piano, just sit, and sit and sit. You'd say to yourself, what the hell is he doing. When I started to write with Dixon, I told the studio I didn't want to write with him because he didn't talk. The studio said, "He'll talk when he's ready."[76]

Warren never made his peace with Hollywood. He missed New York and he hated the way the studios treated their songwriters. In 1930, he went back to work in his old Remick office in Manhattan until Warner Bros. beckoned him West again to write a new musical called *42nd Street*. When he arrived in New York, he learned that Rose had been doing very well for himself. He was in a position to invite Warren to collaborate on some songs for *Sweet and Low*, a new Broadway revue he was producing. Rose had initially called the show, *Corned Beef and Roses*. Everybody told him it was a lousy title but it took a long time to convince him to change it.

When *Sweet and Low* opened, it had three songs by Warren and Rose, including "Would You Like to Take a Walk?" co-written with Dixon, and "Cheerful Little Earful," co-written with Ira Gershwin. When composer Burton Lane asked him why Rose's name appeared on the sheet music, Ira answered, "Well, he came in one day and he made a suggestion about changing a line . . . I didn't feel like fighting."[77]

When Rose asked Warren to work with him again on his next project, a revue called *Billy Rose's Crazy Quilt*, he joined right in. The score had four of their songs, including its most important number, "I Found a Million Dollar Baby," which they had written in 1926. Tony Thomas rightly calls it "a uniquely American song, expressing a style and sentiment that could not have originated elsewhere."[78] Rose had written a lyric with this title some time earlier and had given it to a different composer, but he had not liked the result. Now he gave the lyric to Dixon to rewrite and asked Warren to write a new melody. The idea behind the song was Barbara Hutton, the Woolworth's heiress whose troubled life included seven marriages. What Rose did was typical. Songwriters rarely discarded anything. They filed unused songs waiting for the right time to revise, reinvent, or simply try again.

# Chapter 9
## 1931–1935

**"Between the Devil and the Deep Blue Sea"** and **"I Love a Parade"**
[*Rhyth-mania*] (1931)
Lyrics by Ted Koehler (1894–1973), music by Harold Arlen (1905–1986)

Each of the four scores that Harold Arlen and Ted Koehler wrote for Cotton Club revues between 1931 and 1934 produced hit songs: "Between the Devil and the Deep Blue Sea" and "I Love a Parade" in 1931; "I Gotta Right to Sing the Blues," and "I've Got the World on a String" in 1932; "Stormy Weather" and "Happy As the Day Is Long" in 1933; and "As Long As I Live" and "Ill Wind" in 1934. The two men also snuck off for a while in 1933 to write their first songs for the movies. With Prohibition over, the Depression deeper than ever, and the Harlem Renaissance fading, the Cotton Club closed its doors in February 1936.

Five years earlier, when *Rhyth-mania*, Arlen and Koehler's first Cotton Club show, opened, Cab Calloway and Aida Ward were the stars. Arlen remembered, "Those opening nights were like no other opening nights in the theater, because even though it was a night club, you'd get everyone there, from the mayor to anybody who was who. It was like a Broadway opening today."[1]

Like most songwriters, Arlen sometimes completed a song very quickly. Usually, he sat at the piano when he composed, but he also wrote songs that came in unusual though matter-of-fact ways. At a party one night, he and Koehler wrote "Stormy Weather" with Cab Calloway in mind. In no more than thirty minutes, each completed his half and, relieved to have another song over and done with, they went looking for a deli to get a sandwich. Because Calloway did not appear in the next Cotton Club revue, it fell to Ethel Waters to introduce the song.

Although its title makes "Between the Devil" sound more reflective and perhaps more troubled than "I Love a Parade," both songs are lively, even vibrant. The character, initially portrayed by Calloway, can't make up his mind about the woman he loves because her behavior is inconsistent, yet he can't tear himself away. Although he feels torn, she keeps "running back for more."

Koehler said that Arlen liked to walk much more than he did, but used to talk the lyricist into going along. Koehler remembered that one day Arlen insisted that they walk from East 86th Street to the Mills Music office on West 46th to "schmooze with the boys." Koehler was appalled, but he went. As they walked, he said, "Why didn't you join the army if you like to walk so much?" On another occasion, they went walking on a very cold afternoon: "To pep me up [Arlen] started to hum an ad-lib march. I guess I started to fall into step and got warmed up." By the end of the walk, they had written "I Love a Parade."[2] It became so popular that thereafter the Cotton Club's revues were called *Parades*.

## "Dream a Little Dream of Me" (1931)
Lyrics by Gus Kahn (1886–1941), music by Fabian Andre (1910–1960) and Wilbur Schwandt (1904–1998)

Many people remember Mama Cass Elliott's 1968 recording of "Dream a Little Dream of Me," but few know that the song goes back to 1931, or that Gus Kahn wrote the words. Kahn was a major lyricist who deserves to be mentioned in the same breath as Sammy Cahn, Howard Dietz, Mack Gordon, and maybe even E.Y. Harburg. Cass and Kahn—the singer and the songwriter—never knew one another; she was born less than a month before he died. Kahn wrote these lyrics because the composers—Fabian Andre and Wilbur Schwandt—somehow got their melody to him soon after they finished it. He had already collaborated with George Gershwin, Walter Donaldson, Vincent Youmans, and Richard A. Whiting, and now with these two men who would never write another hit even though they had successful careers, mainly as arrangers of Latin-American music for dance bands. The two composers had met when they played in a band touring the Midwest and apparently wrote the song during an intermission in Milwaukee or the village of Paw Paw, Michigan.

On vacation in Mexico City in 1950, Andre met a family named Gilliam and their 6-year-old daughter, Michelle. When Michelle grew up, she married John Phillips and became one of the two women in The Mamas and the Papas. She remembered that "Fabian was just a fabulous rake"[3] and a drunk. During a rehearsal in 1968, she learned that he had died by falling down an elevator shaft. As she talked about him to Philips, Elliot, and Denny Doherty, they began to play around with the old song he had written with Schwandt and Kahn.

Kahn was a charter member of the school of lyricists whose spiritual father was Irving Berlin, who once referred to simplicity as "the first and last rule of writing songs."[4] His easy mastery of the tricks of the lyricist's trade keeps the song bouncing along effortlessly. They appear in the first line with alliteration ("stars shining") and assonance ("shining bright"), continue in a combination of the two in line three ("birds singing," "sycamore"), and add internal rhyme to the mix in the second chorus ("nighty-night" and "hold me tight" along with the subtler "tell me you'll" and "alone and blue"). To balance the verbal tricks, Kahn keeps repeating the central word, "dream," that marks off the steps of the song's pleading invitation. Donald Kahn said of his father, "He always tried to keep his lyrics simple. He also said that young men and women don't know how to say 'I Love You' to each other, so we say it for them in 32 bars."[5]

## "It Don't Mean a Thing (If It Ain't Got That Swing)" (1931)
Lyrics by Irving Mills (1894–1985), music by Duke Ellington (1899–1974)

Irving Mills was aggressive, relentless, savvy, and successful. A combination manager, publisher, and lyricist, he parlayed Duke Ellington's talents into success for both Ellington and himself. Ellington thought in terms of musical compositions rather than songs. Mills was often the one who saw a new piece's potential as a hit and either added words himself or assigned one of his publishing firm's lyricists to add them—and then cut himself in for a portion of the royalties.

Ellington wrote "It Don't Mean a Thing" during intermissions when he was appearing at the Lincoln Tavern in Chicago in August 1931. In addition to its lasting popularity, it is important partly because it is probably the first song to use the word "swing" in its title. Written a few years before what became known as the Swing Era, its lyric features of lot of "ooh-wahs" to simulate an orchestra's brassy sound. Mills may have picked up the idea for the title from a favorite saying of trumpeter James "Bubber" Miley, who was with the band at the Cotton Club in the 1920s. Another trumpeter, Cootie Williams, insisted that he often used the expression. A third possibility, and perhaps the most likely, is that Mills, himself, used it spontaneously when he once complained to Ellington that customers were not dancing to his music.

## "Just One More Chance" [*Monkey Business*] (1931)
Lyrics by Sam Coslow (1902–1982), music by Arthur Johnston (1898–1954)

Although crooning was the dominant style of popular singing by the late 1920s, it recast itself in the early 1930s as something more insistent, from something friendly to something smoldering. Songwriters who had been writing for the high, light voices of Gene Austin, Nick Lucas, and Whispering Jack Smith began to write for the deeper, more masculine baritones of Bing Crosby and Russ Columbo. The second batch of crooners could sing with great intensity (as in Crosby's recording of "I Surrender, Dear"), but more often their style was quiet yet ardent, restrained yet intimate, warm yet seductive. Audiences—especially female audiences listening to the radio—found crooning irresistible. During those same years, songwriters also wrote several songs about crooning: "I'm Crooning a Tune About June" by J. Fred Coots and Benny Davis (1929), "Crosby, Columbo, and Vallee" by Joe Burke and Al Dubin (1931), "Learn to Croon" by Arthur Johnston and Sam Coslow (1933), and "My Kid's a Crooner" by Marion Harris and Reg Montgomery (1935).

Soon after sound pictures arrived, Sam Coslow sold his music publishing business to become a songwriter at Paramount, where he met composer Arthur Johnston. During the early years of Bing Crosby's film career, they wrote several of the hits he introduced in movies. In the midst of collaborating on more than a dozen movies, Johnston asked Coslow, "Do you ever squeeze in just a plain, ordinary pop song? Something that's not in a picture?" He asked because he had come up with a title he liked, "Just One More Chance." He said he also had a four-note musical phrase for it but didn't know where to go next. Almost immediately, the next four notes "popped" into Coslow's head. He said, "I could finish this with you like rolling off a log, but what do we do with a song and no picture—just hold it and put it in the trunk?" Their problem was that most bands on the radio were playing only songs that had appeared in movies. Johnston said they needed to entice Crosby to record it because "it sounds perfect for him." They finished the song that afternoon, tailoring it to what Coslow called "Crosby's croony ballad style."[6] It became the crooner's first solo hit.

### "When the Moon Comes Over the Mountain" (1931)
Lyrics and music by Harry Woods (1896–1970), Howard Johnson (1887–1941), and Kate Smith (1907–1986)

Decades after her first radio show began in 1931, Kate Smith described how terrified she had been before it went on the air. It was to be a simple program, she explained: "just my voice and a five piece band." Once she and Collins had chosen four of the five songs they needed to fill the time, he said, "Well, we need one more and it ought to be a sort of theme song—you know, a bit at the beginning and a bit at the end." He looked over the sheet music they had chosen—"By the River Ste. Marie," "I Surrender, Dear," "Please Don't Talk About Me When I'm Gone," and "Dream a Little Dream of Me"—and said, "I don't like any of these for it. It ought to be something new, something we can identify with you." In a story that feels too pat to be quite believable, Smith then goes through her own sheet music and pulls out a song. She sings it and, when he says he likes it, she tells him, "You know, I helped to write that song . . . I've just carried it around with me, hoping to use it one day."[7]

She wrote in one of her autobiographies, "We decided to rescue a little song on which I had collaborated some years before, and which had been lying on the shelf because nobody seemed to care about it." Then her writing turned coy:

> Maybe some of you will remember that song . . . I've sung many selections over the air in the past seven or eight years, but no song ever calls up such tender memories for me as that one. Every time I sing it, my mind goes back to those first days when I was getting my start in radio. It seems as much a part of me, almost, as my name.[8]

How odd then that she never mentions the two men who did most of the writing. Composer Harry Woods and lyricist Howard Johnson did the bulk of the work, while Smith did just enough to justify a cut-in to collect royalties.

## "Where the Blue of the Night (Meets the Gold of the Day)" (1931)
Lyrics by Roy Turk (1892–1934) and Bing Crosby (1903–1977), music by Fred E. Ahlert (1892–1953)

Sometimes it takes a while to get a song exactly right, even if you're as adept as Fred Ahlert and Roy Turk, two underrated songwriters. They had already collaborated on "I'll Get By," "Mean to Me," and "Walkin' My Baby Back Home" before they came up with a song they first called "When the Gold of the Day (Meets the Blue of the Night)," then "When the Blue of the Night (Meets the Gold of the Day)," and then got it right before they published it. In something as small as a song, a change in a single word can matter—as it does in Ahlert's subdued waltz. The shift from "When" to "Where" as the first word in the refrain is a change from time to place, anticipation to mystery, a question you can answer to something suggestive and uncertain. Despite the lyric's sometimes purple language, it suited Bing Crosby's youthful but romantic baritone, plangent and seductive.

**FIGURE 9.1**    Jack Benny (center) checks out composer Fred Ahlert (at piano) and lyricist Roy Turk, while composer Fred Fisher watches from behind. Courtesy of Photofest.

When the newly popular Crosby needed a theme song for his radio program, he chose "Where the Blue of the Night" because he may have worked on the lyric with Turk. Turk gave Bing a cut-in as co-lyricist because he chose the song as his theme. Crosby's friend Harry Barris was bitterly disappointed when Crosby did not choose "I Surrender, Dear," Barris' big ballad that became one of Crosby's first major recordings. Crosby and Barris had been two of the three members of The Rhythm Boys, the singing group within Paul Whiteman's Orchestra that first brought Crosby to public notice.

Crosby was to introduce his new theme on the radio on August 31, 1931, but the announcer told his listeners that Bing would not appear that night. He ducked out a second time and finally sang "Where the Blue of the Night" a few nights later. Among the rumors to explain his absence—he had laryngitis, he was hung-over, he had stage fright, he had nodes on his vocal cords. Crosby explained that he had been singing at several clubs and his voice was exhausted. He told one interviewer, "The pipes just gave out, and I couldn't produce hardly a sound. Just hoarse. Tired."⁹ Crosby sang the song throughout his career and recorded it once every decade, but he wasn't all that impressed even though he'd had a hand in writing it: "I really think I'd trade anything I've ever done if I could have written just one hit song."¹⁰

## "Don't Blame Me" (1932)
Lyrics by Dorothy Fields (1905–1974), music by Jimmy McHugh (1894–1969)

Jimmy McHugh and Dorothy Fields first collaborated in 1928. By 1932, they had a string of successful songs to their credit. As McHugh said of his success, "When I was an office boy in Boston, I was a hep kid with a beat. I'm still a hep kid with a beat."¹¹ They also had their method of working together down pat. Fields usually started a song by giving Jimmy a title, even though he always had notebooks cluttered with scraps of melody he had jotted down. She described what happened as she waited for him to form a tune: "You listen to him make noises on the piano for a couple of days until he gives you a piece of paper scrawled over with markings which look as though they had been made by a fly fresh from the ink well."¹²

Then it was her turn—she would take the scrawl home where she sat with a yellow legal pad looking, as she said, for inspiration: "You figure out that this is meant to be music, and learn to play it. Then you hum over the melody and the title and start writing the chorus. When you have that done, you start on the verse, being careful to avoid polysyllabic words and to use a theme dear to the hearts of all, ie: love." Fields, who wrote the greatest of all sarcastic love songs, "A Fine Romance," was equally capable of sarcasm about her own work: "When this is done, you take your beautiful, beautiful lyrics to Mr. McHugh, and then he arranges the melody to correspond more exactly with the words." Finally, the collaborators ran through the song together, McHugh embellishing the melody and she singing the words in what she referred to as her "cigarette contralto."¹³

Even though McHugh had a reputation as a great song plugger, "Don't Blame Me," arguably the best torch song that he and Fields wrote, had a slow start. He couldn't get it recorded but managed to interpolate it in the Chicago run of a successful English revue called *Clowns in Clover*. It was also in the movie *Dinner at Eight* the next year, and that's what brought it to the public's attention. Years later, cabaret singer Mary Cleere Haran said that only one lyricist got right what the hormones were about. She was talking about Dorothy Fields and went on to say that "Don't Blame Me" and "I Can't Give You Anything but Love" are "flat-out assertions of desire."¹⁴ The song's persona is "forthright and self-assured, making the lyric just about as sexy as it can be." Fields' lyric ends suggestively, "And blame all your charms /

That melt in my arms," thereby meeting the mandate of nearly every music publisher, "Get 'em in bed by the last eight."[15]

**"Eadie Was a Lady"** [*Take a Chance*] (1932)
Lyrics by B.G. DeSylva (1895–1950), music by Nacio Herb Brown (1896–1964) and Richard A. Whiting (1891–1938)

*Humpty Dumpty* was supposed to be a Broadway revue about putting on a Broadway revue, but it was such a mess that even its out-of-town run in Pittsburgh closed after a few performances. Lyricist Buddy DeSylva, also one of the show's producers, rallied the cast: "Oh, hell, let's take a chance."[16] To see if it would help, DeSylva changed the show's title to *Take a Chance*. He was right—it succeeded, mainly because it had some fine songs, including "Eadie Was a Lady," and Ethel Merman and Jack Haley starred.

Even so, composer Richard A. Whiting, burdened with a bad heart that would lead to his death in 1938, wanted out. The pressure of trying to fix a seriously flawed show wore on him, and he missed his family back in California. "I've never gone through a thing like that," he recalled afterwards, "where everything was falling apart." When DeSylva and Merman insisted that he remain with the show, he refused to change his mind and suggested that they replace him with Vincent Youmans: "I've given you three or four good songs. Let me go." Youmans composed five additional songs as cast members were fired and scenes rewritten. Meanwhile, when Merman let the writers know that none of the songs suited her brassy style, her accompanist, Roger Edens, reminded them that "Buddy DeSylva had an idea for a number . . . but it's been shelved." Overnight, he expanded and arranged Whiting, DeSylva, and Brown's "Eadie Was a Lady" to make the song funnier and more biting than before.[17] The extensive rewriting and revising was enough to turn *Take a Chance* from a turkey into a hit. Soon audiences were calling it "the 'Eadie Was a Lady' show."

It was said that blonde bombshell Jean Harlow used to play Merman's recording to get in the mood for her sex-tiger movie roles. Yet Merman's character as a tough bruised romantic is what comes through as she sings about two old hookers, Maud and Mabel, who remember their pal Eadie, whose "past was shady" but who "had class with a capital K."

**"Lover"** [*Love Me Tonight*] (1932)
Lyrics by Lorenz Hart (1895–1943), music by Richard Rodgers (1902–1979)

Gerald Mast calls *Love Me Tonight* "one of the best original scores ever written for films."[18] With such songs as "Lover," "Isn't It Romantic," and "Mimi," it is not hard to figure out why. The plot is a fairy tale about a princess (Jeanette

MacDonald) who falls in love with a tailor (Maurice Chevalier). Rodgers explained in his autobiography that the song was never reprised because:

> Jeanette sang it in an outdoors scene while riding in a horse-drawn cart. Still yearning for an unknown lover, our lonely princess sings the romantic lyric with sincerity, except that certain words and phrases are directed to her very frisky horse: "Lover, when you find me / Will you blind me with your glow? / Make me cast behind me all my—WHOA!"[19]

Yet when Rodgers played his new song for Darryl F. Zanuck, the studio head told him to "make it better."[20]

Although MacDonald's version altered what Rodgers and Hart had written, it did not seem to bother them, despite their reputation for disapproving of changes in their songs. They even wrote a song about their concern—"I Like to Recognize the Tune," for *Too Many Girls*, a Broadway success in 1939. Rodgers wrote that he and Hart thought it was hard enough for a song to catch on "without being subjected to all kinds of interpretive manhandling." Early in his career, David Raksin was given one night to complete some arrangements for a Rodgers and Hart score. At one point, he discovered two chords that appeared to be in the wrong order. With the approval of the head orchestrator, he reversed them so they could easily be changed back, depending on Rodgers' reaction. When the composer heard them the next morning, Raksin said later, he "came charging up the aisle. I tried to tell him I had written it so it could easily be reversed, but he didn't want to hear any of that and so I finally lost my temper. Rodgers said, 'What have you done to my music?' so I replied coolly, 'What music?'"[21]

Because Rodgers wrote a lilting melody to which Hart set breathlessly impassioned words, Peggy Lee's 1952 recording of "Lover" tested the composer's insistence that his melodies be performed exactly as he wrote them. Despite Rodgers' complaints about what she did to his "little waltz," Lee believed that "he must have liked it" because he gave a talk "in which he made the point that without different interpretations, a song won't last as long as it otherwise might. And he gave me permission to do any of his songs."[22] But when he was asked about the recording, he said, "I don't know why Peggy picked on me when she could have fucked up 'Silent Night.'"[23]

### "Soft Lights and Sweet Music" and "Let's Have Another Cup of Coffee" [*Face the Music*] (1932)
Lyrics and music by Irving Berlin (1888–1989)

America was so deep into the Great Depression by 1932 that giddy songs about rouged knees and raccoon coats already felt like museum pieces.

Although they didn't always feel quite natural, love songs after the Crash could sing about landing a job, organizing a union, and running for office. The Gershwins nominated John P. Wintergreen and Alexander Throttlebottom as the standard bearers at the top of the "Love Party" in *Of Thee I Sing*. A few years later, Harold Rome wrote "It's Better with the Union Man" and "One Big Union for Two," so *Pins and Needles* could nudge the Great White Way to the left without leaving romance behind, and Irving Berlin and librettist Moss Hart had a satiric show called *Face the Music* on the boards.

Although Hart's sassy but thin plot is a send-up of crooked cops, pols, and plutocrats, the score's two best songs range from the romantic to the cheery. The love ballad has a rich yet restrained melody, with a lyric that alludes to the "moan of a cello," "velvet lights," and "sweet music" without losing its conversational directness. That unlikely combination keeps the song connected to the simplicity that Berlin told an interviewer was "the first and last rule of writing songs."[24]

"Let's Have Another Cup of Coffee" could not be a more different kind of song. In the 1930s, when the rich lost their bundles, they might have eaten lunch in a cafeteria like the Automat. Stick a coin in the slot, flip the glass door open, and remove your egg salad on white. These places were like a penny arcade for grown-ups with nothing but a few dimes in their pockets. In fact, Berlin liked going to Automats, and his oldest daughter, Mary Ellin Barrett, speculates that, like everyone else, he "enjoyed putting in his nickel and taking out his piece of pie." She added that it was one of the first of her father's songs she knew, because he used to sing it to her.[25]

Early in *Face the Music*, the young man and woman who will be the show's love interest meet one another. She is a young performer, he is the son of a banker, and there's talk of a possible show if a producer can find the money. The producer leaves as the boy and girl agree to work on the project together. They slide naturally into a song that comes too early in the show for a love duet but whose tone fits the wisenheimer 1930s. Berlin focuses on the young people in a song that is both an upbeat Depression anthem and an ironic take on upbeat Depression anthems. There may be "a rainbow in the sky," but one had better be cautious when "Mr. Herbert Hoover says that now's the time to buy." The tone of Berlin's song suits the time (and thus the audience's sensibility), as well as the circumstances in which the two characters find themselves.

**"The Carioca"** [*Flying Down to Rio*] (1933)
Lyrics by Edward Eliscu (1902–1998) and Gus Kahn (1886–1941), music by Vincent Youmans (1898–1946)

*Flying Down to Rio* was Vincent Youmans' last score. The composer of "I Want to Be Happy," "Tea for Two," "Great Day," and "More Than You Know" was washed up at the age of 35. Soon after he finished the songs, he tried to negotiate a contract with RKO to write more movie scores but learned that he had tuberculosis. He did not die until 1946, but he never again had a song in a movie or show. He was not an easy man, but he deserved better than he got, and his songs were an essential part of the outlook and mood of the 1920s and 1930s.

Youmans wrote the songs for *Rio* sitting by the swimming pool of his hotel. Typically, contracts with songwriters required them to write a specific number of songs but, given the cavalier way in which the studios treated them, most composers and lyricists were smart enough to submit twice the number called for. Youmans, untried in the ways of Hollywood, and stubborn to boot, turned in the four songs he had signed to write—and not a note more. The studio was horrified but had no choice: it had to pay Youmans to write extra songs. For "Music Makes Me," he collected $2,500, thereby nearly doubling his pay for the movie. The score's other songs included the title number and "Orchids in the Moonlight."

*Flying Down to Rio* matters mainly because it is the first movie in which Fred Astaire and Ginger Rogers dance together. Astaire said, "I was under the impression that we weren't doing anything particularly outstanding in 'The Carioca.' I had thrown in a few solos, too, in the limited time given me, but I never suspected that they would register so well. However, everything clicked."[26] After the movie's success and the appeal of the fourteen-minute dance scene that evolved from Fred and Ginger's brief dance, the attempt to turn "The Carioca" into a popular new Latin Dance Craze fizzled because it was too hard for the average person.

### "Did You Ever See a Dream Walking?" [*Sitting Pretty*] (1933) and "With My Eyes Wide Open, I'm Dreaming" [*Shoot the Works*] (1934)
Lyrics by Mack Gordon (1904–1959), music by Harry Revel (1905–1958)

Harry Revel and Mack Gordon wrote the songs for the movie *Sitting Pretty*, about two New York songwriters who head for Hollywood to write for the movies. The story was not autobiographical, even though Revel and Gordon were a couple of New York songwriters who had moved to Hollywood to write for the movies just a few years earlier. One of the differences: in the movie, the two songwriters travel west with a pretty blonde who works in the lunch wagon at the corner. The actress was 22-year-old Ginger Rogers.

Revel and Gordon got the job because Lou Diamond, who ran the business side of Paramount Pictures, heard their songs when he was in New York and recommended them to the studio. As Diamond was dictating his letter, producer Charles Rogers back in California realized that he needed songs for a movie he was about to start shooting. Rogers asked Jack Haley, one of the movie's stars, and bandleader Abe Lyman for a recommendation. They supposedly yelled out at the same time, "See if you can get Gordon and Revel!" A few days later, Diamond's letter arrived, urging Rogers to sign the two men to a contract for the one picture. The first song they wrote, "Did You Ever See a Dream Walking," became a hit and was instrumental in making the picture a success.[27] Revel and Gordon wrote together at Paramount for the next six years. The following year, for a movie called *Shoot the Works*, they wrote another dream song with an unusual title, "With My Eyes Wide Open, I'm Dreaming." Gordon wrote several dream lyrics that start out with a hyperbolically surreal approach that changed in the course of the song as the dream of love becomes attainable. In addition to "Did You Ever See a Dream Walking" and "With My Eyes Wide Open, I'm Dreaming," he and Revel wrote such songs as "I've Got a Date with a Dream," "I Never Knew Heaven Could Speak," and "I'm Walking with Moonbeams, Talking to the Stars."

Gordon lacked the wit of such lyricists as Dorothy Fields and Frank Loesser, but he had their ear for ordinary American talk. "Did You Ever See a Dream Walking" sets up a series of questions and answers that culminates in a happy ending. A dramatic monologue, its questions suggest an observer rather than a participant. The lyric becomes personal only in the answer. To the slightly surreal questions Gordon poses about seeing a dream walking or hearing a dream talking, he replies, "Well, I did," to suggest a kind of self-satisfied one-up-manship.

### "Who's Afraid of the Big Bad Wolf?" [*Three Little Pigs*] (1933)
Lyrics and music by Frank Churchill (1901–1942), additional lyrics by Ann Ronell (1908–1993)

You never predict what song will become the next hit. In the case of "Who's Afraid of the Big Bad Wolf?" what sounds like a children's song became one of the best-known popular anthems of the Great Depression. After composer Carl Stalling left the Disney Studios in the early 1930s, Walt Disney hired Frank Churchill to write music for the animated shorts called Silly Symphonies. When Churchill wrote "Big Bad Wolf" for the Disney version of the *Three Little Pigs* (with additional lyrics by Ann Ronell), the song became the company's first hit song, unlikely as that may seem. Churchill wrote it to express the carefree personalities of two of the pigs as they tease their hard-working brother. In the end, a song that celebrated the underdog pigs' victory over the wolf touched a responsive chord during the Depression.

"Big Bad Wolf" was so successful that songs became an important part of Disney's moviemaking. The problem was that the company had no songs at its disposal, and using a copyrighted song meant paying royalties at a time when Disney was stretched financially. Occasionally, Walt would ask a songwriter to compose something that suggested a popular song without plagiarizing it. For a baseball scene in a short involving a tortoise and a hare, for instance, Churchill wrote some music entitled "Battin' the Balls Around" that resembles Albert Von Tilzer and Jack Norworth's "Take Me Out to the Ball Game."[28]

**"Cocktails for Two"** [*Murder at the Vanities*] (1934)
Lyrics by Sam Coslow (1902–1982), music by Arthur Johnston
(1898–1954)

Prohibition took effect on January 19, 1919. For a few years before and after, songs about drinking were common. At first, they were comic laments that commiserated with those who looked ahead to January 19th with dread, and then they became comic celebrations of those who got around the law successfully—from "How Are You Going to Wet Your Whistle (When the Whole Darn Town Goes Dry)" to "I Married the Bootlegger's Daughter." By the middle of the decade, Prohibition had become a fact of life in America; in 1925, there were 30,000 speakeasies in New York City alone. Drinking soon became a much less important subject, although it continued to appear in passing in such songs as Ray Henderson, Lew Brown, and B.G. DeSylva's "Button Up Your Overcoat" ("Keep away from bootleg hooch / When you're on a spree") and Joe Meyer, Irving Caesar, and Roger Wolfe Kahn's "Crazy Rhythm" ("What's the use of Prohibition? / You produce the same condition").

When the repeal of Prohibition neared, lyricist Sam Coslow realized that drinking songs would quickly become a thing of the past, but he also realized that repeal would provide a short-lived opening. He told his collaborator, composer Arthur Johnston, that they should beat everyone to the punch by writing the first of the new drinking songs. They would use the number they called "Cocktails for Two" in Paramount's big new musical, *Murder at the Vanities*.[29] The relevance to the end of Prohibition stops just short of being explicit in the verse: "Oh what delight to be given the right / To be carefree and gay once again."

Coslow and Johnston played the song for Earl Carroll, the Broadway producer whose naughty annual revue, *Earl Carroll's Vanities*, provided the setting and the selling point for the movie. He turned them down flat, but they had previously played it for Carl Brisson, the movie's leading man. Paramount (erroneously) considered him the new Maurice Chevalier. Brisson loved the song and went to the Studio's top brass. One of them said, "I think Carroll's out of his mind. The song stays in."[30] Although Brisson sang it with Kitty Carlisle as part of an extravagant production number, almost nobody knows any version besides Spike Jones's, complete with klaxons, raspberries, and hiccups.

### "The Continental" [*The Gay Divorcee*] (1934)
Lyrics by Herb Magidson (1906–1986), music by Con Conrad (1891–1938)

Composer Con Conrad got to Hollywood early; he was one of the first songwriters to write for the movies. He had already written the music for "Margie" in 1920, "Ma, He's Making Eyes at Me" in 1921, and "Barney Google" in 1923. He got work in Hollywood but wrote few hits. Because he thought he might do better with Herb Magidson, his lyricist friend from New York, he urged him to join him in 1934, so they could land a movie contract as a team. RKO producer Mark Sandrich was interested but told them he had a specific assignment in mind. "All we want you to do," he said sarcastically, "is to invent a new dance that will sweep the country—like Vincent Youmans did last year with 'The Carioca'." The Oscars had just added a new Best Song category, so Sandrich was, in effect, telling them to win the first Oscar—and do it in a week.

With no guarantee in hand, they went to work but made no progress. It may not have helped that they were writing a new song for a movie adaptation of Cole Porter's Broadway hit *Gay Divorce*, to be retitled *The Gay Divorcee*, apparently on the premise that it was okay for a divorcee to enjoy herself but not for a divorce to be enjoyable. The studio dropped all the Porter songs except "Night and Day," probably to avoid paying royalties for previously published songs and to allow their publicity machine to promote the new songs in the hope of making them into lucrative hits. But the decision put Conrad and Magidson in the position of replacing Cole Porter.

The new collaborators struggled with one particular song until Conrad and his wife left Los Angeles to drive to San Francisco. As they drove, Conrad tried to work out a melody in his head, but only when he began to think about dancers did he begin to find his way. He kept whistling until he finished the song. As soon as he reached San Francisco, he called Magidson and whistled the tune to him. By the time he returned to Hollywood, Magidson had finished the lyric.

The song did win the first Academy Award for Best Song, perhaps because it provided the music for a seventeen-minute production number. Dozens of couples whirled around a huge dance floor with Fred Astaire and Ginger Rogers at the center of it. A typical 1930s number, it was more a case of overkill than anything else—grandiose rather than grand. To Conrad's blaring Latin beat, Magidson's lyric invited dancers to try something daring but subtle, nonchalant but intimate, "an invitation to moonlight and romance." The bodies are swaying, the lovers are gliding, and lips are whispering. For every allusion to something romantic there is an erotic counterpart. There's hardly a lyrical base Magidson doesn't touch, even though he was constrained by the new Hollywood Production Code and the Hayes Office's strict enforcement.

**"Fun to Be Fooled"** [*Life Begins at 8:40*] (1934)
Lyrics by E.Y. Harburg (1896–1981) and Ira Gershwin (1896–1983),
music by Harold Arlen (1905–1986)

Yip Harburg thought that writing the hit revue *Life Begins at 8:40* was "joyful," but Harold Arlen called it "a pretty hard job." Since 1930, the composer had been writing the all-black revues at the Cotton Club with lyricist Ted Koehler, but now he had a chance to break out on his own by writing the music for a Broadway revue. Harburg and Ira Gershwin collaborated on the lyrics, but Arlen said, "I did the music alone. And to be asked to do it, and to take it on, took guts. So, I proved I could come out of the Cotton Club."[31] Like his best lyricists, he detested the familiar. Harburg said that Arlen "threw everything out. He was frightened of everything that sounded like something else . . . He will labor on one phrase, sometimes for weeks, exploring every musical possibility with the patience of a chess champion."[32]

Harburg and Gershwin had become friends in high school when they realized they both loved light verse. One day, Ira took Yip (whose birth name was Isidore Hochberg) home so he could hear recordings of the lyrics of W.S. Gilbert. His nickname was a shortened form of Yipsel, from YPSL, the acronym for the Young People's Socialist League, to which he belonged. As a socialist opposed to World War I, he spent three years in Uruguay, but returned to the United States to marry and open an appliance business. When the company went broke soon after the Crash, Harburg took Ira's advice that he write lyrics instead. He liked to say that he "gave up the dream of business and went into the business of dreams."[33] That kind of wordplay was pure Yip. He used a figure of speech the Greeks called *chiasmus* throughout his career, most notably in the song title, "When I'm Not Near the Girl I Love, I Love the Girl I'm Near." He once published a book of light verse that included the lines:

To let a fool kiss you is stupid,
To let a kiss fool you is worse.

Of his collaboration with Ira, he said, "It was like doing a crossword puzzle—one making up one line one day, the other making up the next line the next day. Ira and I have a similar sense of humor. We shy away from the sentimental."[34]

Harburg discovered the catchphrase that became the song's title in a cigarette advertisement. Under a headline, "It's fun to be fooled, but it's more fun to know," the ad exposed the secrets of elaborate magic tricks. By 1934, the expression was familiar enough for Harburg and Gershwin to use it in the score's most direct love ballad, though, even there, they wrote with a sense of whimsy. Harburg commented, "I was saying life is all being fooled. We are all being fooled by it, but while it's happening it's a lot of fun. I think it's a lot of fun. I think it's a lovely excursion and I'm glad I got a ticket for this short cruise, and that's all."[35]

The score also includes "Let's Take a Walk Around the Block," "What Can You Say in a Love Song," and "You're a Builder-Upper." Arlen called Harburg and Gershwin "two interesting guys," because they were always "using the language, twisting it, bending it."[36] Especially in "Builder-Upper," Arlen's edgy, snappish music matches their words; it's constantly hopping, skipping, and jumping, as if nothing is settled. The method in the lyric is to add suffixes to keep the words busy in a song that picks you up and then slaps you down, that says you make "me feel like I'm Clark Gable" and in the next breath says "you make me feel I'm something from the zoo."

**"I'll String Along with You"** [*Twenty Million Sweethearts*] (1934)
Lyrics by Al Dubin (1891–1945), music by Harry Warren (1893–1981)

During the twenty-five years that composer Harry Warren worked at Warner Bros., 20th Century Fox, MGM, and Paramount, he never stopped missing New York City and only rarely took a break from writing for the movies. He was always busy, at least partly because he was one of the few songwriters who did not have a trunk, "the file or box where songwriters keep the good songs they did not get to use . . . Dubin and I were so busy that we didn't have time to write anything other than the song we had to do for the pictures—and almost every song was used."[37] He routinely complained that the studios "usually ask for the song that you haven't got. Say we're going to start shooting Monday, and the scene is the one that Dick Powell or Fred Astaire comes in the room and they have this conversation and he sings the ballad. Well, that's the one we haven't got written yet. Never fails."[38] He had a healthy dislike for the attitude of studios and producers toward songs. Watching the filming of one of his songs:

**FIGURE 9.2**    Composer Harry Warren (seated) and lyricist Al Dubin created the musical sound of the Great Depression. Courtesy of Photofest.

I mentioned to the producer, Hal B. Wallis, that they were doing the lyrics wrong. He said, "What's the difference? Who knows the right lyrics?" . . . Little did I realize that this would be typical of the attitude of movie producers toward music and that I would run into this sort of thing time and time again in the years to come.[39]

When he was writing at Warner Bros., he once told Jack Warner that it usually took him three weeks to write a song. Warner exploded, "Three weeks! Three weeks to write one lousy song!" "No," Warren explained, "Three weeks to write one good song!"[40]

Warren said that his songs came to him "subconsciously" because he thought about writing them all the time:

I often wondered what would happen on the next picture if I didn't get anything but it always came. And I think that's it, the secret of subconsciously thinking about what you want to write or putting yourself in the mood or sometimes it's the artist himself or a woman, or a band. You fit 'em like a tailor . . . I've always written music the way I felt it. I write for the public because I feel like the public, the way they would write if they could. You don't need to know anything about music to understand what I write.[41]

"I'll String Along with You" begins with a catchphrase that lyricist Al Dubin latched onto. Warren said, "I think he heard it in a movie, and once he had the first couple of lines of the lyric, I was able to do the whole melody. That was an easy one." What wasn't easy was shooting it for the movie, *Twenty Thousand Sweethearts*. Dick Powell's character is singing it on the radio but he becomes so hoarse that Ginger Rogers' character has to take over. Rogers had trouble hitting her cue and, Warren remembered, "after twenty-four takes I couldn't stand it any more and left."[42]

### "Miss Otis Regrets" [*Hi Diddle Diddle*] (1934)
Lyrics and music by Cole Porter (1891–1964)

Cole Porter said to Bricktop in her club one night, "Brick, I've written a song for you."[43] It was "Miss Otis Regrets," one of the few Porter songs not intended for a show or movie. Songs that tell melodramatic stories were not common in the 1930s; maybe that's why Porter supposedly wrote it for the red-headed, cigar-smoking singer and café owner whose real name was Ada Smith, but whose Parisian joint was one of the essential watering holes for the expatriate *cognoscenti* in the 1920s. Such an audience would have relished the tale of a right sort of mannerly young woman who loved not wisely but too well and who, as a result, came to a bad end. Her servant greets a visitor to explain why "Miss Otis regrets she's unable to lunch today." Seduced and then abandoned, Miss Otis had been arrested, convicted, imprisoned, and finally lynched after hunting down her lover and shooting him. On one hand, she had perfect manners; on the other, she gunned down a no-good man. Only a few years after the emergence of such blues giants as Gertrude "Ma" Rainey and Bessie Smith, and such great torch singers as Helen Morgan and Ruth Etting, the servant's exquisitely formal telling of the tale gives the torch-like story a wry Porteresque twist.

One version of the song's beginnings says that Porter bragged to his good friend, actor Monty Woolley, that he could write a song about anything. When Woolley came up with the title, Porter went to work. Five years later, in 1939, Porter couldn't remember how the idea came to him, except that he'd been leafing through the Social Register and had come upon the name of Otis. He recalled that since he wasn't in the mood to write about elevators, he turned to a song about Miss Otis. This explanation sounds like an especially contrived version of the unlikely stories that bad movies used for years to portray the writing of songs. "You haven't heard anything," Porter added, "until you've heard Monty Woolley sing it."[44]

A variant on the story says that Porter was at a party thrown by a Yale classmate when he heard a cowboy song on the radio that he thought sounded so dreadful he improvised a comic lament on the living room piano. As he imitated the weepy tune, "Miss Otis" began to take shape. Woolley immediately jumped in to help by donning a morning coat and imitating a butler as he sang along. Woolley performed "Miss Otis" at parties for years afterwards.

Of the many stories that surround the song, the bawdiest concerns a tryst between Porter and a waiter who worked in a popular restaurant nearby. Everyone called the young man "Dixie" because he was from the south of Italy. One day, Porter invited him to his apartment on the pretense that he needed help installing a new wine cellar. He kissed Dixie on the cheek and asked what that would cost. Dixie said, "Five hundred dollars." Porter rubbed his leg. Dixie said, "A thousand dollars." At that point, Porter unzipped the man's fly, took out his penis, and asked what would be the full price for the use of that. Dixie answered, "Two thousand dollars." Porter wrote a check for the full amount, handed it to him, and said, "Miss Otis regrets she's unable to lunch today. Now get out."[45]

## "On the Good Ship Lollipop" [*Bright Eyes*] (1934)
Lyrics by Sidney Clare (1892–1972), music by Richard A. Whiting (1891–1938)

Both Richard A. Whiting and Jule Styne had Shirley Temple stories to tell, but at least Whiting didn't have to be in the same room with her. Temple introduced "On the Good Ship Lollipop" in the 1934 movie *Bright Eyes* after Whiting finally came up with an idea for the song. He was struggling at the piano when his daughter Margaret arrived, holding a big lollipop that threatened to get everything in the room sticky. Margaret told the story in her memoir many years later: "He said, 'Get away from me, where did you get that lollip. . .' He stopped in mid-sentence. 'That's it!' He rushed to the phone, called Sidney Clare, and announced, 'I've got the title!' "[46]

Styne worked with Temple at 20th Century Fox in 1937, before he emerged as an important composer of movie songs. Hired as a vocal coach, he was assigned to "America's darling" and was given the bungalow across from hers. He knew it was hers because he could hear her frequent temper tantrums. Styne said, "Listen, I was afraid of that kid." His job was to polish her voice and write her arrangements, but he hated walking across the street because "you'd never know what mood she'd be in when you got there."

Fox once sent Styne to the Temple home to rehearse Shirley, even though no one from the studio went near the place. The morning always started with badminton in the hot sun. Finally, when Styne said that it was time to start rehearsing, Shirley's father told his daughter, "Honey, you have to stop playing now." She screamed at him, "Look, I earn all the money in this family. Don't tell me what to do." Styne waited inside until she was ready to rehearse.[47]

### "Stompin' at the Savoy" (1934)
Lyrics by Andy Razaf (1895–1973), music by Benny Goodman (1909–1986), Edgar Sampson (1907–1973), and Chick Webb (1905–1939)

The first hit for Chick Webb's band was almost immediately forgotten even though Harry Warren and Mort Dixon called it, "I Can't Dance (I Got Ants in My Pants)," but the band's second hit became a Swing classic. When the twenty-five-year-old alto saxophonist Edgar Sampson joined Webb, he

**FIGURE 9.3**    Major lyricist Andy Razaf. Courtesy of Photofest.

began to do more composing and arranging than before. Eventually, he wrote a riff as the basis for an instrumental, and called it "Stompin' at the Savoy" because Webb's was the Savoy Ballroom's house band.

Located between 140th and 141st Street on Lenox Avenue in Harlem, the Savoy began to sponsor competitions between bands in 1927, a year after it opened. After Webb and his band at the time, The Harlem Stompers, won the first competition, they continued to outswing the bands led by Count Basie, Fletcher Henderson, and Benny Goodman. The Ballroom was one of the few truly integrated places where blacks and whites were free to dance together.

Webb and Goodman both cut themselves in for a share in the song's royalties when they agreed to record Sampson's riff. It was an all-too-typical practice through the 1920s and 1930s. But it was still an instrumental. Andy Razaf had earned a reputation for putting novelty lyrics to Swing instrumentals that caught the spirit of the original—everything from soaring brass to crashing cymbals. His words enhanced whatever it was that made the piece swing. For "Stompin' at the Savoy," he used call-and-response, borrowed from the practice of the black churches, dating back into slavery, when the preacher lined out the hymns orally because it was against the law for slaves to learn to read and write. He also found more recent allusions in such songs from the Dance Craze as "Alexander's Ragtime Band" and "Darktown Strutters' Ball," but he found his most immediate inspiration from the sign outside the Ballroom that read "Savoy—The Home of Happy Feet." He repeated the name "Savoy" throughout the lyric as a kind of verbal rim shot. "Savoy" was the "home of sweet romance" where dancers—and lovers—could stomp away the night.

### "What a Diff'rence a Day Makes" (1934)
Spanish lyrics and music by Maria Grever, English lyrics by Stanley Adams (1907–1994)

Tin Pan Alley was incredibly competitive. Songwriters were always looking for a new angle to try to find the elusive formula that produces a hit. Yet songwriters also insisted that they were helpful to one another—to young men and women trying to break in, to a composer who needed a lyric, or a lyricist trying to find just the right word. As Stanley Adams put it, "Composers and lyricists thrive on helping one another . . . We always sought advice, input, or suggestions from anyone. The altruism is a fantastic thing. The pride we take in everybody in the business and the pleasure we take in someone else's success—you don't see much of this in industry or the business world."[48]

When Adams was in his mid-20s, he was trying to put English words to a tune by Mexican composer Maria Grever. It had what he called "a tango tempo." Adams' new lyric traced the way in which one life can change in the twenty-four hours when you fall in love. He said of the English version he called "What a Diff'rence a Day Makes": "I wrote it exactly to the feeling of the tune. A blues touch, then happy, a contrast of delirious joy, then sorrow. Actually it was the sequence of how one felt during the course of a day." Although his words had no similarity to Grever's original Spanish lyric, Adams also talked about lyric writing, "Some of it's inspiration, but most of it is good, hard work, and some sweat. A writer digs down and tries to interpret what the composer is trying to say."[49]

## "About a Quarter to Nine" [*Go Into Your Dance*] (1935)
Lyrics by Al Dubin (1891–1945), music by Harry Warren (1893–1981)

After Al Jolson introduced Harry Warren and Al Dubin's "About a Quarter to Nine" in the movie *Go Into Your Dance*, he added it to the list of songs he performed for the rest of his career. Warren and Dubin, like most songwriters, knew how to design a song to suit the voice, singing style, and public personality of a star—and Jolson was a distinctive performer. "It wasn't a problem to write for him," Warren said. "He always liked what we did and never offered any criticism, but he was dying to get his name on the sheet music. He asked if he could write a verse or two. He'd done this with other songwriters, but Dubin and I were determined his name wouldn't be on ours. It was great to have Jolson do your songs—he really knows how to put them over—but he liked people to think they were all his."[50] After they had finished writing the entire score for *Go Into Your Dance*, Warren and Dubin drove down to Palm Springs to hear Jolson introduce "About a Quarter to Nine" at a benefit. The audience liked the songs, and on the way back to Los Angeles, with Warren and Dubin in the back seat, Jolson's driver turned to the performer: "Gee, Al, those were great songs. Who wrote 'em?" Jolson stretched out his arms and answered, "Who *wrote* 'em?"—as if to suggest he had.[51]

Warren and Dubin labored under great pressure at Warner Bros. because they were usually working on more than one movie at a time. At one point, they were writing *Go Into Your Dance* while they were also writing *Gold Diggers of 1935* ("Lullaby of Broadway"). With the producers of both movies demanding songs, Jack Warner invited the songwriters to lunch. "That was a bad sign," Warren explained. "Whenever the bosses call you in and tell you you're 'one of the family' and how they appreciate your work, you can guess they're in trouble." One day, when the lights went up after they had watched a work print of scenes from *Go Into Your Dance*, they discovered that Warner was in the booth. He was surprised to see them. "He told us we had been laid off," but no one had bothered to tell them. "We didn't quite feel we were one of the family," Warren said.[52]

The studio shot *Go Into Your Dance* as quickly as it could so it could pair Jolson with Ruby Keeler, its top female star and Jolson's wife at the time. She happened to be between pictures. Jolson's career was on the skids, and Ruby was the studio's insurance policy. Complicating the matter was Jolson's massive ego and Al Dubin's prickly sensitivity. Warren described him as looking:

> like the foreman of a road gang, but he was really a very sensitive man, very well read and a great lyricist. He took offense easily . . . I remember telling him the lyrics he had written for "A Quarter to Nine" didn't fit the melody. He was incensed and stormed out, but he came back a couple of days later with a new set.[53]

### "It's Easy to Remember" [*Mississippi*] (1935)
Lyrics by Lorenz Hart (1895–1943), music by Richard Rodgers (1902–1979)

Even songwriters as firmly established as Rodgers and Hart had trouble finding work on Broadway during the Great Depression, and soon returned to writing for the movies. They hated the way the studios treated them, but like so many of the New York songwriters, they liked the combination of warm sunshine and absurdly high pay. Paramount had assigned them to write three songs—two for Bing Crosby to croon—in *Mississippi*, a 1935 melodrama with songs in which a disgraced Bing must restore his name to claim his beloved Southern belle. Once Dick and Larry finished their work, they returned to New York, but the studio asked them to write one more song for Bing. Although it took them only a day to complete "It's Easy to Remember," they stalled while they figured out the best way to present it. They had learned the hard way that a producer's first reaction was usually crucial to a song's future, and they had also learned Harry Warren's movie truism, "Out here in Hollywood, a songwriter was the lowest form of animal life."[54] Hart said, "If we send the manuscript, somebody out there will play it and sing it the way we don't want it." Rodgers added, "If we send a record, they'll play it in some executive's office with the doors banging and the telephones ringing and nobody paying any attention."[55] Eventually, they walked over to Paramount's offices on Broadway. With Rodgers at the piano and a hired radio singer to perform it, they made a short sound film and sent it to Hollywood, special delivery.

The next year, 1936, Rodgers learned that Pandro Berman, the head of RKO, wanted a new story for Fred Astaire. He concocted a brief synopsis in a couple of hours—a story of a hoofer mixed up with the Russian ballet. Although Berman liked it, the rest of the RKO brass nixed the idea. This wasn't the Fred of white tie and tails that they felt audiences wanted to see. "It didn't matter much," Rodgers recalled, "since we had invested so little time." A few weeks later, he and Hart encountered theatrical producer Lee Shubert, who was struggling to find a vehicle for Ray Bolger, a young performer with the potential for stardom. Rodgers wrote, "Standing on the corner of Forty-fifth Street and Broadway we told Mr. Shubert . . . the story of the hoofer and the Russian Ballet. They liked it, and this time there were no associates to be consulted. We concluded the deal [for *On Your Toes*] standing there on the corner."[56]

When someone once tried to talk to the ever-practical Rodgers about the sources of his inspiration, he replied:

> That's a bad word for what happens to me when I write. What I do is not as fancy as some people may think. It is simply using the medium to express emotion . . . Mine happens to be notes . . . Your job is to translate this situation and these people into musical terms. This isn't a question of sitting on top of a hill and waiting for inspiration to strike. It's work. People have said, "You're a genius." I say, "No, it's my job."[57]

That same sense of detachment darkened considerably when Rodgers spoke privately about Hart. In public, the composer often portrayed himself as responsible and rational, while Hart was his mercurial but beloved friend. When Rodgers finished writing his own lyrics for *No Strings* in 1962, almost twenty years after Hart's death, the man who also wrote *The Sound of Music* told his star, Diahann Carroll, "You just can't imagine how wonderful it feels to have written this score, and not have to search all over the globe for that drunken little fag."[58]

### "Last Night When We Were Young" (1935)
Lyrics by Yip Harburg (1896–1981), music by Harold Arlen (1905–1986)

Years after they wrote "Last Night When We Were Young," Harold Arlen and Yip Harburg both said it was their favorite song, but, Arlen added, "no one's ever heard of it."[59] He was wrong about that, but not about the excellence of his choice. In 1935, he and Harburg had signed contracts to write for Warner Bros., and were assigned to work together. Many of the songwriters hired by the studios were arbitrarily assigned to one another

**FIGURE 9.4**   Collaborators E.Y. Harburg and Harold Arlen. Courtesy of Photofest.

and then figured out ways to collaborate successfully. For their first song together, Yip set a lyric to a melody that Harold had written in New York. Arlen didn't tell Harburg that he had been unable to find anyone able to write words for it or even speak well of it. Composer Jerome Kern found it too esoteric, and George Gershwin told him that people could not sing it. Johnny Mercer said, "I don't think I could write a lyric to that."[60]

But Yip Harburg said, "My particular psyche happened to be on his vibe at the time and the title and lyric came out of the tune completely." He called it "Last Night When We Were Young," but he added that he had no idea where the title came from: "I suppose the tune opened it up . . . The whole pathos of the human situation, of the human race, is in that musical phrase. Old Harold gave it to me. I rode in on the coattails of his genius."[61] Arlen, however, had no idea where the melody had come from. He wrote a six-syllable phrase, then another eight, and he was on his way, and Harburg's lyric captured what Edward Jablonski called "the resigned melancholy" of the music.[62]

When he first heard the song, Metropolitan Opera star Lawrence Tibbett was so enthusiastic about it that he had it included in *Metropolitan*, a movie he was making. Although the song was cut before release, Tibbett recorded it and, a few years later, young Frances Gumm found Tibbett's version in a pile of used records. She fell in love with it and, soon after MGM changed her name to Judy Garland, she recorded it. Arlen and Harburg tried repeatedly to place it in a movie, but producers either rejected it or cut it before the release because they thought it was too sad. Only when Frank Sinatra recorded it for Capitol in the 1950s did it become a success.

"Last Night" is the only Harburg lyric in which the loss of love is irrevocable. He wrote it soon after his wife suddenly left him and his father died. It is also one of the few songs that feels inevitable, as if no other words were possible for that melody. The paradox in the title suggests how quickly time has flown as the lyric looks back longingly yet tenderly on a hopeful time when everything felt possible, including love. Harburg uses recurring hyperbole to reinforce the paradox as well as the preciousness of time: "Life was so new . . . / Ages ago last night."

# Chapter 10
## 1936–1940

**"Down in the Depths"** [*Red, Hot and Blue*] (1936)
Lyrics and music by Cole Porter (1891–1964)

A wealthy woman looks down on Fifth Avenue and Central Park from her ninetieth floor penthouse. Dressed in her "pet pailletted gown," she laments the loss of her lover, who has just walked out on her. "Pailletted" is a word that only Cole Porter could have used in a song, as he implicitly contrasts the shimmer of her beaded gown with the "million neon rainbows" down on the street. It also appears in a song that only Porter could have written, especially during the Depression, when a penthouse usually appeared in lyrics as an image of desire rather than reality. If you haven't got a nickel to your name, you can still dream of a penthouse, as in Val Burton and Will Jason's "Penthouse Serenade," Sammy Fain and Lew Brown's "Our Penthouse on Third Avenue," and Irving Berlin's "Castles in Spain (On a Roof in Manhattan)." While it is true that many songs are intuitively classless—everybody gets to fall in love—a sense of class did appear during the 1930s in such songs as Berlin's "Slumming on Park Avenue," Herman Hupfeld's "I Gotta Get Up and Go to Work," Jay Gorney and E.Y. Harburg's "Brother, Can You Spare a Dime?" and even Frank Churchill and Ned Washington's "Whistle While You Work." But where Berlin, Hupfeld, Harburg, and Washington were writing about those who trudge off to a job every day, Porter stuck with the penthouse crowd.

Porter was reportedly working on the score to *Red, Hot and Blue* under great stress, but he said, "I've never worked on a play in which everything has gone so smoothly." During the out-of-town run in Boston, everyone agreed that the score needed an additional song. "It had to be done in a hurry, of course," Porter recalled, "but I didn't have any difficulty as I knew

**FIGURE 10.1**   Ebulliently confident Cole Porter. Courtesy of Photofest.

the situation in the show perfectly. I got my song in mind on Tuesday, worked on it that night and Wednesday, and it was in the show orchestrated and sung by Ethel Merman on Thursday night."[1] Porter loved writing for Merman; she was his favorite because, he said, "Her voice, to me, is thrilling. She has the finest enunciation of any American singer I know. She has a sense of rhythm which few can equal . . . And she is so damned apt."[2] Although her reputation rested largely on her belting and her brass, Merman understood—as did Porter—that she was capable of a lot more. She demonstrated her emotional range in "Down in the Depths": "What Cole has done is analyze my voice and turn out songs which showed off its variety."[3] The *New York Times* noted that, in "Down in the Depths," Merman "eats out her heart fortissimo."[4]

During rehearsals for *Red, Hot and Blue*, Porter walked past co-author Russel Crouse at least a dozen times without acknowledging him, all in a single day. By six o'clock, the flummoxed Crouse was about to ask how he had offended Porter, when the songwriter placed a hand on his shoulder in a friendly way and said in a firm voice, "In my pet pailletted gown." He had spent the entire day trying to find just the right words for the lyric. Ray Kelly said of Porter, "He just sort of carried around a little soundproof room of his own that no one could seem to penetrate. His work was constant."[5] Protesting the accusation that he was remote, Porter said that he was working: "I've done lots of work at dinner, sitting between two bores. I can feign listening beautifully and work." It was easier for him because he didn't work at a piano. "First," he said:

> I think of an idea and then I fit it to a title. Then, I go to work on the melody, spotting the title at certain moments in the melody, and then I write the lyric—the end first—that way it has a strong finish . . . I do the lyrics like I'd do a crossword puzzle. I try to give myself a meter which will make the lyric as easy as possible to write without being banal.[6]

Only after he wrote down both the words and the notes did Porter go to the piano to revise. If he liked the result, "he sings it with a relish that is handsome to see, throwing his head back and closing his eyes. If he is not yet sure about it, he leans forward tensely and listens to each word as it comes out of him."[7]

## "The Glory of Love" (1936) and "The Last Round-Up" (1933)
Lyrics and music by Billy Hill (1899–1940)

Billy Hill is far from being the best-known songwriter of his time, but despite his unlikely background, his equally unlikely career, and his impulsive behavior, he produced a number of hits and standards, especially impressive when you consider that almost nobody has heard of him. Maybe that's because he was holed up in Tin Pan Alley in Midtown Manhattan, writing what was then called Hillbilly music. His cowboy songs include "Wagon Wheels," "Empty Saddles," and his first hit, "The Last Round-Up." It was initially sung, not in Texas or Oklahoma, but on the stage of the Paramount Theater in Times Square. Hill did not fit easily into smooth round holes. His father was a sea captain and his mother a Latvian Jewish immigrant. He played violin in the Boston Symphony until he ran off to work as a cowboy in Montana when he was 17.

Looking for female company one day, he walked into a hotel lobby and saw an out-of-work showgirl named Dedette Walker. He proposed marriage; she laughed until he said he was on his way to becoming a famous songwriter. They married that day and headed for a Yuma honeymoon, but when all four tires on his Model T blew out, they spent their wedding night in a ditch along an Arizona highway. Waiting for the sun to rise, he wrote "The West, A Nest and You"; it became his first published song. To avoid being categorized as a writer of Hillbilly songs, he wrote and published them as George Brown and often sold them outright for as little as $10. He barely survived the lean years by working as an elevator operator. When she went into labor, the hospital wouldn't admit Dedette because she and Billy were broke; while he chased down some money, she gave birth in the hospital elevator.

Finally, in 1933, he had his first hit. He almost sold "The Last Round-Up" for $25, but songwriter Gene Buck thought it was so good that he loaned him $200 to tide him over until he could find a publisher. He had been nursing the idea for the song for a long time. While he was working as a ranch hand in Montana, he asked an old-timer why cowboys continued their arduous work when they got older. The cowboy said that there was a time when they had to stop; he called it their "last round-up." Soon after, the man was trampled to death when his horse threw him. Hill remembered the incident and used it as the basis for the song about an aging cowboy who reflects on his approaching death.[8]

Despite Hill's success with Hillbilly songs, "The Glory of Love" is his best song. The lyric is about the variety within a love affair and the need to keep your balance. You give "a little" and you take "a little"; you even let your heart break, but only "a little." Therein lies love's story and its glory—the capacity to keep it alive even though it changes. Ironically, the money the song earned did not hold Hill's marriage together. He and his wife were also drinking heavily. They separated and, on Christmas Eve 1940, Hill died alone in a Boston hotel room at the age of 41.

### "In a Sentimental Mood" (1935)
Lyrics by Irving Mills (1894–1985) and Manny Kurtz (1911–1984), music by Duke Ellington (1889–1974)

The writing of "In a Sentimental Mood" resembles other Duke Ellington songs: a musician in the Orchestra played a major role in its composition, and Irving Mills, who was a lyricist as well as Ellington's manager and publisher, was involved in adding words to the melody some time later. As James Lincoln Collier wrote, "the central melodic ideas of virtually all of Ellington's best-known songs originated in somebody else's head."[9] In this case, Duke adapted a melody by alto saxophonist Otto "Toby" Hardwick.

Ellington often told anecdotes about how he wrote his most famous songs. He wrote "In a Sentimental Mood" under the gun in no more than twenty minutes. "Zhwoop!—Just like that," he said.[10] He and the members of the Orchestra were at a party after an appearance in Durham, North

Carolina, when a fight broke out between two women: "One girl had been engaged to this young man for a long time, and suddenly her best friend was now going to take him away from her." Ellington played the role of peacemaker: "So I had the two chicks, one on each side of me, and I said, 'Just listen to this. You girls are too good friends to let something like this come between you.' And this is what I played for them. I played it and I remembered, and then I put it down."[11] Hardwick was the soloist whose improvised melody Ellington adapted, even though he also said on another occasion, "To pacify [the two women], I composed this there and then, with one chick standing on each side of the piano."[12]

### "Goody, Goody" (1936)
Lyrics by Johnny Mercer (1909–1976), music by Matty Malneck (1903–1981)

### "Bob White (Whatcha Gonna Swing Tonight?)" (1937)
Lyrics by Johnny Mercer (1909–1976), music by Bernie Hanighen (1908–1976)

A surprisingly upbeat song about a scorned lover's delight in revenge, "Goody, Goody" was inspired in a Chinese restaurant in New York. Sitting at a table, Johnny Mercer jotted down the idea for a lyric and later filed it away in his trunk. Every songwriter has "trunk songs" that may eventually turn into hits—songs completed but so far unused. At that point in his career, Mercer was a singer and songwriter struggling to establish himself and make a living. He had auditioned for Paul Whiteman but the orchestra leader didn't hire him for a year. Whiteman wanted to use Mercer for a new vocal trio modeled on the old Rhythm Boys. He changed his mind a week after the hiring but kept Mercer to sing duets with trombonist Jack Teagarden. "I was kind of like a utility ball player," Mercer said. "I would write lyrics, or I would sing songs; I'd go the store for sandwiches, whatever."[13]

During the two years he worked for Whiteman, Mercer wrote songs with Matty Malneck, a violinist and arranger in the band. In need of a hit song to keep his career going, Mercer pulled out a sheet with his jottings on it. Between sets one night, he and Malneck turned it into "Goody, Goody" in fifteen minutes. Eventually, they convinced Benny Goodman to give it to his band singer, Helen Ward, even though she wanted no part of it. She called it "that damn' song," but Mercer said, "It's a phrase that everybody said, but I just, I don't know why I got that particular approach to it."[14] Despite her disdain for it, Ward's recording with Goodman was the hit version.

After he left Whiteman, Mercer found work as a singer in California with some of the many New York jazz musicians who were moving to the West

Coast to perform. Among them was Bernie Hanighen, with whom Mercer had previously collaborated ("Fare Thee Well to Harlem"). This time, in Hanighen's swinging, jazz-flavored melody, Mercer heard the sound of bob whites from his Georgia boyhood, but he transformed it into a jazz-laced lyric about all the other birds who find the bob white's "corny trill" square. Buddy De Sylva, by then a Hollywood producer, liked the song so much that he hired Mercer to work at Paramount.

### "Let's Face the Music and Dance" and "Let Yourself Go" [*Follow the Fleet*] (1936)
Lyrics and music by Irving Berlin (1888–1989)

In 1933, soon after the success of his and Moss Hart's revue, *As Thousands Cheer*, Irving Berlin set out to write a sequel to be called, *More Cheers*. By the time he decided against it, he had already written two songs, "Cheek to Cheek," a longer than usual ballad he soon used in *Top Hat*, the first movie score he wrote for Fred Astaire and Ginger Rogers, plus "Let Yourself Go," a rhythm tune that Rogers performed in *Follow the Fleet*. The fifth of the nine Astaire–Rogers' movies, *Follow the Fleet* was far from a blockbuster. In the populist 1930s, Astaire played a sailor on leave and Rogers was his ex-dancing partner. As a result, both an elegant dance ballad ("Let's Face the Music and Dance") and a syncopated dance tune ("Let Yourself Go") were performance numbers with little connection to the plot. What turned Berlin's seven songs into a score was an overriding Depression sensibility.

Whenever he worked with Astaire, Berlin would consult with him before he completed a song. They cooperated so closely because they were good friends and because Berlin held Astaire in such high esteem. Astaire would visualize Berlin's idea and then "pace it out in steps on the floor." He would say, "I'd change just that little bit. You know—dum-di-di-dum not de-de-dum-de-dum." Berlin would reply, "Yeah, I think you're right," and retreat to a small office he had made for himself on the RKO lot. There he would play with the idea until it took form as a finished song.[15]

Astaire said of Berlin, "Irving is always thinking up new song ideas." The two friends often played gin rummy for hours when Berlin was in Hollywood working on a movie: "In the middle of our gin games he would often sing and throw lyric ideas and rhymes at me to test them out." One night, when Berlin was out West for *Follow the Fleet*, he left Astaire's house at 3 a.m. The cab driver didn't know Beverly Hills very well, so he kept driving around, trying to find Berlin's destination. Berlin reported to Astaire the next day, "I wasn't paying any attention to the driver—my mind was on a tune. When I looked at my watch I found I'd been riding around for two hours."[16]

On another occasion, Berlin was keeping Astaire company at the hospital while the dancer waited for his wife to give birth. They were playing cards to pass the time. In the middle of a game, Berlin asked, "What do you think of this for a tune?" Astaire listened and said, "I like it." "Good," Berlin replied. "Gin."[17]

### "Smile" (1936)
Lyrics by John Turner (1932–) and Geoffrey Parsons (1910–1987), music by Charles Chaplin (1889–1977)

In its simplicity, clarity, and touching emotionalism, "Smile" is worthy of Irving Berlin. Yet three men wrote it rather than one, and did so over a span of eighteen years. Charlie Chaplin, the great silent movie comedian, was also a composer who wrote the score to his movie *Modern Times*, and oversaw the movie's use of sound effects. He said in his later years, "One happy thing about sound was that I could control the music, so I composed my own. I tried to compose elegant and romantic music to frame my comedies in contrast to the tramp character, for elegant music gave my comedies an emotional dimension. Musical arrangers rarely understood this. They wanted the music to be funny. But I would explain that I wanted no competition, I wanted the music to be a counterpoint of grace and charm, to express sentiment." Sometimes a musician would try to discuss the technical side of music with him, but "I would cut him short with a layman's remark, 'Whatever the melody is, the rest is just a vamp.'"[18]

Typically, Chaplin assigned specific melodies or musical themes to specific characters and situations. One untitled melody accompanied the story's love affair between Chaplin and Paulette Goddard. It did not emerge as an individual song—and a hit—until 1954, when John Turner and Geoffrey Parsons gave it a title and a lyric that reflected the melody's sweet melancholy in its admonition to "smile, though your heart is breaking." A spurned lover, it suggests, can survive even heartbreak. Although the song became popular in the United States when Nat "King" Cole recorded it, Turner and Parsons were English.

### "(I've Got) Beginner's Luck" [*Shall We Dance*] (1937)
Lyrics by Ira Gershwin (1896–1983), music by George Gershwin (1898–1937)

All lyricists have to learn the techniques and tricks of the trade. Then each writer gives them a distinctively personal stamp and develops a singular way of working. While the process of songwriting is not deeply introspective, it does have a less obvious inner component intensified by the demands of a looming deadline. Ira Gershwin described the struggle to fin-ish a lyric as "working incommunicado, trying to solve the riddle of a lyric for a tune." Even after working on a single song until after sunrise, the song runs through his head while he is asleep and stays with him at breakfast—a kind of aural dream. No matter what else he was doing, it keeps popping up as if to say, "Work on me now or you'll never get through." Fortunately, over time, newer tunes became "less tenacious and more tractable."[19]

Yet Ira's actual working method was much more precise and systematic than waiting around for something to pop. He didn't read music, so a lead sheet was not much help. A lead sheet is what a composer usually gives a lyricist. It contains the melody, maybe with chords indicated above, but nothing more; it is the bare bones of a song. Ira preferred to get the melody in his head and hum it endlessly to himself until he found the words. He would divide a huge sheet of paper into sections, one for the first line, another for the bridge, and so on. He often wrote the last line first and worked backwards, and he went through reams of paper when he was working on a score. Michael Feinstein, who as a young man worked as his secretary and archivist, said that writing was "torture" for Ira: "If it hadn't been for George's ambition, Ira wouldn't have produced nearly as much."[20]

Fred Astaire sings "Beginner's Luck" to Ginger Rogers near the start of the movie *Shall We Dance*. Its approach comes from its title: a matter of luck to be found at a gambling table, along a trout stream, or—less confidently—in his love life. Although Astaire does not dance, George's melody feels like a dance tune with its quirky, punctuated rhythms and its inserted exclama-tions, and Ira's monosyllabic lyric matches George's snappy rhythms: "The first time that I'm in love I'm in love with you," along with the explosive, "Gosh, I'm lucky!" and "Gosh, I'm fortunate." It feels as if they wrote it for Astaire to tap dance to.

### "Bei Mir Bist du Schoen" (1937)
Lyrics by Saul Chaplin (1912–1997), Sammy Cahn (1913–1993), and Jacob Jacobs (1890–1977), music by Sholom Secunda (1894–1974)

It is hard to imagine a more unlikely hit than "Bei Mir Bist Du Schoen." First written with a Yiddish lyric, it started on a Long Island beach, moved back to the Lower East Side, jumped up to Harlem, and became an interna-tional hit when three singers from Minnesota recorded it. Sholom Secunda and Jacob Jacobs, songwriters in New York City's Yiddish theater, wrote *Bei Mir Bist du Schein* for the 1933 Yiddish language musical *Men Ken Lebn Nor Men Lost Nisht* (*I Would if I Could*). Jacobs was on the beach one

**FIGURE 10.2**    Saul Chaplin and Sammy Cahn when they wrote "Bei Mir Bist du Schoen." Courtesy of Photofest.

afternoon when some pretty girls recognized him. To reassure his wife, he said, "*Bei mir bist du schein*"—"You're beautiful to me." And there was the start of the song.

Several years later, Saul Chaplin and Sammy Cahn were at Harlem's Apollo Theater with their agent, Lou Levy. That's where they first heard the song—performed in Yiddish by a black duo, Johnny and George, who said that Jenny Grossinger taught it to them when they appeared at her Catskill Mountain resort. Chaplin, Cahn, and Levy couldn't get over the audience's enthusiastic response. Afterwards Cahn remarked, "Imagine how much more the audience would enjoy it if they understood the words."[21] By the time they got home, they had decided that an English version would be perfect for Tommy Dorsey, who was about to open at the Paramount Theatre in Times Square. When Cahn ran into Dorsey a few days later, he tried to sell him on the song, "You do this song at the Paramount Theatre, where you get an occasional Jew, you'll kill them." The bandleader replied, "You're out of your goddamn mind!"[22]

Cahn once described the way he wrote this particular lyric as well as many of the songs that followed: In this case, he started by translating each Yiddish word into English. "Now when I write a lyric," he explained, "I always start at the top. I never know where it is going." He contrasted himself to Johnny Burke, perhaps because he and Burke both wrote successfully with Jimmy Van Heusen: "Johnny Burke always started at the bottom. He'd lay out a key idea, and then he'd write from the line backwards." For Cahn, though, beginning at the beginning meant "that I will go where I need to go. It will always be there if I just stay with it. And the minute I got '*Bei Mir Bist Du Schoen, please let me explain*,' that was the key to the whole song."[23]

In addition to Chaplin and Cahn, Levy represented a trio of unknowns called the Andrews Sisters. Levy got them an audition with Dave Kapp at Decca Records, who said he would record them if he found the right material. The three young women, who started hanging around Chaplin and Cahn's apartment, came across the "Bei Mir Bist du Schoen" sheet music and taught themselves to sing it. When Kapp heard them, he agreed to record it.

That's the basic story, but then you start adding the variants, all from people who were there. Chaplin says a New York newspaper reported that two gentile songwriters bought it from a poor Jewish songwriter for a few bucks and then earned $90,000 in royalties. Chaplin writes, "No matter how drastically we changed our names, we could never be gentile. We weren't from the Bronx. And until we wrote our version of the song we had never even met Sholom Secunda or Jacob Jacobs . . . The $90,000 figure was ludicrous because [the song] hasn't amassed that amount of royalties for us in the forty five years since it was first published."[24] Maybe not, but it did earn enough for Cahn to buy his parents a new house.

Another story says that Levy brought the Secunda–Jacobs song to the Andrews Sisters because he thought that having three gentile girls sing in Yiddish might go over in New York. Halfway through the recording session, Kapp insisted that they sing it in English. Levy persuaded Cahn and Chaplin to write a new lyric: "I asked [Sammy] to do it, and he sent the lyric back over the telephone."[25]

The song's popularity spread even to Nazi Germany, where the title was assumed to be a South German dialect. When authorities learned that the writers were Jewish, they banned it.

### "Down with Love" and "Buds Won't Bud" [*Hooray for What*] (1937)
Lyrics by E. Y. Harburg (1896–1981), music by Harold Arlen (1905–1986)

Long after he left for California, where sunshine and money spread across the landscape with equal abundance, Yip Harburg considered himself "a New Yorker down to the last capillary."[26] Despite his successes in Hollywood, he made a point of returning to New York every couple of years to write a show. Some of them soared, others flopped, but he kept going back. "The goal, the dream," he said, "was the Broadway show. Those of us who came periodically to the stage were always honored, envied, and rewarded. In the movies the target was the mentality of a twelve-year-old."[27] Harburg and Harold Arlen teamed up in 1937 to write a comic anti-war musical in which a chemist played by the irrepressibly silly Ed Wynn accidentally discovers a poison gas that would enable someone unscrupulous to dominate the world.

Arlen and Harburg agreed that the music should come first, but the composer wrote with a sense of the person who would provide the words: "Each lyricist is an individual and I have to work with each in his own way." He called "Down with Love," the kind of lighthearted number he wrote mainly with Harburg, a "lemon-drop" song.[28]

Harburg typically wanted the music for the score to come first because a good melody stimulated him. "I'm a chameleon," Harburg told an interviewer. "I love putting myself into everyone else's shoes—and each composer lends me a pair."[29] He believed that songs generally were better when the music came first: "A great song requires a great melody that comes right out of the heart and brain of the composer without any constrictions imposed by a lyric. Feeding him an idea, a title, is fine, but usually if you give him a complete, immutable lyric first, he'll start underscoring and usually a banal melody results."[30]

Harburg was an acrobat with words. They are always in motion, twisting and tumbling wherever his irreverent romanticism takes them. It's a breathtaking game: will he fall flat with all the words lying around him in a jumble, or will they and he soar? He never threw a good lyric away; he always tried to find another opportunity to use it. He told an interviewer, "I doubt that I can ever say I love you head on. It's not the way I think. For me the task is never to say it—to think in a curve, so to speak."[31] In 1930, he first wrote what would become "Buds Won't Bud" to a tune by Jay Gorney. Its second chorus begins: "Oh the buds won't bud / The dew won't do." He reworked it two years later in two similar songs, "'Cause You Didn't Do Right By Me" with Lewis Gensler, and "You Didn't Do Right By Me" with Dana Suesse. Two years after that, he tried again with a Morgan Lewis melody called "Cause You Won't Play House." The fourth try was the charm, as he and Arlen wrote "Buds Won't Bud." Suesse had said of their earlier effort, "It's not a very good tune, really. It's just a throwaway tune. It's the lyric that's darling."[32]

The score's distinctiveness lies in Yip's combination of punning wordplay ("Dew won't do," "knicks won't knack") and romantic upheaval ("Give

it back to the birds, / And the bees and the Viennese"). These characteristic Harburgian cautionary lyrics fit Arlen's irrepressible rhythmic drive
perfectly.

**"The Folks Who Live on the Hill"** [*High, Wide and Handsome*] (1937)
Lyrics by Oscar Hammerstein (1895–1960), music by Jerome Kern
(1885–1945)

After the ornate romanticism of the operetta songs he wrote with Rudolf
Friml ("Rose Marie") and Sigmund Romburg ("Lover, Come Back to Me,"
"The Desert Song"), and even Jerome Kern in *Show Boat*, Oscar Hammerstein had begun to write with the touching simplicity that characterized
his work with Richard Rodgers. One biographer suggests that his tender
lyric for "The Folks Who Live on the Hill" is no more than "a step away"
from *Carousel*'s "When the Children Are Asleep,"[33] as a young wife sits on
a hilltop with her new husband to imagine their life through the years, an-
ticipating how they will over time become known to all as "the folks who
live on the hill."

FIGURE 10.3    Collaborators Oscar Hammerstein II and Jerome Kern. Courtesy of Photofest.

The song's simplicity expresses a new and more natural stance for Hammerstein. The style is direct and, in Hugh Fordin's word, "uncluttered"[34] as the lyricist expresses a personal point of view that also fits the character who sings it. Despite his preference for simplicity, he did make one tricky rhyme—"veranda" will "command a (view)." Although he admitted to using a rhyming dictionary from time to time, he said that he turned to it only as a last resort when he had exhausted every possibility. He knew that it would not help with the new words, colloquialisms, and unconventional rhymes so important to lyrics. "In fact," he said, "it may be a handicap when one is writing a song which makes a feature of rhyming." His ultimate advice was "never to open a rhyming dictionary. Don't even own one!"[35]

### "Love Walked In" [*The Goldwyn Follies*] (1937)
Lyrics by Ira Gershwin (1896–1983), music by George Gershwin (1898–1937)

George and Ira Gershwin often argued as they were writing a new song, but they always worked out their differences; the bond between them was too deep to let disagreements fester. This time it was over a melody George scribbled in a notebook dated September 1931. Ira didn't add lyrics until 1937, when they were working on *The Goldwyn Follies*, their final project before George died. George was already ill when Sam Goldwyn asked him to audition his songs to be sure they were commercial, what the movie producer called "hits like Irving Berlin." Gershwin was furious, but Goldwyn liked what he heard, including "Love Walked in."[36] Ira, on the other hand, called the song "too pop" and said they should not use it. George answered, "What's wrong with a pop song? This is a movie and it should have a pop song." George called his melody "Brahmsian"; Ira said it was churchy.[37] Eventually they called in lyricist Yip Harburg to referee. He said, "It did not have the blaze of the Gershwin trademark, but it was a brave sweep of melody, effective and appropriate. Unfortunately, it cried out for that sentimental love lyric, a theme that always sent Ira scurrying. The love song was his bête noire."[38]

Ira gave in eventually, even though he had no specific place in the plot to anchor the song. He found himself "wallowing in a swamp of vague generalities" until he came up with a lyric based on what he referred to ironically as the song's "ambulatory lyric."[39] Ira originally called it "Love Walked Right in" but dropped "Right" because he thought it was nothing more than padding. Ira was correct about that but dropping "Right" also meant that the song lost an element of assertiveness. With "Right" in the title, "Love" didn't merely enter, it "walked right in and drove the shadows away."

Ira recalled that the lyric took him two or three weeks to write, and was eventually sung by the movie's hero as he cooks hamburgers in a restaurant.

Several months after the movie opened, Ira and his wife were driving through the Donner Pass when a drunken driver sideswiped them. No one was hurt, and they listened to the radio as they waited for a tow truck. The program was *Your Hit Parade*, and its Number One song was "Love Walked In." It had been on the Top Ten list for some weeks: "We didn't know it was still on the list. That more than made up for a badly busted fender."[40]

### "Some Day My Prince Will Come" [*Snow White*] (1937)
Lyrics by Larry Morey (1905–1972), music by Frank Churchill (1901–1942)

Even Walt Disney wasn't free from the controversies that arise over the authorship of a popular song. In the mid-1930s, he insisted that the songs for *Snow White*, his first full-length animated film, "should set a new pattern, a new way to use music. Weave it into the story so somebody just doesn't burst into song." In this way, Disney seems to have anticipated the integration of songs into plot that became commonplace after the success of *Oklahoma!* in 1943. "Some Day My Prince Will Come" was originally supposed to be part of a dream sequence in which Snow White and the Prince dance among the clouds surrounded by animated stars. When the movie opened, it had become a lullaby that Snow White sings for the dwarfs after a party, an accompaniment when she bakes a pie, and finally in a fuller version when the Prince carries her away at the end.

A year after the movie's release, an article in the *New Yorker* observed:

> On the day after Yale beat Navy in the final quarter, we read in the claim of T.W. Allen Co., music publishers that "Some Day My Prince Will Come," the torch song of *Snow White*, was just "Old Eli" in waltz time. We like to think that the whole gamut of human emotions is only a matter of timing of a metronome, and that such widely divergent things as love and hate can hang on the springs of the same little ditty. Under the sweater of each varsity man is a Prince on a horse; there is probably more than a trace of Red Grange in every Snow White.

The judge in the ensuing lawsuit concluded that "there is no proof that Mr. Churchill ever saw it. He has testified that he did not [and] that he composed by thinking of a tune in his mind, and then writing it down on a piece of paper."[41]

It is unlikely that Churchill would have plagiarized. Despite his heavy drinking and his bouts of depression (leading to his suicide in 1942), he was used to having his songs cut. For *Snow White*, he and lyricist Larry Morey wrote twenty-five songs, of which eight were used, including "Heigh-Ho" and "Whistle While You Work." He was a reserved, quiet man who never complained when someone decided that one of his songs did not quite fit. He said that he could always come up with another dozen. When he died, Disney said that he would "never find anyone to replace the man from Rumford, Maine who grew up playing with piglets and had a talent for jaunty tunes."[42] Morey was as versatile as Churchill was resilient. In addition to writing lyrics, he was the screenwriter who adapted Felix Salten's novel, *Bambi: A Life in the Woods*, into the 1942 Disney movie.

## "They Can't Take That Away from Me" [*Shall We Dance?*] (1937)
Lyrics by Ira Gershwin (1896–1983), music by George Gershwin (1898–1937)

Because *Porgy and Bess* took so long to write, and because not much money was coming in after its mixed reviews, George and Ira Gershwin decided to return to Hollywood to write for the movies. After a while, though, George's agent reported that there were no offers. Since he had written an opera, he was now considered highbrow. He immediately wired the studios, "I have written hit songs and I expect to do so in the future."[43] He and Ira were soon at work for RKO on the next Fred Astaire–Ginger Rogers movie, *Shall We Dance*.

For years at parties, George would bound enthusiastically from conversation to conversation, stopping only to pound out his own songs on the piano. Hoagy Carmichael described him as "a dapper lean shark of a man."[44] Meanwhile, Ira would stand quietly in the corner watching his brother. Joan Peyser believes that this close observation "generated his lyrics. And they proved to be a virtual diary of George's life."[45] Ira was writing what he believed George should have been feeling in the varied circumstances of his life. When Ira wrote the words to "They Can't Take That Away from Me," he used Paulette Goddard for inspiration—the way she wore her hair, sipped her tea, and sang off-key.[46] She and George were involved in an affair at the time, even though she was married to Charlie Chaplin. When they first began to work on the song, George had a simple but haunting rhythm in mind. After he played it several times, Ira suggested, "If you can give me two more notes in the first part, I can get 'The way you wear your hat.'" George tried it and liked it. Ira said that George was almost always obliging that way.[47]

Soon after *Shall We Dance* opened, writer S.N. Behrman told George "how marvelous it was of Ira to have added singing off-key to the list of the heroine's perfections—how it bathed nostalgia in humor. George agreed.

We got together on how extraordinary Ira was."[48] That was something of a deflection for George, for whom the song called up strong emotions. Arranger John Green took the test pressings for George and Ira to hear. "I put the recordings on and when George heard 'They Can't Take That Away from Me,' he broke down. He reached his hand out to me, and came close to tears. He kept saying 'Thank you' and I don't know why. That song must have meant something special to him." George wrote in a letter that he and Ira had written "a song called 'They Can't Take That Away from Me,' which I think has distinct potentialities of going places."[49] He was very disappointed when its performance in the movie was so brief, but it soon went on to do very well on the pop charts. Within two months of the movie's opening, George Gershwin was dead.

As Astaire and Rogers ride a Hudson River ferry between New Jersey and Manhattan on a foggy night, he sings "They Can't Take That Away from Me," because they're about to end a marriage of convenience. The lyric lists off the small things—"the way you wear your hat, the way you sip your tea"—that have contributed to his falling in love with her. The song blends joy and sadness in its anticipation of parting. Like Cole Porter's "You're the Top," Ralph Rainger and Leo Robin's "Thanks for the Memory," and Richard Rodgers and Lorenz Hart's "I Wish I Were in Love Again," "They Can't Take That Away from Me" is a list song, defined by William Zinsser as a song that uses "some kind of enumerating device to catalogue affairs of the heart."[50]

## "Flat Foot Floogie (with a Floy Floy)" (1938)
Lyrics and music by Slim Gaillard (1916–1991), Slam Stewart (1914–1987), and Bud Green (1897–1981)

Jive talk was all the rage in the 1930s and 1940s. It was what the hepcats said. And then there was Slim Gaillard, songwriter and musician, who invented his own surreal version of it. He called it "Vout" or "Vout Oreenie," a weird but often funny concoction of gibberish and double talk that paralleled his mastery of several foreign languages. "Flat Foot Floogie," a good example of "Vout" in action, made no sense at all but that hardly mattered. It is as close to inspired as a nonsense song gets. Gaillard originally entitled it "Flat Foot Floozie," but a floozie was a slang term for a prostitute and "floy floy" was slang for venereal disease.[51] When Gaillard changed "floozie" to "floogie," the song became nonsense and allowed radio stations to air it during those more circumspect times. The sheet music to "Floogie" was included in a time capsule that represented American culture, circa 1939. It was to be opened in 1939. There was "Flat Foot Floogie," side by side with *Finlandia* and "Stars and Stripes Forever."

Among Gaillard's other songs were the hit "Cement Mixer (Put-ti, Put-ti)" and "Yep Roc Heresy." One radio station banned "Heresy," calling it degenerate, although it was actually nothing more than a recitation of the menu from an Armenian restaurant.

Gaillard was a genuine eccentric. In 1952, a young man took his date to hear him play at a Manhattan jazz club. As they entered, Gaillard segued from whatever he was playing into "Here Comes the Bride." He then introduced the next number with an announcement, "We would like to dedicate this next number to our newlyweds here spending their honeymoon at Birdland. What a drag! If that was me I'd go somewhere and lock the vouty and throw the reeney away." A few days later they happened to pass one another on Broadway. The young man said, "Mac Vouty!" Without missing a beat, Gaillard replied, "O rissimo reeney!"[52] When Bob Hope once asked his radio guest Marlene Dietrich what she thought of Gaillard, she answered, "Vout."[53] Gaillard once had a band he called Henry Sausage and his Pork Chops. He would say of it, "We fry, man."[54]

### "Heart and Soul" [*A Song Is Born*] (1938)
Lyrics by Frank Loesser (1910–1969), music by Hoagy Carmichael (1899–1981)

In 1938, Paramount assigned Hoagy Carmichael to work with young Frank Loesser. A dozen years had passed since the laconic Carmichael's first major song ("Washboard Blues"), and he had already written "Georgia on My Mind," "Lazy Bones," and "Star Dust," among dozens of others. Despite his affection for jazz when it was still young, and his choice to become a musician and songwriter rather than a lawyer, Carmichael was essentially conventional and conservative. He said of himself, "Change always upsets me. My music is often about things lost to me. Simple things like rocking chairs, the weather of my childhood, moods and memories, and landmarks."[55] Loesser was outspoken and assertive, but he was eager to learn from such an accomplished writer. For several years, the laid back Hoosier collaborated with the excitable New Yorker, and mentored him as well. Carmichael remembered that Loesser "had a tendency to want to write things 'way out.' This may be because he was so packed full of ideas then that he was overlooked." Over time, though, Carmichael realized that his initial judgment of Loesser as "zany" and not "serious enough about the matter of writing songs" was wrong: "Then one day, sitting at the piano, [Loesser] said, 'How's this?' I said, 'Follow it with this—.' We reeled off a few stanzas and I realized this was the lyricist I'd hoped he'd be. All the time we worked together, Frank never violated the rules of construction or what it takes to make a hit song."[56]

As they finished their first collaboration entitled "Heart and Soul," Carmichael and Loesser thought they had written a number that would appeal to a broad public. It had a tripping melody helped along by a strong beat, so much so that piano teachers gave it to their beginning students as a two-hand duet that they could master. Its particular chord progression, eventually known as the "Fifties progression," became common in doo-wop songs twenty years later. Before long, even people who couldn't play piano could pound out "Heart and Soul," usually in combination with "Chopsticks." Loesser's daughter Sarah and her friends played the two songs together at parties. "I never knew my father wrote 'Heart and Soul,'" she said. "I thought whoever wrote 'Chopsticks' wrote it."[57]

Although neither Loesser nor Carmichael had any such intention in mind, the two songs soon became an exercise in counterpoint. After Irving Berlin, no one wrote as many contrapuntal duets as Loesser, including "Make a Miracle" (*Where's Charley?* 1948), "Baby, It's Cold Outside" (*Neptune's Daughter*, 1949), "Fugue for Tinhorns" (*Guys and Dolls*, 1950), and "Inchworm" (*Hans Christian Andersen,* 1952).

### "I Let a Song Go Out of My Heart" (1938)
Lyrics by Henry Nemo (1909–1999), John Redmond (1906–1947), and Irving Mills (1894–1985), music by Duke Ellington (1899–1974)

Duke Ellington wrote the music for "I Let a Song Go Out of My Heart" when the Orchestra was on tour in a "little hotel [in Memphis] owned by an old friend of mine . . . and I had a certain amount of inspiration. I'm seldom alone. I'm extremely partial to extremely pretty people."[58] When he returned to New York, he asked Henry Nemo, a musician and sometime songwriter, to add a lyric. It was the thirteenth song Ellington had written for the score to the *Cotton Club Parade of 1938,* but because he was superstitious he cut it.

The decision to add lyrics usually came from Irving Mills, Ellington's manager and music publisher. He would commission a lyricist when he heard a melody that he thought would appeal to a large audience. Irving's bother, Paul, said that Duke:

> might've voiced an opinion on a lyric . . . but he was not a lyric writer by any means . . . Most times he'd call up the day after the [recording] sessions and say, "What's the name of my song?" He didn't know. He liked the tune but had no idea what the title should be . . . There was no real picture in the song that led you into a particular title. They just had to pick things out of the air.[59]

As usual, Irving Mills cut himself in as co-lyricist, although his contribution was negligible. George Simon said of Mills' house, "I want you to notice one thing and that's the huge expanse of red carpeting that covers the ground floor. That's Duke's blood."[60]

Mills exploited Ellington, but Ellington may also have exploited members of his Orchestra. When he needed a song but had no ideas, he would gather the band after performing. They would sit in with him, improvising, until he finished writing. The Orchestra was his easel, the musicians his paints. Some of the musicians resented Duke's taking the songwriting credit. As trumpeter Cootie Williams said, "People stopped doing things like that because they wasn't paid for them properly."[61] For years, when the Ellington Orchestra played "I Let a Song Go Out of My Heart," saxophonist Johnny Hodges would roll his fingers to make the sign for money as a way of complaining silently about the royalties he never received.[62]

**"Take the 'A' Train"** (1938)
Lyrics and music by Billy Strayhorn (1915–1967)

**FIGURE 10.4** Mitch Miller (left) clowns with Duke Ellington and Billy Strayhorn. Courtesy of Photofest.

Billy Strayhorn and Duke Ellington first met when the younger man was still living at home in Pittsburgh and working in a drugstore. After they met backstage, Duke invited Billy to play for him. Because he was shy, short, and wore thick glasses, everybody called him "Swee' Pea." First he played "Sophisticated Lady" exactly as Duke had. Then he said, "I might do it like this"[63] and played it again with syncopations, frills and flourishes, and Duke was impressed enough to send for some of his musicians to hear the young man. As Strayhorn played "Solitude," Duke stood with his hands on Billy's shoulders.

Ellington wanted to hire Strayhorn but he obviously didn't need a second piano player. Billy wrote a few arrangements for him over the next several days and then Duke was gone, but not before he paid Billy $20 for his work and drew him a map to his Harlem apartment. Weeks later, with no word from Ellington, Strayhorn borrowed money to get to New York as he continued to read the note over and over again. The directions began, "Take the A train to Sugar Hill." He knew he needed to impress Duke a second time with his music. He said the song came to him effortlessly as he ran errands and made deliveries. By the time he sat down at the piano, it was formed: "It was like writing a letter to a friend," he said. When Strayhorn finally caught up to Ellington in Newark, New Jersey in January 1939, Duke didn't remember his name but he did remember his playing. Billy performed his new song about the subway and then called home: "Guess what? I'm going to work for Duke. I played that tune ' "A" Train' for him, and he liked it. I'm moving to New York."[64]

Another version of the song's composition is less romantic but perhaps more grounded in actual events. The following year, ASCAP insisted that the radio networks increase royalty payments. When they refused, ASCAP called a strike. Ellington could no longer play his hits on the air. Because he needed new songs, he turned to Strayhorn and his son, Mercer. With a bottle of wine and a couple of cartons of cigarettes between them, they set to work. During the marathon that followed, Mercer Ellington found a draft of "'A' Train" in a garbage can after Strayhorn had thrown it away because it sounded too much like a Fletcher Henderson arrangement. Mercer was smart enough to rescue it.

"Take the 'A' Train" marked Strayhorn's breakthrough as a composer. It became a hit recording for Ellington, who used it as his Orchestra's theme from 1941 until his death in 1974. As jazz composers often do, Strayhorn built the tune on the harmonies of an earlier song, in this case Jimmy McHugh's "Exactly Like You." Once he was satisfied with it, Strayhorn called it "a swinging riff tune"[65] about the Eighth Avenue subway, and said that its lyric consisted of subway directions. Once Ellington was using the song, vocalist Joya Sherrill added a revised lyric that has been used most often in the years since.

### "Day in, Day Out" (1939) and "Fools Rush in" (1940)
Lyrics by Johnny Mercer (1909–1976), music by Rube Bloom (1902–1976)

The short-lived collaboration between composer Rube Bloom and lyricist Johnny Mercer produced several hit songs that have endured as standards, including "Day in, Day Out" and "Fools Rush in." Bloom had written them as he always did, composing on the piano. Because he was self-taught, he memorized his melodies and a helper wrote them down for him. Mercer had returned to New York from California in 1939 to work with Bloom on some songs for a Broadway revue, *Lew Leslie's Blackbirds of 1939*. The show ran only nine performances but Bloom also played some other melodies for Mercer. After hearing them, Mercer promised to write lyrics when he had time and added, "If you play these for anyone else, I'll never talk to you again."[66] Mercer eventually kept his word with a lyric—"Day in, Day Out"— that suggests boredom in a contradictory way to create intensity.

Bloom had also written an instrumental called "Shangri-La," inspired by the classic 1937 Ronald Coleman movie *Lost Horizon*. Mercer gave the melody a new three-syllable title—"Fools Rush in"—but tried to keep the mystical spirit of Bloom's inspiration. Simple—almost every word is a monosyllable—yet suggesting that falling in love is like entering an enchanting and possibly dangerous new world, the lyric gives a new twist to the adage that "Fools rush in where wise men fear to tread," a line Mercer borrowed from the eighteenth-century poet Alexander Pope. "I think it's one of my better lyrics," Mercer once said; "a simple way to a very big, almost operatic kind of tune."[67]

"Fools Rush in" added another title to the string of successful songs Mercer wrote during the 1940s. It was featured on the popular weekly radio program *Your Hit Parade*, which performed the Top Ten songs of the week. A vocalist as well as a songwriter, Mercer was often invited on the show and sometimes got to sing his own hits. On one program, his songs held the Number One, Two, and Three positions; on another he had written the lyrics to five of the Top Ten songs. "Imagine that," he said; "one half of the Hit Parade!"[68]

### "If I Didn't Care" (1939)
Lyrics and music by Jack Lawrence (1912–2009)

After he finished writing the blues-influenced "If I Didn't Care," Jack Lawrence got up enough nerve to play his new song for several of his musician friends, even though he didn't tell them that he had already mailed it to Dave Kapp at Decca Records. Playing it for friends was tougher than it sounds, because Lawrence had been turning out movie hits in collaboration with composer Peter Tinturin. Now he was tackling both words and music on his own. Between assignments, he said, he had a lot of time to spend "noodling on the piano, going back to my beginnings, writing my own words and music."[69] The most important outcome of that noodling was "If I Didn't Care."

The reaction of Eliot Daniels, Rudy Vallee's piano player, to Lawrence's songs was typical: "Jack, you know I'm your friend. You know I think you're a helluva lyricist. You know I wouldn't lie to you . . . Jack, forget it. It stinks!" Arranger Archie Bleyer told Lawrence that, while the song was probably commercial, he had made "a terrible musical mistake" by beginning in one key and ending in another. Lawrence immediately sent a revised version to Kapp, who replied, "Too late. Song already recorded by new group called the Ink Spots. You have a smash hit." When Lawrence ran into Daniels a few months later, the piano player shook his head and said, "I still think it stinks."[70]

The Ink Spots' recording sold nineteen million copies and made the group into recording stars with a distinctive style recognized today as a precursor to rhythm and blues, rock 'n' roll, and doo-wop—a strongly rhythmic guitar riff or vamp, followed by Bill Kenny's high tenor solo, a free-form recitation of the release by bass Hoppy Jones (characterized by the use of the words "Honey Chile," as if he were talking directly to someone he loved), and then a final chorus by Kenny. Lawrence's lyric lends itself to Kenny's glossy, romantic style. Each chorus begins with the same conditional phrase, "If I didn't care," followed by three unanswered questions that describe the state of the lover's emotions. The lyric doesn't go farther or deeper than the initial intense moment that concludes with an understated final question, "Would all this be true if I didn't care for you?"

## "I Get Along Without You Very Well" [*Las Vegas Story*] (1939)
Lyrics and music by Hoagy Carmichael (1899–1981)

That's almost what the sheet music says except for a subtitle that reads, "Except Sometimes," and names Hoagy Carmichael as both composer and lyricist. The complete story of its composition is more complicated than that. Before *Life*, the large-format magazine that was so popular through the 1950s, there was another magazine also called *Life* that resembled the English humor magazine *Punch*. In 1924, the original *Life* published a poem entitled "Except Sometimes." It began, "I get along without you very well, /

Of course I do." The poet was identified only as "J.B." A friend of Hoagy's thought the composer might like its treatment of lost love, so he clipped it out and mailed it to him. Carmichael filed it away and didn't rediscover it until 1938. He wrote a melody along with several versions of J.B.'s lyric. When he believed the song was ready to publish, the lyrics were still so closely based on the original poem that he felt he needed to get permission from the original writer. But all he had were the two initials.

Under pressure to find the name, because he had already scheduled the song's radio debut, Carmichael turned to the fast-talking radio commentator, Walter Winchell. Winchell read an on-air item about J.B.: "Hoagy Carmichael, whose songs you love, has a new positive hit—but he cannot have it published. Not until the person who inspired the words communicates with him and agrees to become his collaborator . . . If you wrote those lines in a poem, tell your Uncle Walter, who will tell his Uncle Hoagy, and you may become famous." After several months of similar announcements and a number of phony claims, Winchell broadcast the news that "Jane Brown claims ownership. She will rate 3¢ a copy on the ditty if her claim holds up."[71] Brown, whose married name was Thompson, was a 71-year-old widow living in Philadelphia. She didn't listen to Winchell and had no telephone, but somehow two staff members from the old *Life* had managed to find her. Through her attorney, she agreed to the terms of the contract Carmichael was offering.

The legend says that Dick Powell introduced the song on his radio show on January 19, 1939, but Jane Brown had died the night before. A more likely story says that the song was broadcast a month earlier, and both Winchell and Carmichael knew it. There was no mention of a mysterious original poet. Either way, the song's wistful melody provides an ideal setting for the lyric's rueful way of putting the best face on the melancholy of loss.

**"Stairway to the Stars"** (1939)
Lyrics by Mitchell Parish (1900–1993), music by Matt Malneck
(1903–1981) and Frank Signorelli (1901–1975)

**"Deep Purple"** (1939)
Lyrics by Mitchell Parish (1900–1993), music by Peter DeRose (1900–1953)

"Stairway to the Stars" and "Deep Purple" are dreamy romantic ballads that helped to confirm Mitchell Parish's reputation as a lyricist who could successfully add lyrics to compositions originally written as instrumentals, even if he did his work years later. By the time he wrote the words to Matt Malneck and Frank Signorelli's "Stairway to the Stars" and Peter DeRose's

"Deep Purple," he had already put words to Hoagy Carmichael's "Star Dust" and Duke Ellington's "Solitude" and "Sophisticated Lady." Malneck and Signorelli were jazz musicians who wrote instrumentals that often had lyrics added later. In 1934, they had collaborated on an extended work, "Park Avenue Fantasy," much longer than a typical thirty-two-bar popular song. Paul Whiteman's Orchestra played it on the radio but it got little public response. Not until 1938, when Malneck used the piece as the theme of his new radio show, did he or Signorelli approach Parish about adding a lyric to its final section. That's what became "Stairway to the Stars."

The lyric Parish wrote ranges from the conversational to the ornate, the familiar to the fantastical, the romantic to the child-like. The very first line begins the contrast, using alliteration to bridge the difference between an ordinary staircase and the elevated stars. It's an engaging, almost amusing conceit. Elsewhere, though, lovers hear the romantic "sound of violins," but they are "out yonder where the blue begins." The downhome and the hifalutin collide in a single line, and, before the end, they will "sail away on a lazy daisy petal."

DeRose, a jazz pianist who appeared on the radio for a dozen years with a ukulele player named May Singhi, wrote an instrumental he called "Deep Purple" in 1933 while he was sitting in his garden. Paul Whiteman had it scored as part of his attempt to make "a lady out of jazz,"[72] but the song became a hit only after Parish added lyrics in 1938. It was eminently fitting for him to use "purple" in the title of one of his songs.[73] As usual in a Parish lyric, moonlight illuminates the dream-like scene as a lover imagines that he and his beloved, though separated, will "always meet / Here in my deep purple dreams."

## "Strange Fruit" (1939)
Lyrics and music by Abel Meeropol (aka Lewis Allen) (1903–1986)

This is a story about a singer, a minor composer, and a left-wing schoolteacher and poet who used a pseudonym—singer Billie Holiday, songwriter Arthur Herzog, and teacher Abel Meeropol, who sometimes published under the name of Lewis Allen. Aside from poems, plays, and musicals that no one remembers, Meeropol wrote the lyrics to "The House I Live in," the basis for a 1945 Oscar-winning short with Frank Sinatra, and "Strange Fruit," an extraordinary 1939 song about lynching. Holiday's name occasionally appears on sheet music covers but she did not write songs. Sometimes she would hum a melody, her piano player would arrange it, and Billie would add lyrics. But then she would check in with a real songwriter, usually Herzog, who would give the result a more singable, more commercial, form.

Between 1890 and 1940, nearly 4,000 people were lynched in the United States. In the mid-1930s, stirred by some especially grisly photographs of lynchings, Meeropol wrote a poem entitled "Bitter Fruit." Before long, he set it to music and it was being performed in left-wing circles in New York. A black quartet performed it during a fundraiser for anti-Fascists during the Spanish Civil War. The program's director, Robert Gordon, was also directing the first-floor shows at the new Café Society, where Billie Holiday was the headliner.

Barney Josephson's Café Society was unusual in that it was a left-wing nightclub whose patrons included union officials, intellectuals, artists, jazz lovers, and celebrities. Performers were integrated and so were audiences. One night, Meeropol sat down at the piano and played "Strange Fruit" for Holiday. He said, "I don't think she felt very comfortable with the song, because it was so different from the songs to which she was accustomed." She asked him one question: "What does 'pastoral' mean?" No one changed Meeropol's lyric, though Holiday would eventually claim, inaccurately, that she wrote it. Holiday said that she, Herzog, and her piano player "got together and did the job in about three weeks." At first, Holiday was afraid to sing it. "There wasn't even a patter of applause when I finished," she said. "Then a lone person began to clap nervously. Then suddenly everyone was clapping."

A few years earlier, Holiday walked into Milt Gabler's Commodore Music Store on 52nd Street. She was upset by the news that Columbia had refused to record "Strange Fruit" because, she said, "They're afraid of the content of the song." Gabler suggested to Holiday that she ask the people at Columbia if they minded if she did a recording for Commodore, the store's small jazz label. Because Commodore was not large enough to be competition and was a good customer, Columbia agreed. "So we went into the studio," Gabler said, "with 'Strange Fruit,' 'Fine and Mellow,' 'I Gotta Right To Sing the Blues,' and Jerome Kern's 'Yesterdays.'"[74]

### "All or Nothing at All" (1940)
Lyrics by Jack Lawrence (1912–2009), music by Arthur Altman (1910–1994)

Music publisher Lou Levy played a melody for Jack Lawrence and asked him to write lyrics for it. Lawrence and the composer, Arthur Altman, had collaborated before, but had had a falling out since the early days when they were struggling for recognition. Lawrence told Levy that he liked the music "with some reservations." He agreed to write the lyrics "if I had carte blanche in making any musical changes that occurred to me." He made a few changes based on "the words I dreamed up," but both Levy and Altman liked the results. Levy arranged for recordings of the romantic ballad by Jimmy Dorsey (vocal by Bob Eberly), Freddy Martin, and Harry James (vocal by Frank Sinatra). Levy, Altman, and Lawrence liked the recordings, especially Sinatra's, but "all three records bombed."[75]

By 1943, Sinatra had become a national phenomenon, the heartthrob of the bobby-soxers. Columbia Records signed him, but the musicians' union's strike against the recording companies was creating panic. Various companies tried a cappella arrangements, harmonica accompaniment, even kazoos. Nothing worked very well. Lou Levy's brainstorm saved the day for Columbia and Sinatra. He suggested that the company dig up Sinatra's 1939 recording of "All or Nothing at All." Unlike most big band recordings of the day, which limited the vocalist to one chorus, usually in the middle of the arrangement, this one was almost entirely a Sinatra solo. Columbia reissued the recording with a new label that downplayed "Harry James Orchestra" and enlarged the name "Frank Sinatra." It was so successful that an MGM cartoon used a skunk dressed as Frankie to croon it to a warren of rabbits.

A year later, Sinatra told gossip columnist Louella Parsons that "All or Nothing at All" got him and James fired from the Sunset Strip club where they were appearing in 1939. The manager complained that James' trumpet playing was too loud "and my singing was just plain lousy. He said the two of us couldn't draw flies as an attraction—and I guess he was right. The room was as empty as a barn." Later, Sinatra used the song when he auditioned for Tommy Dorsey.[76]

**"Blueberry Hill"** (1940)
Lyrics by Al Lewis (1901–1967) and Larry Stock (1896–1984), music by Vincent Rose (1880–1944)

It sounds like a double play combination—Autry to Armstrong to Domino. Mainly, though, it shows how a song can get around. How could Vincent Rose, the composer who wrote "Whispering," "Avalon," and "Linger Awhile" in the 1920s, be the same man who wrote "Blueberrry Hill" for rhythm and blues singer Fats Domino in 1956? Domino's version rose to second on the Top Forty list and first on the R&B list, and *Rolling Stone* listed it as one of the 500 greatest songs of all time. The explanation is simple: Rose, along with lyricists Al Lewis and Larry Stock, wrote the song in 1940 for a Western starring Gene Autry. The most important of the singing cowboys was the first to sing it. Lewis also wrote the words to the Eddie Cantor number "Now's the Time to Fall in Love," but he was better known as a character actor than a songwriter. In the 1960s, he played Grandpa on *The Munsters* and Officer Schnauzer on *Car 54, Where Are You?* Stock, who also wrote the

Dean Martin hit "You're Nobody 'Til Somebody Loves You," remembers that "one important publisher turned down 'Blueberry Hill' because, he claimed, blueberries don't grow on hills. I assured him I had picked them on hills as a boy, but nothing doing."[77] The publisher that eventually issued it failed to notice the sexual implications in the word "thrill," as a now-separated couple remembers the night they spent on top of the hill in the moonlight.

Once the song appeared, it kept reappearing. After Autry's movie performance, Glenn Miller's Orchestra had the hit recording. Louis Armstrong recorded it in 1949, but his recording went nowhere until Domino's hit version. It helped to lift Armstrong's version to a spot on the Billboard Top Forty. Yet Domino recorded it only because he ran out of material during a studio session. He insisted on doing it, even though producer-arranger Dave Bartholomew objected strongly. Then, during the recording, Domino forgot the words. A studio engineer had to piece the final version together from bits of several different takes.

One more performance deserves mention: Vladimir Putin sang it at a 2010 charity event. He had learned the lyrics as part of his study of English.[78]

**"I Hear Music"** and **"Dancing on a Dime"** [*Dancing on a Dime*] (1940)
Lyrics by Frank Loesser (1910–1969), music by Burton Lane
(1912–1987)

A 1936 revue called *The Illustrators Show* opened and closed on Broadway in four nights, but the two songs by lyricist Frank Loesser and an early collaborator named Irving Actman were good enough to earn them a short-term contract to write for Paramount Studios. They were at the bottom of the songwriting barrel but, beginning in 1936, they wrote songs for twenty movies before they separated—such forgotten songs for such forgotten films as "Hot Towel" and "Let's Have Bluebirds on All Our Wallpaper" for *Post Office* and "Bang! The Bell Rang" for *Flying Hostess*. The two novices were learning about assembly-line songwriting in Hollywood. Loesser wrote back to his wife on the East Coast, "Right now Irving and I are in the throes, trying to knock off a hit out of a situation where the producer orders a certain title, the musical director orders a certain rhythm, the dance director orders a certain number of bars and the composers order a certain number of aspirins."[79] Between these songs and the writing of "I Hear Music" and "Dancing on a Dime" with Burton Lane in 1940, Loesser had begun to earn a reputation for such songs as "See What the Boys in the Back Room Will Have," "Two Sleepy People," and "The Lady's in Love with You."

In the late 1930s and early 1940s, Lane and Loesser wrote songs for a half-dozen movies that established Loesser and finally allowed him to make a decent living. At first, he couldn't afford a car, so Lane used to drive him everywhere. He once drove to Loesser's house to pick up Frank just as they were sitting down to a dinner of baked beans and half an apple each. Lane remembered, "They were so broke that Frank only had one suit that he had to keep cleaning." None of this kept Loesser from concentrating on his work. He would have Lane play a melody over and over until he remembered it well enough to put a lyric to it. "Now Frank was very secretive," Lane said:

> He would sit across the room from me, a pad held very high so that all I could see was his eyes. He would write very small, and then he would suddenly start to smile, and I'm dying to know what he's writing. I would say, "Frank, what is it, what did you get, what made you laugh, what's tickling you?" And he'd go on writing till he'd finished, and then he'd put what he'd written up on the piano.[80]

Sometimes, Loesser preferred to go off by himself to write for the few weeks it took him to finish the lyrics to Lane's tunes. In all the time they worked together, he never made a suggestion about changing a melody or even a note. As a result, Lane was surprised when Loesser began to write both words and music for *Guys and Dolls*. He didn't know that Loesser had that ability with music, even though Frank used to say, "You know, someday I'd like to write a musical comedy, and I'd like to try writing the music myself."[81]

**"In the Mood"** (1940)
Lyrics by Andy Razaf (1895–1973), music by Joe Garland (1903–1977)

**"Moonlight Serenade"** (1939)
Lyrics by Mitchell Parish (1900–1993), music by Glenn Miller (1904–1944)

**"One O'Clock Jump"** (1937)
Music by Count Basie (1904–1984)

**"Let's Dance"** (1934)
Lyrics by Fanny May Baldridge, (1893?–1961), music by Josef Bonime (1891–1959) and Gregory Stone (1900–1991)

In the 1930s and 1940s, big bands covered a lot of the hits of the day with arrangements for dancing. It was pretty straightforward work, especially for the bands that used singers regularly—Frank Sinatra with Tommy

Dorsey, Helen Forrest with Harry James, and Bea Wain with Larry Clinton, among many others. But the instrumental jump tunes (fast songs with a strong beat) that originated with a specific band were often a different matter. According to the law at the time, a song not written down and registered for copyright had no legal protection. Any musician could transcribe and use it.

Years before Glenn Miller formed his successful Orchestra, he had supposedly written a brief musical theme called "In the Mood" that he never used. The real composer was jazz trumpeter Wingy Manone, who, in the late 1920s, had written the riff as the basis for a recording he called "Tar Paper Stomp." Soon, the riff became part of the common musical currency of the time. Two years later, Horace Henderson used it for "Hot and Anxious," recorded by his brother Fletcher's orchestra. And, in 1935, sax player Joe Garland had written a variation on the theme for the Mills Blue Rhythm Band. By 1938, Garland had done a full-length arrangement, called it "In the Mood," and took out a copyright in his own name. After Artie Shaw decided not to record it because it was too long for a 78 r.p.m. record, Garland sold it to Miller. Garland and lyricist Andy Razaf appear on the sheet music as co-writers.

Because Miller thought that his recording of the song would be a hit, he had hired Razaf ("Ain't Misbehavin'," "Honeysuckle Rose") at the last minute to put words to Garland's arrangement. Razaf revised a lyric to an unpublished Razaf-Fats Waller song called "Whatcha Got on for Tonight," leading David Jasen to observe that he fitted "the recycled tune with a recycled lyric."[82] Razaf's lyric invented a conversation between a couple on the dance floor as the music gets her in the mood for a kiss. When he finished, the song's publisher paid him $200, which he assumed was an advance. In fact, Razaf's agent had told Miller that the lyricist would do it for a flat fee, but never told Razaf. Despite the song's huge profits, he never got another penny and was forced to write the double-entendre lyrics ("Kitchen Man," "My Handy Man") he detested to earn some money.

The riffs that jazz musicians tossed off for their own use without bothering with copyrights often led to confusion, but also indicate something about the informal way jazzmen composed. In 1936, Count Basie's band was performing regularly at a Kansas City club called The Reno, and was broadcasting late at night on a local station whose signal reached Chicago. One night, with only ten minutes left in the broadcast, Basie couldn't think of another song for the band to play. He told the show's director that they'd do a "head arrangement," an improvisation in which each section makes up its part based on what the others are playing. The announcer insisted on a name to announce. Aware that they needed to play until the top of the hour—1 a.m.—Basie said, "Call it 'One O'clock Jump.'" Another version of the story says that the title was "Blue Ball," but the announcer was too timid to use it.[83]

Despite the popularity of "In the Mood," Miller's theme song was a different untitled composition that he had written as a young trombonist with Ray Noble's Orchestra. He asked lyricist Edward Heyman ("Body and Soul," "I Cover the Waterfront") to add words. Miller disliked Heyman's title—"Now I Lay Me Down to Sleep." Big band historian George T. Simon also tried unsuccessfully with "Now I Lay Me Down to Weep" and so did Mitchell Parish with "Wind on the Trees." By this time, Miller had his own successful orchestra. Parish had already acquired a reputation for adding successful lyrics to old instrumentals, so Miller asked him to try again. The result was a lyric, and a song, entitled "Moonlight Serenade," inspired by Miller's recording of Frankie Carle's "Sunrise Serenade." Parish described someone in the moonlight waiting for the touch of his lover's hand.

The only band close to Miller's in popularity was Benny Goodman's. In 1934, before it was well known, the Goodman band was signed for *Let's Dance*, a new Saturday night radio program that began at 10:30 and ran for three hours in different time zones. With one Latin band, one sweet band, and one swing band rotating on the show, Goodman's swing arrangements sounded particularly exciting to young listeners and gave Goodman his first taste of national recognition. In need of a theme song for the program, Goodman, who had classical training, took a melody he entitled "Let's Dance," based on a piano piece from "Invitation to the Dance" by the early nineteenth-century German composer Carl Maria von Weber.

### "It's a Lovely Day Tomorrow" [*Louisiana Purchase*] (1940)
Lyrics and music by Irving Berlin (1888–1989)

On the same 1938 trip to England that led to "God Bless America," Irving Berlin wrote a second song that took on a particular resonance as events unfolded over the next year and a half.

When Berlin was in London for the September premiere of his latest movie, *Alexander's Ragtime Band*, the news of the Munich Pact upset him terribly. Among the people he was talking to was his friend Alexander Korda, a Hungarian-born British film producer. The two men were taking a cab down Fifth Avenue and had reached 58th Street when Korda asked Berlin why he hadn't yet written a new war song. A block later, Berlin had begun to hum. Ignoring Korda, he was completely caught up in the task. By the time they got to 52nd Street, he nudged Korda and said, "Say, listen to this. Do you think this'll do?"[84] He called his first "war song" of World War II, "It's a Lovely Day Tomorrow." One unnamed source, quoted in an English newspaper, reported that the song was first performed in London: "For the first time an American song is a success here before it is over there. In fact, it has not been heard in America."[85]

Back in the United States, Berlin was writing the score for a new musical, *Louisiana Purchase*. By the time the show opened on May 25, 1940, the War in Europe had begun and Berlin was still so troubled by events that he added the song he had written for Korda to the score. The day after the opening, the battle for Dunkirk began as British and French forces fell back to the English Channel and were eventually rescued. The star of Berlin's show was petite, chic Irene Bordoni, for many Americans the embodiment of Gallic charm. Her big number in the show was "It's a Lovely Day Tomorrow." As the German army rolled through France, she sang the words night after night—"Just forget your troubles and learn to say / Tomorrow is a lovely day"—with tear-filled eyes and a breaking voice, because she did not know if her family and friends were safe or even alive.

Berlin's opening reference to the bad news to be found on the front page of a newspaper leads to a suggestion that "there's consolation in the weather report." Like many "pollyanna songs" of the previous twenty years, it promises sunshine after gray skies, but given the state of the world and Berlin's own somber mood, it never quite manages to escape its inner sadness. Its lyric, set to a melancholy melody, urges the listener not to lose hope. That's a far cry from the bouncy optimism of such earlier pollyanna songs as "Look for the Silver Lining" and "Keep Your Sunny Side Up."

### "Java Jive" (1940)
Lyrics by Ben Oakland (1907–1979), music by Milton Drake
(1912–2006)

It's just possible that the best jive tune is the one that makes the least sense. Even its lyricist can't figure out why it "took off like rockets." Ben Oakland knows that the lyric "means nothing." He said to composer Milton Drake, "Why don't we do a satire on the word jive, and that's when we came up with lyrics which have become the mainstay of every coffee joint in the word . . . I ask you. What the hell is java jive? No sense whatsoever." One night, when he was playing it at a party, a record producer named Jack Kapp told him that the Ink Spots were going to record it the next morning. Oakland continues the story, "He says, 'It's sensational!,' I said. 'You're outta your mind, Jack! It's pure nonsense! It's a gag!' He was adamant. 'No, it isn't,' he says, 'get it over to me.' All I can say is bless him."[86]

### "We'll Meet Again" (1940)
Lyrics by Hughie Charles (1907–?), music by Ross Parker (1914–1974)

### "A Nightingale Sang in Berkeley Square" (1940)
Lyrics by Eric Maschwitz (1901–1969), music by Manning Sherwin (1902–1974)

### "(There'll Be Blue Birds Over) The White Cliffs of Dover" (1941)
Lyrics by Nat Burton (1901–1945), music by Walter Kent (1911–1994)

### "When the Lights Go on Again (All Over the World)" (1942)
Lyrics by Bennie Benjamin (1907–1989), music by Sol Marcus (1912–1976) and Eddie Seiler (1911–1952)

During the twenty-seven months between Germany's invasion of Poland and the Japanese attack on Pearl Harbor, growing numbers of Americans grew concerned that the United States would enter the war; they believed that it was only a matter of time. They were clearly on the side of the English, who soon stood alone against Hitler's forces. Part of the American people's emotional response lay in their embrace of songs that had first become popular in England (even when Americans had written them) and also of a young singer named Vera Lynn, who recorded most of them. The "love affair" started with one of the War's great love songs, the bittersweet but ultimately hopeful "We'll Meet Again," which lyricist Hughie Charles thought would be perfect for Lynn. Somehow, this singer with the rich but slightly sultry voice and a straightforward singing style, captured—even embodied—the mood of the British people during the War, much as Kate Smith did in the United States. "I always tried to choose cheerful songs," Lynn said in 2009, "that soldiers missing their wives and sweethearts could relate to. We weren't psychologists, but we understood that it was important to express the right meaning, and we put a lot of effort into getting the songs right."[87] "We'll meet again," the song insisted, even if we don't yet know the time or place.

Also in 1939, Eric Maschwitz and Manning Sherwin wrote "A Nightingale Sang in Berkeley Square," an equally optimistic and even more romantic affirmation of the survival of love. Once again, Vera Lynn recorded it. Maschwitz and Sherwin wrote it in the small French village of Le Lavandou in the summer of 1939, only a month or two before Hitler's armies crossed into Poland. Maschwitz confesses that they "stole" the title from a story by Michael Arlen. Since there are no nightingales anywhere near Berkeley

Square—something few Americans would have known—the title affirms the magical quality of the lovers' meeting in a slightly surreal setting, with "angels dining at the Ritz" when "the streets of town were paved with stars." Manning first played the song on a piano in a local bar, helped out by a resident saxophonist, while Maschwitz sang the words holding a glass of wine.

The next two songs are unusual in that neither is a love ballad. They resemble anthems in their ability to express the mood of a people during difficult days and, at the same time, project optimism about the future—not only victory but a restoration of the meaning of peace in terms that ordinary people will embrace: "Jimmy will go to sleep in his own little room again." Walter Kent and Nat Burton wrote "Bluebirds" at a time when the RAF and the Luftwaffe were fighting the Battle of Britain in the skies over the white cliffs of Dover, yet the song looked ahead to a time when the iconic cliffs would become a setting for a peaceful, even idyllic, life. The lyric's unintentional irony lies in the fact that bluebirds are not native to Britain. Perhaps Burton made the mistake because he, too, was an American songwriter and had never been to England. He and Kent were inspired by newspaper reports of the courage of ordinary Londoners during the Blitz, but they may also have borrowed the idea for the song from *The White Cliffs of Dover*, a book-length poem by Alice Duer Miller that was enormously popular in both countries once it appeared in 1940. It traces the sentimental story of a woman through both World Wars, but its unstated theme was Miller's desire to promote Anglo-American unity at a time when many Americans distrusted England. Miller was annoyed that Burton and Kent did not consult with her before publishing the song but she chose not to sue for their use of her title.

Like Burton and Kent, Bennie Benjamin, Sol Marcus, and Eddie Seiler were American songwriters even though their most important World War II song, "(When the Lights Go on Again) All Over the World," became popular first in Great Britain. They wrote it, Benjamin said many years later, because "it was a very bleak time and the lights had gone out. Darkness swept over the United States. That's where the idea came from." The three men had first met at a music-publishing house four years earlier when Seiler and Marcus asked Benjamin if he was songwriter: "I told them, 'Absolutely I'm a writer.' So they said, 'Let's hear what you've got.' I play them a couple of things and we hit it off. That night I took them up to Harlem and three or four hours later we had written 'I Don't Want to Set the World on Fire,'"[88] their first song together and their first hit.

# Chapter 11
## 1941–1945

**"Boogie Woogie Bugle Boy"** (1941)
Lyrics and music by Don Raye (1909–1985) and Hughie Prince (1906–1960)

**"I'll Remember April"** (1942) [*Ride 'Em, Cowboy*]
Lyrics by Gene de Paul (1919–1988) and Patricia Johnston (?), music by Don Raye (1909–1985)

**"Don't Sit Under the Apple Tree (With Anyone Else But Me)"**
[*Private Buckeroo*] (1939)
Lyrics by Lew Brown (1893–1958) and Charles Tobias (1898–1970), music by Sam H. Stept (1897–1964)

Collaborating was tough for Don Raye and Hughie Prince, because Raye had gone to Hollywood to write for the movies while Prince remained behind in New York. Universal Studios had signed them to write songs for *Buck Privates*, a movie starring the comedy team of Bud Abbott and Lou Costello, and featuring a young female singing trio, the Andrews Sisters. When the girls said they liked Raye and Prince's previous hit, "Beat Me, Daddy, Eight to the Bar," the songwriters tried to write a boogie-woogie variation on the same theme. They wrote "Boogie Woogie Bugle Boy" early in 1941, nearly a year before the United States entered World War II, but after the peacetime draft had begun.

Raye liked to base his songs on the hepcat styles and slang of the day. The Andrews Sisters liked "Bugle Boy" but Universal Studios wasn't sure that audiences would accept a female group singing boogie-woogie. Because the draft was a contentious political issue, the studio also feared that the public might resent treating it as a musical joke. The song told the story of a trumpeter who was the "top man at his craft," but was reduced to playing reveille in the army until his company commander wised up and drafted more musicians to form a band. From then on, every morning "the company jumps when he plays reveille." Maxine Andrews remembered that the sisters also wanted to add choreography, but Universal refused: "They didn't like the idea of the gals dancing at all . . . we had to learn the routines at night! We were busy shooting during the daytime, and we were not allowed to learn dancing on Universal's time." Without doubt, Patti, Maxene, and LaVerne's distinctive sound and energetic performing style contributed to the song's success. Maxene said that singing groups in those days "never moved, but we never could contain ourselves."[1]

Raye had more trouble selling a song the following year when he collaborated with composer Gene de Paul and co-lyricist Patricia Johnston on "I Remember April." Raye wrote the lyric after meeting Johnston and falling in love with her. A lyricist herself, she helped him polish what he had written. Because Raye had a reputation for boogie-woogie songs, the studios were not receptive to his writing a ballad. He and Gene de Paul had written three different songs that the studio rejected. When they took their fourth try to the producer, Raye made a point of saying that they had written the kind of song he wanted. But the producer turned it down again because it wasn't what they were looking for. The next day, Sam Goldwyn called a meeting at his house with the songwriters, the director, the producer, and the assistant producer—not the sort of meeting a couple of lowly songwriters often attended. Goldwyn did the talking: "I want you should write me a song that the first time you hear it, it should feel like an old favorite. I want it by four-thirty tomorrow afternoon." De Paul took Goldwyn at his word; he borrowed a melody from Antonin Dvorak's *New World Symphony* and took it to Goldwyn before the deadline. "I think you'll recognize it," he said. "It's got that 'old familiar' sound."[2] The studio placed the song in the Abbott and Costello vehicle *Ride 'Em, Cowboy,* but it still took three years and recordings by Kitty Kallen and Bing Crosby before it became a hit.

A lot of the Andrews Sisters' records were set to a boogie-woogie beat, commonly called "eight to the bar" because it is written in 4/4 time. Although composer Sam H. Stept had initially written a melody he called "Anywhere the Bluebird Calls," Lew Brown and Charles Tobias put new words to it to reflect what was on people's minds in the early days of World War II. Now called "Don't Sit Under the Apple Tree (With Anyone Else But Me)," it portrayed a soldier away from home, who pleads with his girl not to go back with somebody else to the place where they fell in love. The title sounds as if it will be a desperate plea, perhaps in the melodramatic style of the 1890s, but Stept's restrained boogie-woogie, and a chorus punctuating the plea for fidelity with "No, no, no, no" gives it an up-to-date jivey feel. It became a hit once the Andrews Sisters sang it in the 1942 movie musical, *Private Buckaroo*.

**"Chattanooga Choo Choo"** [*Sun Valley Serenade*] (1941)
Lyrics by Mack Gordon (1904–1959), music by Harry Warren
(1893–1981)

Harry Warren had a take on collaboration: "Ya know, when two fellas are sitting in a room it doesn't make any difference who wrote what. It's a wedding of two guys trying to write a song. A lyricist might contribute three or four lines of music." But he also had his own way of doing things. When Harry Warren left Warner Bros. for 20th Century Fox, his new studio assigned him to work with lyricist Mack Gordon, who had recently ended his collaboration with Harry Revel. Warren said that when Gordon hummed suggestions he would reply, "Mack, I'm not Harry Revel. Don't hum in my ear. It drives me crazy to have someone humming a melody when I'm trying to write one . . . It's tough trying to do your job, and I'd say, 'Don't worry about doing mine! I'll worry about the tune.'"[3] All in all, though, the change required relatively little adjusting on Warren's part, even though Gordon "was just about the opposite in temperament and style to me. He was a socializer and enjoyed the Hollywood life."[4]

More importantly, working with Gordon was similar to working with Al Dubin. The ideas and most of the titles came from Gordon, after which both men worked separately from the same lead sheet. Gordon would return with a complete lyric. "Dubin was the better-educated man," Warren said, "with a marvelous vocabulary. Mack didn't have the vocabulary, but he had an innate sense of song . . . What bothered me about working with him was his wanting to hear melody over and over, until I was sick of hearing my own music. We got around this by hiring a pianist . . ."[5] In 1940–1941, when their collaboration was brand new, they wrote the songs for seven movies; *Sun Valley Serenade*, featuring "Chattanooga Choo Choo," was the sixth.

Glenn Miller introduced the song in *Sun Valley Serenade* and then had the hit recording. Singer Margaret Whiting, the daughter of composer Richard Whiting, had a distinctly personal memory about the song. Cookie Warren, Harry's daughter, was her best friend: "One night, Warren told me that Glenn Miller was going to come to hear a song that Harry had written for him." Cookie had gotten dates for the two girls, but Margaret wanted to meet Miller: "So Harry sat at the piano and Glenn ended up picking up his trumpet and playing along to the song, which was 'Chattanooga Choo Choo'! I got to be one of the first people to hear it!"[6]

**"Let's Get Away from It All"** (1941), **"Everything Happens to Me"** (1940), and **"Violets for Your Furs"** (1941)
Lyrics by Tom Adair (1913–1988), music by Matt Dennis (1914–2002)

During his career as a songwriter, arranger, pianist, and singer, Matt Dennis wrote six standards, three of them in a single year. When Jo Stafford was singing with Tommy Dorsey's Orchestra, Dennis went to the Hollywood Palladium one night in December 1940 to hear her. Afterwards, she introduced him to Dorsey, who asked to hear some of his songs, liked what he heard, and offered Dennis a job: "How would you like to write for me? We'll record them."[7] Dennis had a problem, though: none of the melodies had lyrics. He contacted Tom Adair, whom he had met the previous year when Adair approached him with a lyric he had written, called "Will You Still Be Mine?" Dennis loved its sophistication and soon set it to music.

Dennis told an interviewer that Adair had been working as an operator handling complaints for the Los Angeles water company, "so we worked a lot over the phone."[8] Adair entitled his two new lyrics, "Everything Happens to Me" and "Let's Get Away from It All." The first is an amusing catalogue about the frustrations of a lifelong victim of Murphy's law. It begins with a golf date but it rains, continues through playing an ace after which a partner trumps, and concludes with a love affair whose end has provoked his complaint: "Your answer was goodbye and there was even postage due. / I fell in love just once, and then it had to be with you."

In that same interview, Dennis said, "We wrote 'Let's Get Away from It All' over the phone in about an hour, back and forth."[9] Instead of the traps into which the schlemiel in "Everything Happens to Me" keeps tumbling, "Let's Get Away from It All" is a cleverly rhymed exercise in escape—everything from taking a kayak to Nyack to a "powder to Boston for chowder." The means of travel vary from the ordinary to the surprising, but what makes them work is the reliance on the internal rhyme and alliteration in a line like "Let's take a kayak to Quincy or Nyack." Both songs make the necessary nod to love, but only toward the end and without losing the humor that makes the songs so appealing: "Let's go again to Niag'ra / This time we'll look at the Falls."

Dennis and Adair's third standard that year came from their visit to New York City to hear Billie Holiday sing at a nightspot called Mr. Kelly's. Dennis later recounted the story: "It was winter and the snow was really coming down," he recalled. "Tom had a date and he bought violets, and Billie was wearing furs, and we were thinking about what she might sing. Tom came up with the title and we scribbled it out, words and music, on the tablecloth. Sinatra recorded it right away."[10]

**"This Time the Dream's on Me"** [*Blues in the Night*] (1941) and **"Hit the Road to Dreamland"** [*Star Spangled Rhythm*] (1942)
Lyrics by Johnny Mercer (1909–1976), music by Harold Arlen (1905–1986)

Johnny Mercer liked to write lyrics about dreams and dreaming, maybe because his method of writing involved something akin to dreaming. Perhaps the strangest story about his working habits came from Harry Warren. When they were working together, Mercer would typically lean back with his eyes closed. Warren wasn't sure if he was asleep, so asked about Mercer's wife, "How's Ginger?" He got no answer, so he looked at his watch. It was lunchtime so he left. When he returned an hour later, Mercer had not moved. Warren sat down at the piano and Mercer, without opening his eyes, said in a matter-of-fact way, "She's fine."[11]

Even Harold Arlen, a gentler soul than Warren, once said about his collaborations with Mercer, "Our working habits were strange." Yet the dapper Arlen was known for coming up with ideas in unlikely places—while being taken for a drive down Sunset Boulevard or walking around the Central Park Reservoir with the dog he named Over the Rainbow. Arlen said:

> After we got a script and the spots for the songs were blocked out, we'd get together for an hour or so every day. While Johnny made himself comfortable on the couch, I'd play the tunes for him. He has a wonderfully retentive memory. After I would finish playing the songs, he'd just go away for a couple of weeks. Then he'd come around with the completed lyric.[12]

When Mercer returned with the lyric for "This Time the Dream's on Me," he wasn't especially pleased with his work. He had built it from a coined catchphrase based on the familiar expression "The drink's on me," but the result felt rushed. "It's one of Harold's nicest tunes. It's kind of a poor lyric, I think . . . I think it's too flip for that melody. I think it should be nicer . . . I could have improved it, too. I really could. I wish I had. But, you know, we had a lot of songs to get out in a short period of time, and we had another picture to do."[13]

For "Hit the Road to Dreamland," Mercer was much closer to the mark. To Arlen's tricky jazz rhythms, he contrived a colloquial lyric that finds the perfect equilibrium for a combination of humor and romance. When the last two customers in a railroad club car look for ways to delay saying goodnight, the waiters grow frustrated because they want to close up shop. Portrayed by the Golden Gate Quartet in the movie *Blues in the Night*, the waiters politely but firmly get the couple, played by Mary Martin and Dick Powell, to leave.

### "I Remember You" and "Tangerine" [*The Fleet's in*] (1941)
Lyrics by Johnny Mercer (1909–1976), music by Victor Schertzinger (1888–1941)

Johnny Mercer said of "I Remember You," "I wrote it very fast, ten minutes, half an hour at most." But he also said, "I wrote it for Judy Garland. I always had such a crush on Garland I couldn't think straight, so I wrote this song."[14] It was a lot more than infatuation, as Mercer biographer Philip Furia makes clear. They had at least two lengthy and intense affairs. In fact, Garland inspired a number of Mercer's lyrics, including "That Old Black Magic" and "Skylark," in addition to "I Remember You." Their relationship had begun in 1941, when Mercer was already married and Garland was engaged to composer-conductor David Rose. Even though Garland married Rose to bring the affair to an end, she continued as the inspiration for a number of Mercer's most ardent songs. He later said that "I Remember You" was his most direct expression of his feelings for her.[15] The song is as immediate an expression of passion as one is likely to find in a popular lyric, yet it is also simple and straightforward: "You're the one who said / 'I love you, too,' I do. / Didn't you know?"

When Mercer died in 1976, a friend suggested to his wife Ginger that "I Remember You" would make a suitable epitaph. She flew into a rage. A posthumous selection of Mercer's lyrics, which she and another friend edited, omitted "I Remember You," even though it is one of his important lyrics. Ironically, at Ginger's memorial service in 1994, the program had a caption beneath her photograph: "I Remember You."

"Tangerine" was more a matter of a songwriter exercising his craft. Looking back, Mercer seemed to be scratching his head as he observed, "I don't know why I called it 'Tangerine,' except that it had a kind of Latin flavor, the melody."[16] Songs with a Latin beat had been popular since the 1930s, when Franklin Roosevelt's Good Neighbor Policy and the arrival of the rhumba, a very successful dance from Cuba, influenced American attitudes. The popularity of Latin rhythms continued through the War years. Mercer said that, once he came up with the title word to provide a rhyme for "Argentine," "the course was set."[17] "Tangerine" becomes the name of an Argentine woman known for her dazzling beauty, "her eyes of night and lips as bright as flame." Here, with the sort of tossed-off ease that demonstrates a master at his work, Mercer fills the line with long "i" sounds to move the lyric along the melody it rests upon.

These songs are two of eight that Mercer wrote with Victor Schertzinger in 1942, all for the movie *The Fleet's In*. By all accounts a truly sweet guy, Schertzinger was also something of a triple threat: a violinist and conductor of symphony orchestras, a composer of popular songs, and a Hollywood director. These songs were Mercer and Schertzinger's only collaboration because the composer died suddenly soon after he finished the movie. Speaking of the way they worked together, Mercer said, "He gave you a tune on a lead sheet, and whatever you brought in pleased him. As they say, a doll to work with."[18]

### "(I Left My Heart at) The Stage Door Canteen"
[*This Is the Army*] (1942)
Lyrics and music by Irving Berlin (1888–1989)

Soon after the United States entered World War II, Irving Berlin gathered a company of professional entertainers who were in the armed forces, wrote a new revue score, and put together an all-soldier show, *This Is the Army*, to raise money for Army Relief—just as he had with *Yip, Yip Yaphank* when he was an enlisted man in World War I. *This Is the Army* had two hit songs: the comic anthem "This Is the Army, Mr. Jones," and Berlin's most important love song from those years, "(I Left My Heart at) The Stage Door Canteen." He wrote very little during the War because he accompanied *This Is the Army* on its post-Broadway tour to cities and army bases all over the country. It was so successful that it (and he) then went overseas to Europe and the Pacific. They did not quit until the War ended. Berlin not only played a significant role in keeping the show going, he also appeared onstage to revive the song he had written and performed in *Yip, Yip Yaphank*, "Oh, How I Hate to Get Up in the Morning." He even fit into his old World War I uniform. One afternoon, after watching Berlin rehearse the number, a stagehand announced, "If the composer of that song could hear the way that guy sings it, he'd turn over in his grave."[19]

In the earliest days of both World War I and II, songwriters turned first to patriotic songs. George M. Cohan wrote "Over There" the day after Congress passed a declaration of war in 1917, and Irving Berlin's original unused version of "God Bless America" was a martial anthem from 1917. Once we entered World War II, though, much of the glamor and romance faded in the aftermath of loneliness and longing, and the deaths in combat. In 1942, the government asked Tin Pan Alley to write only patriotic songs, but most of them had little appeal. The public wanted love songs that reflected the time, and songwriters and publishers were happy to comply. The songs' deepest appeal came from a melancholy strain that crept into most of them.

Because Berlin's show portrayed the soldiers who left rather than the women who stayed behind, the character in "Stage Door Canteen" is a young soldier. He has fallen in love with one of the hostesses at the Canteen but must leave to return to duty and, the song implies, combat. The show opened on July 4, 1942, only seven months after Pearl Harbor; emotions were still raw and close to the surface. Listening to a soldier who does not have time even to say goodbye to the woman he loves would have been emotionally trying for audiences. Berlin did not diminish the emotion but he contained it by adding an amusing secondary story to the lyric. The soldier describes how he kept her serving him coffee as he sat, dunking donut after donut "until she caught on."

### "I'm Old-Fashioned" [*You Were Never Lovelier*] (1942)
Lyrics by Johnny Mercer (1909–1976), music by Jerome Kern (1885–1945)

You don't expect to find the names of Jerome Kern and Johnny Mercer on the same piece of sheet music. Kern was thirty-four years older than Mercer; he grew up in New York City and was shaped by operetta and Broadway. Mercer grew up in Savannah and was shaped by jazz and the blues. Yet Mercer once told lyricist and Mercer biographer Gene Lees, "I can't remember when I didn't love a Jerome Kern or Victor Herbert melody. To grow up with these tunes coloring my youth was one of the greatest gifts anyone could have."[20] Kern and Mercer collaborated on the score for one movie, *You Were Never Lovelier*, starring Fred Astaire and Rita Hayworth. When they met, the normally shy Kern played several of his songs, Mercer recalled, "but he did play me this song . . . and I had an idea for it. I brought it in, and he played it over. And he got to that note '*stay* old-fashioned' and he got up and he *hugged* me."[21] Then Kern, who was as demanding as he was shy, called his wife. Mercer continued, "She ran downstairs and he kissed me on the cheek and he said, 'Wait'll you hear this lyric!' Well, of course, you know, that makes you feel like a million dollars. It's just a fair lyric, but he was pleased."[22]

Soon after, Kern invited singer Margaret Whiting to come to his home to hear the score. He had heard that she was a good judge of songs and knew that she and Mercer were close through her father, composer Richard Whiting. When Kern played the score for her, he paused after "I'm Old-Fashioned" to tell her that Mercer was a genius.[23]

### "(I've Got a Gal in) Kalamazoo" [*Orchestra Wives*] (1942)
Lyrics by Mack Gordon (1904–1959), music by Harry Warren (1893–1981)

Early in the twentieth century, when Dixie songs were all the rage, L. Wolfe Gilbert made the mistake of setting "Waiting for the Robert E. Lee" "Way down on the levee / In old Alabamy." Gilbert did not know that Alabama had no levees, because he had never been there. Songs were more interested in atmosphere and romance than accuracy. As Harry Warren put it:

I've had a lot of titles about places that I've never been to. I think everybody around in those days was writing about far-off places they'd never been to. A lot of fellas wrote southern songs about Dixie and they'd never been down there, they didn't know anything about it. But they wrote them just the same. I've written songs like "Shuffle Off to Buffalo." I've gone through Buffalo but I never stayed in Buffalo. Like Kalamazoo. The city of Chattanooga, I'm an honorary citizen, but I've never been there.[24]

As for the writing of "Kalamazoo," Warren explained that he had "written the complete melody as a kind of rhythmic exercise, with no thought of lyrics."[25] He said:

I had a dum-dum-dum-dum rhythm going in my head, which was why Johnny Mack [lyricist Mack Gordon] and I decided to spell out the name. And I had been in Kalamazoo when I was very young and had carved my name on the wall of the railroad station there. I guess maybe that was the basis for the lyric. It wasn't the first song to spell out its title, but it was an angle that worked.[26]

He also admired Gordon's skill at fitting "his words to the music, and I've always thought that was a very neat and clever piece of writing."[27]

Two years later, in the middle of the War, Warren and Gordon wrote "No Love, No Nothin'" for Alice Faye to sing in *The Gang's All Here,* but most people remembered Carmen Miranda's performance (along with Busby Berkeley's orgasmically surreal staging) of "The Lady in the Tutti-Frutti Hat." It was one of several Latin numbers that they wrote for the tiny Brazilian star, including "Chica Chica Boom Chic" and "I Yi Yi Yi (I Like You Very Much)," as well as a Brazilian styled "Chattanooga Choo-Choo." Miranda once asked Warren how he wrote all those Brazilian melodies for her. "Honey," he answered, "they're not Brazilian—they're Italian, but don't tell anybody."[28]

## "Road to Morocco" [*Road to Morocco*] (1942)
Lyrics by Johnny Burke (1908–1964), music by Jimmy Van Heusen (1913–1990)

For Jimmy Van Heusen and Johnny Burke, writing songs for the Bing Crosby–Bob Hope "Road" pictures was the end of the beginning. In 1939, Van Heusen was a 26-year-old composer in New York who had written a few hits, mainly with lyricist Edgar DeLange. Burke was an up-and-coming piano player in Hollywood, except he preferred to write lyrics. They met by chance in New York when Burke went East for a vacation. Even though Burke was outgoing and Van Heusen quiet, both men were in need of new collaborators. Burke wandered into Van Heusen's office one day to shoot

**FIGURE 11.1**   Jimmy Van Heusen (seated) and Johnny Burke. Courtesy of Photofest.

the breeze, Van Heusen remembered long afterward: "He asked, 'Got any tunes?' I said, 'Sure!' "[29] That led to their first song together, "Oh, You Crazy Moon," a minor success. Then they wrote one of Frank Sinatra's biggest early hits, "Polka Dots and Moonbeams." Their fourth song together was "Imagination," shaped by a series of graceful questions and associations that borders on humor ("Starts you asking a daisy, / What to do, what to do?") set to an engagingly easy melody by Van Heusen. Although sheet music usually makes it clear which collaborator is the composer and which the lyricist, the reality is often not that simple. As Burke said, they sat together at the piano, "where Jimmy Van Heusen and I wrote practically simultaneously."[30]

The two men soon had a reputation as a couple of young songwriters to watch. When producer Mark Sandrich listened to a recording of "Imagination" on the radio and found that he couldn't get the melody out of his head, he yelled to one of his flunkies to "get that guy!"[31] In Hollywood, Van Heusen was the newcomer. Burke had already written several hits with composers Arthur Johnston ("Pennies from Heaven") and James Monaco ("On the Sentimental Side"). Their first movie collaboration was the score for the third of what would eventually total seven "Road" pictures, a series of comedies starring Crosby, Hope, and Dorothy Lamour. In these broad spoofs of the film genres of the day, the main characters travel from Singapore to Zanzibar to Rio to Bali. The gags were zany and often ad-libbed, the girls gorgeous, the dancers silly, and the songs usually topnotch. Burke's lyric for the title song managed to conclude by combining the silly with the topnotch in a memorable pun: "Like *Webster's Dictionary*, we're Morocco-bound."

Unlike most songwriters, Burke spent almost his entire career at a single studio, Paramount. He worked on forty-one different movies, twenty-five of them starring Crosby. With Burke and later with Sammy Cahn, Van Heusen wrote songs for twenty-three movies with Crosby in the lead.

### "Comin' in on a Wing and a Prayer" (1943)
Lyrics by Harold Adamson (1906–1980), music by Jimmy McHugh (1894–1969)

During World War II, the federal government's Office of War Information urged songwriters to set aside love and romance for patriotism. Most of the resulting songs flopped because the public knew what it wanted. Before long, Tin Pan Alley was back to providing love songs that suited

**FIGURE 11.2.** Lyricist Harold Adamson stands between a studio executive and movie actress Carole Landis; composer Jimmy McHugh (right) sits next to crooner Dick Haymes. Courtesy of Photofest.

the time—songs about parting, separation, loneliness and longing, and the dream of return. But Jimmy McHugh had already accepted a government commission to write patriotic songs. "Comin' in on a Wing and a Prayer" was his first and "Say a Prayer for the Boys Over There" (with lyricist Herb Magidson) his second.

McHugh and Sonny Bragg, a student and football player at Duke, had begun an occasional correspondence after they met at a reception when the Duke team played USC in the Rose Bowl in 1939. In 1943, after a long absence, Bragg wrote apologetically to announce that he had been drafted and was flying missions over Europe from a base in North Africa. He wrote, "On my last trip, half a wing was shot away, but we managed to return on one wing and a prayer."[32] McHugh saw in that sentence an idea for a song and a stirring title that he loved: "Comin' in on a Wing and a Prayer."

He approached Frank Loesser about working on the song together. McHugh knew that Loesser was beginning to write both words and music, so he expected the collaboration to last for only a short time, but Loesser's response to McHugh's title was succinct: "I don't like it." On the spot, McHugh bet him that the song he hadn't written yet would outsell Loesser's recent wartime hit, "Praise the Lord and Pass the Ammunition," and contacted his old collaborator, Harold Adamson, to write the lyrics. Once the song became a hit, McHugh told reporters that the melody came "like a bolt from the blue," and then Adamson polished off the lyrics in a few minutes.[33] Although they wrote dozens of songs together over the next five years, McHugh called it one of the quickest songs they ever wrote—the story of a crew's struggle to return to their base after a successful bombing run. Adamson responded to McHugh's staccato musical line with words that sound like a truncated message: a missing plane two hours overdue; the radios humming, waiting for word; and then the pilot's reassuring message that they were "comin' in on a wing and prayer."

**"Der Fuehrer's Face"** [*Der Fuehrer's Face*] (1943)
Lyrics and music by Oliver G. Wallace (1887–1963)

**"Mairzy Doats"** (1943)
Lyrics and music by Milton Drake (1912–2006), Al Hoffman (1902–1960), and Jerry Livingston (1909–1987)

Among the great successes of 1943 were "As Time Goes By" (originally written in 1932, but a hit ten years later because of its inclusion in

*Casablanca*), "Don't Get Around Much Anymore," "Jukebox Saturday Night," "Comin' in on a Wing and a Prayer," "You'll Never Know," and—oh, yes— "Der Fuehrer's Face" and "Mairzy Doats." They are as unlikely a pair of hits as popular music has ever produced, especially in the same year. It shouldn't surprise anybody to learn that Spike Jones—he of the maniacal sound effects—had hit recordings of both songs.

Songwriter Milton Drake's 4-year-old daughter came home one day singing an English nursery rhyme, but she garbled the words. "Cows eat wheat and sows eat wheat and little sharks eat oysters" came out as "Cowzy tweet and sowzy tweet and liddle sharksy doysters." Drake realized that there was a song hidden in there. When he got together with Al Hoffman and Jerry Livingston, they kept the same rhythm but had to come up with a tune for their new words. Once they finished it, though, nobody would publish it; it was too silly. Finally, Hoffman took "Mairzy Doats" to his friend, bandleader Al Trace. Trace and his band, the Silly Symphonists, were the first to perform and record it.

Composer Oliver Wallace, who worked for the Disney Studios from 1936 until his retirement in 1956, was the musical director for five full-length Disney movies—*Dumbo* (1941), *Cinderella* (1950), *Alice in Wonderland* (1951), *Peter Pan* (1953), and *Lady and the Tramp* (1955). Mostly, though, he wrote the music for nearly 150 animated shorts, including *Der Fuehrer's Face,* a satiric Donald Duck cartoon. One day, Wallace ran into Disney in a corridor. "Ollie, I want a serious song," Disney told him, "but it's got to be funny." Disney explained that it was going to be used in a cartoon about what Wallace later called "Donald's adventures in Naziland." He asked for more information. "Suppose the Germans are singing it," Disney said. "To them it's serious. To us it's funny." And he walked away, leaving Wallace with no clue about what he needed to write.[34]

Wallace finally wrote the chorus to "Der Fuehrer's Face" as he rode his bicycle to the grocery store with his wife. The next day he sang it all over the studio, complete with shpritzing punctuation: "Heil [shpritz], heil [shpritz], right in the Fuehrer's face!" Eventually, Disney walked out in the hall to say, "Let's hear it." Wallace tried to stall because he didn't know what Disney would think of a robust Bronx cheer. Could he use such a sound in a Walt Disney picture? Disney insisted and, Wallace said, "I let loose. Walt laughed. The rest is history."[35] When Oscar Hammerstein heard the song, he called it "the great psychological song of the war."[36]

### "Happiness Is Just a Thing Called Joe" [*Cabin in the Sky*] (1943)
Lyrics by E.Y. Harburg (1896–1981), music by Harold Arlen (1905–1986)

In 1940, Vernon Duke and John La Touche wrote the rich score for the all-black Broadway musical, *Cabin in the Sky*, including "Taking a Chance on Love," "Honey in the Honeycomb," and the title number. Ironically, E.Y. Harburg had turned down Duke's invitation to collaborate with him, but in Hollywood three years later, producer Arthur Freed told Yip that the score needed some "Southern songs" and asked him to write them, "and I got Harold [Arlen] and we rewrote the score." Harburg had declined Duke's offer because the original score consisted of "smart, charming, sophisticated songs" that Harburg thought were wrong for the material. Duke, who had a hot temper, "got mad at me and never talked to me again for a long time."[37]

By "Southern," Freed meant black, so there could have been no better choice than Arlen, with his passion for the blues and his awareness of the melancholy of Jewish liturgical music; his father was a cantor with a gift for improvisation, but his music, according to critic John S. Wilson, was "jazz-based" and "blues-rooted." It placed him "alongside Duke Ellington rather than Richard Rodgers or Jerome Kern or Irving Berlin."[38] Arlen told interviewer Michael Whorf with uncommon modesty:

> I have been able to capture the feeling, and only the feeling of the black experience in my music . . . "Happiness Is Just a Thing Called Joe" is wistful and poignant but it's not the blues . . . I was enormously impressed by the blues and it would seem that being influenced by them, I had inherited some sort of mantle which is not altogether legitimate. There are a number of blues strains in my songs . . . There's a rapport there . . . but technically you can't really call that the blues either.[39]

Harburg thought that Arlen's combination of what he called Negro rhythms and Hebraic melodies made "a terrific combination, a fresh chemical reaction."[40] The movie also gave audiences a chance to see another kind of chemistry: black performers who were often denied mainstream opportunities because of race. The cast included Ethel Waters, Eddie "Rochester" Anderson, Lena Horne, John W. Bubbles, and Rex Ingram.

Arlen and Harburg did not replace the score's standards but they added five new songs, including "Li'l Black Sheep," "Life's Full of Consequences," and "Happiness Is Just a Thing Called Joe." Arlen thought that a melody he tentatively took from his trunk for "Happiness" was too ordinary, but Harburg had always loved it. Arlen was reluctant to use it until Harburg listened to it again and said, "Happiness is just a thing called Joe." Then, the lyricist said, "He began liking the tune, and he let me use it. And he was going to throw it away. Harold had a lot of tunes that I would love to resuscitate."[41] "Happiness" was the only important movie song Harburg wrote after *The Wizard of Oz.*

Even though "Happiness" was the score's major love ballad, Harburg knew that he was writing it for a specific character: a religious, middle-aged black woman living in the rural South with her lovable but conniving husband. Harburg's lyric plays off contrasting images of poverty ("Sometimes the cabin's gloomy and the table's bare") and images of hope ("He's got a way that makes the angels heave a sigh"). Yet as a lyricist, he understood the importance of rhyme, not only as a way of enforcing the song's rhythm and its musical structure, but as a way of propelling the song forward. He said, "You want to rhyme as many places as you can without the average ear spotting it as purely mechanical."[42] His biographers selected examples from "Happiness Is Just a Thing Called Joe": "He's got a *smile* that makes the *lil*ac wanna grow" and the subtler "Sometimes the *ca*bin's gloomy *an'* the table bare."

### "I Couldn't Sleep a Wink Last Night" [*Higher and Higher*] (1943)
Lyrics by Harold Adamson (1906–1980), music by Jimmy McHugh (1894–1969)

Tin Pan Alley cranked out large numbers of songs about telephones. The difference between most of the others and "I Couldn't Sleep a Wink Last Night" is that most of the others appeared before 1920, when the telephone was new and exciting. The earlier songs, rooted more in behavior ("Call me up some rainy afternoon") than emotion ("I thought my heart would break the whole night through"), became less popular when songs became moodier and more reflective beginning in the 1930s.

In 1943, Jimmy McHugh's major challenge was composing melodies that suited Frank Sinatra. When he and Harold Adamson got the script for *Higher and Higher,* the crooner's first movie, they followed McHugh's standard approach to writing movie songs. First, they identified the music cues in the story so they could rough out ideas for songs. Then McHugh would return to the piano. In *Higher and Higher,* they found a scene with a lover's quarrel that they wanted to open into a production number. Adamson called McHugh at 3 a.m. to say he had been listening to an overnight music program that suddenly cut away for the news. "There's our title for the production number," he announced, "The Music Stopped." McHugh immediately went to work. He said later, "I began concentrating on the lovers' spat and came down with insomnia. As the thousandth sheep jumped over the fence, both tune and title landed: 'I Couldn't Sleep a Wink Last Night.'"[43]

When McHugh and Adamson got together the next day, they finished the song in thirty minutes.

McHugh always believed that "the best tunes come fast. You wait until an idea hits you and then get it down fast." He had a habit of jotting things on whatever was at hand—menus, gin rummy score sheets, even telegrams. On one occasion, several years before he wrote "I Couldn't Sleep a Wink Last Night," an idea for a melody had awakened him late at night, but he couldn't find any manuscript paper. He scribbled the notes on the bed sheet, but by morning had forgotten all about it. By the time he remembered, the sheets were on their way to the laundry. It took several frantic phone calls to get the sheet—and the song—back to him.

### "I'll Be Home for Christmas" (1943)
Lyrics and music by Kim Gannon (1900–1974), Buck Ram (1907–1991), and Walter Kent (1911–1994)

Songwriters had produced popular songs for Christmas long before Irving Berlin's "White Christmas," but once Berlin redefined the setting for America's Christmas as an idealized, snow-covered New England, and defined it emotionally as a nostalgic but tremulous time of sweet memory combined with loneliness and longing, Christmas songs took on a new resonance, especially during the remaining years of World War II. Perhaps Bing Crosby had an advantage because he had the most popular recording of "White Christmas"; within a year, he also sang Kim Gannon, Buck Ram, and Walter Kent's "I'll Be Home for Christmas," the most successful recording of 1943. Unfortunately, its promise of fidelity and return did not match well with the song's history, both before and after its popularity.

One night during the Christmas season of 1942, Kent, Ram, and fellow songwriter Nat Burton were trading stories in a New York City diner. Kent knew Burton well because they had collaborated on "(There'll Be Blue Birds Over) The White Cliffs of Dover" the previous year. Ram talked about a song he'd written twenty years earlier about leaving home and missing his mother. He happened to have it with him. Kent, who was Jewish, started to laugh at the irony: Ram had written a Christmas song for his Jewish mother. In the midst of general laughter, Ram reminded them of "White Christmas" and said his song also had the stuff to become a hit. The conversation soon moved on to other things.

When Kent and Gannon collaborated again the following summer, they began by jotting down several ideas. The one they liked best was "I'll Be Home for Christmas (If Only in My Dreams)." They recognized the similarity to what Ram had written but believed it was limited to the two titles. They copyrighted their song in August, and again in September after revising both the music and words. Ram was stunned when he learned that Crosby had recorded a song with the same title as his, but nothing would have come of it if he hadn't seen Kent and Gannon's names on the recording. Although he had not heard it, he believed that they had stolen his idea from that night in the diner. Furious, he hired a lawyer and sued.

Kent claimed that he thought his and Gannon's song was different in both its melody and its words, so the use of virtually the same title should not have been an issue. Gannon said he had completely forgotten the earlier song and found his inspiration in the emotions of people separated by the War. The judge found no similarities in the two songs beyond the title. Since you cannot copyright a title, there would have been no legal case except for that conversation in the diner. The judge ordered the publisher to add Ram's name and to pay him a third of the royalties.

**"Speak Low"** and **"That's Him"** [*One Touch of Venus*] (1943)
Lyrics by Ogden Nash (1902–1971), music by Kurt Weill (1900–1950)

Kurt Weill went at things nonstop. He wrote to his parents after the opening of *One Touch of Venus*, "During the seven weeks before the show's

**FIGURE 11.3**   Mary Martin sings Kurt Weill and Ogden Nash's "That's Him" in *One Touch of Venus*. Courtesy of Photofest.

opening I never slept more than two or three hours a night, because I had to be at rehearsals during the day and had to orchestrate at night."[44] He also suggested the key line to Ogden Nash from Shakespeare's *Much Ado About Nothing*—"Speak low, if you speak love"—for the score's major love ballad. His intensity troubled his wife, singer Lotte Lenya, because he had high blood pressure (and eventually died at the young age of 50).

Producer Cheryl Crawford liked the show's plot about a statue of Venus, the goddess of love, who comes to life and falls overwhelmingly in love with an ordinary fellow, a barber named Rodney. In it, she saw a contrast between "the world as we see it and as the goddess sees it . . . I thought it could have social bearing and also be amusing."[45] Based on librettist Bella Spewack's first draft, Crawford, Weill, and Nash thought that Marlene Dietrich would be perfect in the part. She was interested but elusive until S.J. Perelman replaced Spewack and recast the character of Venus as what Dietrich called "too sexy and profane."[46] Four or five actresses later, Crawford and Weill settled on Mary Martin. To convince her to take the part, the composer sang the score for her and her husband, producer Richard Halliday. Martin was especially taken by his singing of "That's Him": "All my life I will remember that man singing Venus' lovely number . . . with a kind of quavery, German sound."[47]

To further reassure Martin, Halliday promised her that she would appear in beautiful clothes. He contacted the couturier Mainbocher. He was reluctant to work in the theater but agreed to listen to her sing the score. As Weill played the introduction to "That's Him," Martin "picked up a little chair and carried it over right in front of Main. I sat on it sideways and sang 'That's Him' right smack into those kind brown eyes." He said when she finished, "I will do your clothes for the show if you will promise me one thing. Promise me you'll always sing this song that way. Take a chair down to the footlights, sing across the orchestra to the audience as if it were just one person."[48] Dressed in a negligee in a hotel room for a night of lovemaking between a goddess and a barber, Martin sang the song with its mix of rapture and absurdity just that way. Agnes DeMille, who choreographed the show, said that Lotte Lenya told Martin to bring her chair to the footlights. "Martin was used to belting things with a high little voice that sounded like a boy soprano. But she whispered 'That's Him' like a girl confessing she was in love for the first time. It was charming."[49]

## "Straighten Up and Fly Right" (1943)
Lyrics by Irving Mills (1894–1985), music by Nat K. Cole (1919–1965)

Nat "King" Cole and his trio had a ten-week stand in Omaha, Nebraska. To pass the time when he wasn't performing, he wrote the melody to

"Straighten Up and Fly Right." It became a hit the next year, partly because its mix of jazz and pop appealed to black and white audiences alike. Mills, the persistent music publisher who both encouraged and exploited African American songwriters, appears on the sheet music as the lyricist, but Cole actually wrote the words. They come from a black folk tale that Cole's father, a Baptist minister in Chicago, had once used as the basis of a sermon. A buzzard takes different animals for a ride but, when he gets hungry, he throws them off before swooping down to eat them for dinner. When he tries the trick one time too many, a monkey wraps his tail around the buzzard's neck and nearly chokes him to death. The lyric mixes a familiar cautionary tale with jive talk, and uses its title as the refrain's memorable catchphrase.

Lyricist Johnny Mercer, the idea man behind the founding of Capitol Records in 1942, asked Cole to record the song for the young label; it sold more than half a million copies and was the Cole Trio's first mainstream hit, even though Cole had sold the song's rights to Mills for $50, a common practice of the day, especially for black songwriters.

### "Sunday, Monday, or Always" [*Dixie*] (1943)
Lyrics by Johnny Burke (1908–1964), music by Jimmy Van Heusen (1913–1990)

Jimmy Van Heusen and Johnny Burke wrote mainly for Bing Crosby from the late 1930s into the 1950s, just as Van Heusen and Sammy Cahn wrote for Crosby and Frank Sinatra after the Van Heusen–Burke and Jule Styne–Cahn collaborations ended. Burke and Van Heusen's last hit together was the mournful "Here's That Rainy Day" in 1953, and among Van Heusen and Cahn's first hits together were "Love and Marriage" and "The Tender Trap" in 1955. Van Heusen and Cahn's songs were slicker and more expansive, Van Heusen and Burke's gentler and more fanciful. Cahn's lyrics were direct, Burke's seemingly made of air. Cahn thought of his lyrics as work and punched them out on a typewriter. On the other hand, Frank Sinatra called Burke "the Poet."[50] Van Heusen called him "a born poet" with an "easy style, pretty but not cloying. That was his trademark."[51]

It is hard to believe that Burke and Van Heusen finished so many songs that became hits, because Burke worked so slowly. He was a painstaking writer who often took weeks to finish a single lyric. "He always started at the bottom," Cahn said of him. "He'd lay out a key idea, and then he'd write the line backwards. [As a result,] the songs were lacier, more fragile."[52] Burke, whose lyrics often had a genuinely poetic strain, explained himself more simply than that. All he had to do, he said, was "to listen to Bing's conversation and either take my phrases directly from him or pattern something after his way of putting phrases together."[53] In "Sunday, Monday, or Always," the combination of the melody's narrow range and Burke's use of simple questions and answers seems perfectly suited to the laconic, laid-back crooner. Of the forty-one movies on which Burke worked, twenty-five starred Crosby. Their association began when he was writing with Arthur Johnston ("Pennies from Heaven"), and continued with Jimmy Monaco ("I've Got a Pocketful of Dreams") and then Van Heusen.

### "Dream" (1944)
Lyrics and music by Johnny Mercer (1909–1976)

Has there ever been a better lyricist than Johnny Mercer? Because he wrote both words and music to "Dream," it's an especially good song for tracing his approach to writing, from the most imaginative and theoretical down to the most specific and practical. Mercer's father always wondered how his son became so interested in jazz and songwriting. When Mercer was in his 60s, he offered an explanation of sorts:

**FIGURE 11.4**   Johnny Mercer and Jo Stafford singing on the radio during World War II. Courtesy of Photofest.

[My father] had probably forgotten how, when I was tiny, three or four maybe, he would sit in front of the fireplace in his rocking chair and sing me songs from an old songbook, written, I think, by Charles Wakefield Cadman, among which were his favorites—"Oh, Genievieve, Sweet Genievieve," "In the Gloaming," and "When You and I Were Young, Maggie." Maybe I was a product of the roaring '20s but I know that a lot of songs that I have written over the intervening years were probably due to those peaceful moments in his arms. Secure and warm, I would drift off to dreams, just as later on, out on the starlit veranda, I would lie in the hammock and, lulled by the night sounds, the cricket sounds, safe in the buzz of grown-up talk and laughter, or the sounds of far-off singing in the distance, my eyelids would grow heavy and the sandman, Japanese or local, was not someone to steal you away, but a friend to take you to the "land of dreams" and another day. There to find another glorious adventure to be lived, experienced and cherished, and— maybe someday—put into a song.[54]

Although his writing methods varied, Mercer was thoughtful about his own abilities: "If I have any gift all, I think it's that I can get the mood of a tune and try to write words for it." He never worked for more than half a day and, if he got tired, he simply quit until tomorrow. "I let my subconscious do the work," he said. "It's a remarkable instrument." Most of the time he began with a title or a simple idea, "and then the rest of the words just seem to fall into place." It was rarely as easy or quick as he makes it sound, but he was understandably reluctant to reduce his words to something mechanical. When he wrote the music as well, as with "Dream," he wrote a few words, used one finger to beat out a melody, and then went back to the next words—back and forth until the song was finished. He says, "It's all as easy as chopping up ten cords of wood per day!"[55]

At the same time, Mercer had mastered the rules of songwriting. For instance, he knew not to begin a line with the same consonant that ended the previous line, and he knew that long vowels best fit the long notes that occur at the end of musical phrases. He knew about the hard consonants like "b" and "k" and the liquid ones like "m" and "n" and "r." So he could write a melody that sustains the "m" at the end of the title word, followed by a brief rest, and then the rest of the line whose lyric illuminates the title word: "Dream, that's the thing to do."

In 1944, Mercer wrote a theme song for a radio show, "The Chesterfield Supper Club," that starred Perry Como and Jo Stafford. "I was just fooling around at the piano," Mercer said, "and I got a series of chords that attracted me." Mercer described what he does as fooling around at the piano, so writing a ballad is much tougher than writing a rhythm tune.[56] The chord sequence he stumbled upon came unintentionally from "Whispering," a John Schoenberger–Richard Coburn–Vincent Rose song from 1920 that Mercer had loved as a child. He built his new song from it, but he insisted the result was different enough so he could rightly claim that he hadn't copied it. As usual with Mercer, the lyric followed the melody. Because he wrote it for a show sponsored by a cigarette company, he included the line, "Just watch the smoke rings rise in the air." He also admitted that he didn't think the words meant a great deal but "just seemed to go with the melody." Maybe so, but the lyrics' theme of searching for a new world was one of Mercer's major themes throughout his career[57] and was especially apt during World War II.

**"It's Been a Long, Long Time"** (1944)
Lyrics by Sammy Cahn (1913–1993), music by Jule Styne (1905–1994)

Songs have always reflected their own time, but during World War II the connection between a song's outlook and its time of composition was often striking. The melancholy ballads "Don't Get Around Much Anymore" and "I Don't Want to Walk without You" could only have been written in 1942, the War's darkest year, and "It's Been a Long, Long Time" had to have been from a time when anticipation was everywhere and returning home only a matter of time. Jule Styne and Sammy Cahn wrote many hits during the War years—those dreamy romantic ballads that so many people hung their hopes on. "It's Been a Long, Long Time," with its romantic yet increasingly erotic repetition—"Kiss me once, then kiss me twice / Then kiss me once again"—appeared when victory and returning home were close. Dreams were about to come true. In fact, Cahn explained that "we tried to stay one step ahead of the generals. One day I looked at the maps and I said to Jule . . . 'You know, I think this war might be coming to an end.'"[58] That observation led to the writing of "It's Been a Long, Long Time." Part of the song's success also rested on Cahn's approach to a ballad. Styne said of their many successes together, "He loved that big-band sound so every song had that big-band sound."[59]

When the ballad became a hit, Jerome Kern told a mutual friend that he'd like to meet Styne. Every Monday night, a group of select songwriters had been gathering at Kern's house—Ira Gershwin, Harry Warren, Harold Arlen, Johnny Mercer, and Hoagy Carmichael. They would chat about what was happening in the business and, if anyone had a new song, he'd play it. Styne was eager to attend. After all, Kern was considered the greatest composer of all of them. When he arrived, Kern greeted him: "I've heard a lot about you. You've got a number one song now. Please play it for us."[60] By the end of the night, they had asked the diminutive but irrepressible Styne to join their group.

The next night, Kern tracked down Styne at a friend's house to invite him to breakfast the following morning. After their meal together, Kern took Styne into his study and reached into a desk drawer. What could Kern want? Styne wondered. Was he going to pull out a script? Instead he pulled out a racing form. "I hear you're the greatest handicapper in town," he said. "Ira Gershwin told me."[61]

### "Saturday Night (Is the Loneliest Night in the Week)" (1944)
Lyrics by Sammy Cahn (1913–1993), music by Jule Styne (1905–1994)

It sounds like a fine title for a romantic lament about separation and longing typical of World War II, but "Saturday Night Is the Loneliest Night in the Week" is one of the few rhythm tunes to become a major hit during those years. What's unusual is that Sammy Cahn wrote the lyric before Jule Styne gave him a melody, but what's fitting is that he did it on a Saturday night. The two songwriters were living at the Gotham Hotel in New York City while they were working on a Broadway musical to star comedian Phil Silvers.

One Saturday night, Cahn was sitting alone in Styne's hotel suite waiting for the composer to return from an evening on the town. At about seven o'clock, Sammy's sister Florence and her husband Jules dropped by. "No girls, no guys, are you feeling okay?" she asked. "Why are you wearing a robe?" Cahn explained that Saturday night is for "civilians," but people in the business who aren't working stay home. For show people, he said, "Saturday night is the loneliest night of the week."[62] Soon after his visitors left, Cahn sat down at the piano. He did not have a new tune from Styne, but he did have the sort of dummy melody that some lyric writers liked to carry around in their heads. Because almost any lyric would fit, it gave a lyricist a way to get started. Cahn played eight bars and then wrote down some words.

By the time Styne returned several hours later, Cahn met him at the door with his newly finished lyric. An hour later, Styne had fashioned a new melody, even though he preferred to write the music first. Despite his success as a composer, Styne believed that the words were more important than the music. "When the music is written first," he explained, "the lyricist will do his best job because he is not writing to his own preconceived rhythmic notions."[63] Once they had finished their new song, the two songwriters rode the elevator to the penthouse where Manny Sachs, the president of Columbia Records, was running his weekly poker game. Cahn asked, "You fellows ready?" When they finished performing the song, Jonie Taps of Shapiro-Bernstein Music Company offered them $1,000 for it. The next morning, though, Sachs called Frank Sinatra, for whom Styne and Cahn wrote a lot of songs, "Your fellows gave away a song last night." Sinatra called Cahn to undo the giveaway and eventually recorded the hit version of the song.[64]

### "Swinging on a Star" [*Going My Way*] (1944)
Lyrics by Johnny Burke (1908–1964), music by Jimmy Van Heusen (1913–1990)

One version of the story has Johnny Burke having dinner at Bing Crosby's house when he got the inspiration for "Swinging on a Star." The other version credits composer Jimmy Van Heusen in a somewhat different telling of the same story.

Crosby, who was about to star in Paramount's *Going My Way*, invited Burke home for dinner to talk about a song to fit a particular slot in the unfinished movie. With the help of an old flame played by opera star Rise Stevens, Father Chuck O'Malley played by Crosby arranges to have his boy's choir audition some songs for a music publisher. The money the songs raise could save St. Dominic's, the rundown church overseen by Father Fitzgibbon (Barry Fitzgerald in an Oscar-winning performance). The boys sing the title song, but the tough-minded businessmen turn it down for being sappy, but when they sing "Swinging on a Star" as an afterthought one of the businessmen says, "That we can use."

In other words, the song was essential to the plot but its content was irrelevant as long as it was lively and felt up-to-date. Although the crooner and the lyricist had a lot to talk about, Crosby's sons claimed his attention until he sent them off to do their homework. Gary, the oldest, complained, "I hate school. I wish I never had to go to school." Bing reacted, "If you don't go to school, you might grow up to be a mule. Do you want to do that?" Or maybe Burke butted in—"Would you rather be a fish than go to school? Or would you rather be a mule?"—before he raced off to Van Heusen's house with his sudden inspiration. The other story has Van Heusen at Crosby's house when Crosby admonished his son. Van Heusen liked the comment about a mule, wrote the melody, and took the idea to Burke.[65]

Van Heusen was gregarious and outgoing, but he preferred to work in a closed room, smoking and drinking milk. He spent all night on the song because Crosby was not easy to write for. His casual exterior covered a strong personality; he knew what kind of song was best for him—something with a natural, conversational style that was neither too sentimental nor too sophisticated.

## "I Fall in Love Too Easily" [*Anchors Aweigh*] (1945)
Lyrics by Sammy Cahn (1913–1993), music by Jule Styne (1905–1994)

The songwriting team of Jule Styne and Sammy Cahn turned from Hollywood to Broadway in 1944. Unfortunately, their show, *Glad to See You*, closed in Philadelphia before it reached New York. It was a disaster from which Styne learned that someday he wanted to succeed on Broadway and Cahn learned that he was content to live and work in Beverly Hills. Although they tried Broadway again, this time successfully, by the end of the decade one of the most successful songwriting teams in the history of the movies had ended. But first they had to return to Hollywood after their failure. Not only did they get blistering reviews, but their fellow songwriters greeted them with teasing that blistered them all over again. Most people thought that Cahn had the sharper tongue, but after being ribbed endlessly Styne faced down his tormenters: "You fellows sit on your ASCAP and go home to your goddam Beverly Hills pools and don't have the guts to take a chance. You write songs about Scranton and you've never been to Scranton. You write songs about ghettos and you've never seen a ghetto. I was born in one. That show was rotten but we tried and we have our self-respect."[66]

By the time Styne and Cahn got back to Hollywood, MGM had signed Frank Sinatra for *Anchors Aweigh*, a new Gene Kelly film they expected to become a major musical. Because Sinatra was so popular and had signed a three-picture contract, the studio wanted him to have its finest songwriters. They offered him Jerome Kern, Harry Warren, or Arthur Schwartz, and told him they would sign Cole Porter if he wanted him. Sinatra replied, "Gentlemen, you don't understand. If Jule Styne and Sammy Cahn don't do this picture, I'm out of it, too."[67] After their failure in New York and the backstabbing in Hollywood, they were especially grateful to Sinatra and were determined to do their best work for him.

Their method of working together was well set by this time. Styne usually did not compose at the piano: "I'm usually away from it. Then it becomes kind of an ego trip for me to sit and play and hear the result. Then I get inspired and try to make it better. Basically, it's hard work and you get on with it."[68] When he and Cahn worked together, Styne fiddled at the piano until Cahn heard a tune he liked. He would tell Styne to play the new melody over and over again, ever more slowly, until the lyric fell into place. What is unusual about "I Fall in Love Too Easily" is that it is only sixteen bars long. Cahn explained its brevity: "This song was written one night in

Palm Springs. When I sang the last line, Jule Styne looked over at me and said, 'So. That's it.' I knew he felt we could have written on, but I felt I had said all there was to say, and if I had it to do over, I would stop right there again."[69] Cahn thought of his lyrics as work; the word he prized above all others was "professional." Yet the songs ached with romantic longing and embracing. Back in the 1990s, a singer who had never heard of Cahn listened to some of his songs and said, "Oh, yeah, the songs you used to listen to just before getting laid."[70]

## "I'll Buy That Dream" [*Sing Your Way Home*] (1945)
Lyrics by Herb Magidson (1906–1986), music by Allie Wrubel (1905–1973)

## "Oh! What It Seemed to Be" (1946)
Lyrics and music by Ben Benjamin (1907–1989), George Weiss (1921–2010), and Frankie Carle (1903–2001)

Composer Ben Benjamin said that:

> [I] was always hearing songs. I can naturally hear songs when I'm writing but, after I'm finished, I can hear the song in its entirety. I hear the artist who sings it; all the parts, the strings, the brass, the rhythm section. I can hear it as loud or as soft as I want to. I would always explain to the arranger and performer what I hear and feel.[71]

This kind of ability must have served him well, because, when World War II ended in mid-1945, songs changed almost overnight. Ballads weighed down with loneliness and longing became optimistic and cheerful. They looked to the future with eager anticipation as the boys returned home to marriage and mortgages. With the coming of peace, people also recognized that Americans would now be redirected to what we soon stopped calling the home front. Unlike songs from the War years, Herb Magidson's lyric to "I'll Buy that Dream" focuses entirely on the future. The title transforms dreaming into something practical and graspable; its title uses "buy," not in the sense of "purchase," but rather of "accept." The woman dreams of being reunited with her beloved, but is also confident enough to have a sense of humor. Once she and her fiancé marry, the rest of the song quickly lays out their idyllic life ahead. It culminates with her at 83 and him at 92, and her final understated affirmation, "It doesn't sound bad, and if it can be had / I'll buy that dream."

At much the same time, no song expressed America's new attitudes more winningly than "Oh! What It Seemed to Be," with its affirmation of promises kept and dreams come true, the joy of the familiar taken for granted once more. The lyric provides a list of things that young people would remember and then experience anew but at a keener level of delight: a "neighborhood dance" becomes a "masquerade ball," and "a ride on a train" becomes "a trip to the stars" because the boy and girl are together at last. Its conclusion is the perfect final step for new and better times: "a wedding in June" that becomes "a royal affair."

# Chapter 12
## 1946–1951

**"Any Place I Hang My Hat Is Home"** [*St. Louis Woman*] (1946)
Lyrics by Johnny Mercer (1909–1976), music by Harold Arlen (1905–1986)

The Broadway musical *St. Louis Woman* is one of those shows with an outstanding score that was taken down by a flawed book—even though, in this case, the librettists were the gifted African American writers Arna Bontemps and Countee Cullen. Fortunately, some of the great songs by composer Harold Arlen and lyricist Johnny Mercer have survived despite the original production's run of only three months. Song after song was remarkable: from the opening number, "Li'l Augie Is a Natural Man," through the comic "Legalize My Name" and the romantic "(I Had Myself a) True Love," to the towering blues anthem "Come Rain or Come Shine." Early in the story, a man's mistress decides to leave him because he is abusive. Arlen and Mercer wrote "Any Place I Hang My Hat Is Home" as the woman's languidly bluesy assertion of independence, although the idea for the song came from an elderly black man that Mercer often encountered in his native Savannah. Mercer would always ask him how he was, and he would invariably answer, "Just fine, Mr. Mercer, any place I hang my hat is home."[1]

Although Mercer usually wanted to be left alone, sometimes for days, until he worked out a complete lyric, with Arlen things were different. Mercer explained that "some guys bothered me . . . I couldn't write with them in the same room with me, but I could with Harold."[2] Despite their friendship, the show seemed star-crossed. Its source—Bontemps' sprawling, often dark novel, *God Sends Sunday*—did not adapt easily to the stage, especially not to the requirements of a Broadway musical. Cullen died before rehearsals started and then the NAACP criticized the show for "offering roles that detract from the dignity of our race." Star Lena Horne agreed and withdrew from the cast, announcing that she had no intention of playing Delia, whom she described as "a flashy lady of easy virtue."[3]

Despite all the problems, on the first day of rehearsal, when Arlen played and Mercer sang the score through, an entirely black cast stood and applauded. Pearl Bailey said of Mercer, "We sat in the room and this man just sat there and sang his whole score . . . This man could sing his songs. He was one of the few people who could sing his songs better than anyone else could sing them, and every one was a masterpiece . . . He wrote his heart, and he sang his heart."[4]

### "Route 66" (1946)
Lyrics and music by Bobby Troup (1918–1999)

The old Route 66 from Chicago to Los Angeles doesn't exist anymore. One of the original U.S. highways dating back to the mid-1920s, it was removed from the U.S. Highway System in 1985, after the Interstate Highway System replaced it. But it remains alive in the song that jazz pianist Bobby Troup wrote in 1966. At the end of World War II, living with his first wife in Lancaster, Pennsylania, Troup decided that, if he was going to make it in the music business, he had to go to Los Angeles. To pass the time during the long drive, his wife suggested that he write a song about Route 40, but he said they would soon be on Route 66. Just outside St. Louis, she leaned over and whispered, "Get your kicks on Route 66." Troup put the lyric together as they drove. They were just about broke by the time they got to LA, but he set the words to music and eventually convinced Capitol, the new record company started by Johnny Mercer, to have its top star, Nat "King" Cole, record it. Within the few weeks, the song sat atop the Hit Parade, and the Troups could afford to buy a house with the royalties from one of the first popular hits that deserved to be called "cool."

### "To Each His Own" [*To Each His Own*] (1946)
Lyrics and music by Ray Evans (1915–2007), music by Jay Livingston (1915–2001)

Jay Livingston and Ray Evans met when they played in the same dance band at the University of Pennsylvania. The band spent summers playing on Caribbean cruise ships. Evans remembered, "One day on our last cruise we were coming up the Hudson River and I said to Jay, 'Let's stay in New York and write songs.' Eight years later it paid off."[5] After they graduated, Evans worked as an accountant, Livingston made $18 a week as a pianist at NBC, and they worked on songs at night. In 1945, after they moved to California, Johnny Mercer heard their work, liked it, and helped them land a contract at Paramount. They were soon assigned to write a title song for a new movie called *To Each His Own*. The studio hated the title but the producer refused to change it. He told composer Victor Young, who was writing the background score, to come up with a title song. Then it was Young's turn to refuse because, he said, the title was a "dumb idea"[6] that nobody would understand. Evans said that when they got the assignment, "We were so eager that we would have written 'Come To Us Jesus in E-Flat' if they has asked us to."[7]

Evans and Livingston had already developed the unusual method of working together that they relied on throughout their sixty-year collaboration. Once Evans had written several sets of lyrics, often with different titles, the two men would go over them together to see if anything fit a situation in the movie they were writing for and could lead to a good melody. Sometimes, Livingston explained, they would use "only a line or two from a page of lyrics, and then we both sit down and write a melody."[8] For "To Each His Own," their first major hit, the song came from Evan's phrase, "Two lips must insist on two more to be kissed." Ironically, the song never appeared in the movie, but, for one week in 1946, five different recordings were on Billboard's Top Ten list—by Eddy Howard, Tony Martin, Freddy Martin, The Modernaires, and the Ink Spots. Some years later, Evans told his business manager, "I'd like to spread out and write with other people." The manager replied, 'When something works, don't mess with it.' "[9]

**"Buttons and Bows"** [*The Paleface*] (1947)
Lyrics by Ray Evans (1915–2007), music by Jay Livingston (1915–2001)

In the movie *The Paleface*, Bob Hope, playing an Eastern dentist named Painless Potter, is driving a covered wagon in the Old West. When he twists around to sing to Jane Russell who's in back, the horses take a wrong turn into an Indian ambush. Russell, as Calamity Jane, takes the reins and fights off the attackers at the same time. After watching Jane in action, Hope has a song that expresses his comic futility. Jay Livingston and Ray Evans called the first number they came up with "Snookum," an actual word that roughly means "OK" in one of the Native American languages. Director Norman MacLeod refused to use it because, he said, the Indians were supposed to be dangerous rather than funny; the song title would blow the scene. Evans and Livingston argued that the movie was a comedy and Hope could get away with anything. MacLeod refused to budge.

After the disagreement, the songwriters stopped by to see Robert L. Welch, the movie's producer. He suggested that they write something that derived from Hope's character, a tenderfoot who hates the West. Evans recalled later that Hope's character wishes he was "back in the East where the girls are pretty and there was civilization and society and everything . . . Somehow in my mind I got the idea of a kind of rhythm: 'Let's go where the girls keep wearing those frills and flowers and buttons and bows . . .' The minute we got to our office, Jay sat down at the piano and went da-da-dah dah da-da-da-da- da-da da-da da-da-da dah." The song's clippity-clop rhythm fit the gait of the horses and the wagon, and the lyric expresses Hope's frustration: "My bones denounce / The buckboard's bounce."[10]

Two years earlier, "To Each His Own," Livingston and Evans' first hit, had established them in Hollywood, but "Buttons and Bows" earned them their first Oscar, even though the hit recording almost didn't happen. Dinah Shore recorded the song at 11.57 p.m. as musicians improvised behind her. At the stroke of midnight, a musicians' strike kept them out of recording studios for a year. "Buttons and Bows" was the last song to sneak in under the deadline. Livingston and Evans wrote often for Hope after "Buttons and Bow," including "Silver Bells" in 1950, their hit Christmas song for *The Lemon Drop Kid.*

## "I Wish I Didn't Love You So" [*The Perils of Pauline*] (1947)
Lyrics and music by Frank Loesser (1910–1969)

Although he began as a lyricist in the mid-1930s, Frank Loesser wrote both words and music during his final years in Hollywood and then throughout his years on Broadway. "I Wish I Didn't Love You So" was one of his last movie songs, with the exception of the 1951 score to *Hans Christian Andersen.* Now that he was a complete songwriter, he developed a somewhat different way of writing. He always wrote the words first and insisted on a highly regimented schedule. He would rise no later than 5 a.m., have a martini, work for four hours, when he would have another drink and a nap, and then return to work from 10 a.m. until the end of the day—except for a second nap after lunch. A restless, energetic man, Loesser never slept for long periods of time.

He had taught himself to write music and play the piano, but he had a dreadful singing voice. Although he knew what he wanted to hear, he couldn't create the sound he had in his head. When singers auditioned or rehearsed for him, he constantly interrupted until what they were singing matched what he knew he wanted. He also wanted singing to be loud; everyone in an audience had to hear every word. Milton Delugg, his first musical secretary, said, "He always had an idea of the melody but actually couldn't notate it. He'd plunk a little bit on the piano and sing it to me. I would write down what he was singing."[11] He especially liked to write while a friend or his wife drove him around in a car, especially when he was working on the lyrics. It let him work without being interrupted.

**"Time After Time"** [*It Happened in Brooklyn*] (1947) and **"Five Minutes More"** [*Sweetheart of Sigma Chi*] (1946)
Lyrics by Sammy Cahn (1913–1993), music by Jule Styne (1905–1994)

Nancy and Frank Sinatra often entertained at home in the years after World War II. According to Jule Styne, "They were amateur theatricals written and performed by some of the highest-priced talent in the world." One Saturday night, with no new sketches or songs ready to perform, everyone agreed to do an off-the-cuff solo. Styne whispered to Sinatra, "Just ask them, 'Has anybody heard the new score to *Annie Oakley*, by Jerome Kern?'" (After Kern's death in November 1945, Irving Berlin wrote the score and Dorothy Fields the book for the Broadway musical eventually renamed *Annie Get Your Gun*.) Styne hadn't heard it either, but he had a melody in mind that sounded to him like something Kern could have written. He announced, "I've only heard a couple of the songs,"[12] and improvised a full-fledged melody from the few notes he had in his head. His friends pleaded for more, but he had to beg off, saying he couldn't remember any more. Later, Cahn remembered what Styne had ad-libbed; he added lyrics and called it "Time After Time."

Even in the lush romantic ballads of the 1940s, Cahn believed:

> a sense of vaudeville is very strong in anything I do, anything I write. They even call it "a vaudeville finish," and it comes through in many of my songs. Just sing the end of "All the Way" or "Three Coins in the Fountain"—"Make it mine, make it mine, MAKE IT MINE!" If you let people know they should applaud, they will applaud.[13]

The same is true even in the muted ending of "Time After Time," where Cahn's lyric, having repeated "So lucky to . . ." three times, now completes the thought begun in the song's second line, "So lucky to be loving you."

Cahn also relied on repetition in "Five Minutes More," so much so that the song is almost a parody of one of the oldest rules of songwriting. Sammy Cahn called what he wrote a case of "lyric-writing chutzpah." When he first showed it to Jule Styne, the often irreverent composer asked, "What's wrong, you got a stammer?"[14]

Styne thought of his writing differently, but also in terms of the way it reached an audience. "When I write music I hear the orchestra," he said. "I don't hear a piano. I play piano orchestrally, too. I hear the brass. I hear the woodwinds . . . Feelings is the whole ball game. If you don't have feelings, you can't compose, you can't sing." He also said on another occasion, "Inspiration is for amateurs."[15]

He also insisted that "Time After Time" was written for a man to sing: "It loses all its power if a woman sings it. It's nice, but it loses all its power. It's a strong song. Even when he sings pianissimo, it has strength to it."[16]

Of all the songs Styne and Cahn wrote for Frank Sinatra, "Time After Time" was Styne's favorite even though he was becoming impatient with writing what he called "Sinatra songs" and was beginning to consider a move to New York to write for Broadway. He told Sinatra:

> "You have to sing other things. It's not good for me . . . I gotta go write for some other people. I have another dimension for me." And that's when he got angry at me. He thought I'm dismissing him. He didn't understand it. I play him "Just in Time," I tell him I'm writing a Sinatra song. I didn't want to tell him it was a Fred Astaire song. I met Fred Astaire at a party once. I said, "Gee, it's too bad I didn't write some of the songs when you were dancing away. You know I've been writing Fred Astaire songs my whole life. Don't tell Sinatra, he thinks they were his songs."[17]

### "A Couple of Swells" [*Easter Parade*] (1948)
Lyrics and music by Irving Berlin (1888–1989)

Irving Berlin oversaw a batch of movies that drew largely on his own substantial songbook—*Alexander's Ragtime Band* (1938), *Blue Skies* (1948), *White Christmas* and *There's No Business Like Show Business* (both 1954), and, by far the best of them, *Easter Parade*. Berlin had originally offered the film rights to Twentieth Century Fox but they refused because he was asking for so much money plus a share of the profits. He then negotiated a very tough deal with Louis B. Mayer at MGM. He got his money and, even though much of the score consisted of old songs, he agreed to write eight new songs as well.

One of the movie's screenwriters, Frances Goodrich, said that Berlin proved very flexible to work with: "Sometimes [Berlin] would come in with an idea with a song to illustrate it . . . and we would say we couldn't work that out . . . and he'd answer, 'That's all right. I'll use it somewhere else.' "[18] One of the rejected songs was "Let's Take an Old Fashioned Waltz," which became the hit song from the 1949 score to Berlin's next Broadway musical, *Miss Liberty*. Berlin originally wrote it to underscore the successful partnership between Astaire and Garland when Fred's character realizes (at last) that Judy's gift is for comic rather than romantic dance. When producer

Arthur Freed told Berlin that he wanted a different kind of song, the songwriter remained unruffled. He said, "Let's have a 'tramps' number," and returned in an hour with "A Couple of Swells."[19] Garland and Astaire appear as hobos who have been invited to dine with upper-crust swells but have no way to take themselves "up the Avenue." What no one but Berlin knew is that he had written the song earlier but had never used it. It was one of his many "trunk songs."

**"It's Magic"** [*Romance on the High Seas*] (1948)
Lyrics by Sammy Cahn (1913–1993), music by Jule Styne (1905–1994)

Doris Day had been the featured vocalist with Les Brown's Band of Renown in the early and mid-1940s, and had done the vocal for the Band's hit recording of "Sentimental Journey" in 1945, but nobody knew who she was when Jule Styne and Sammy Cahn brought her to director Michael Curtiz (*Yankee Doodle Dandy*, *Casablanca*) at Warner Bros. Before the audition, Cahn told Day that Curtiz was expecting a singer like Betty Hutton. Day replied, "I don't bounce around. I just sing." After Curtiz heard her, Cahn reported that the director walked over to her, put his hands on her hips, and moved her as she sang the song again. He then ordered a screen test and cast her in his forthcoming movie, *Romance on the High Seas*, for which Styne and Cahn were providing songs.

Cahn liked to say that, when he heard a tune, words popped into his mind. Styne liked to say that he was a patient man. Two years earlier, he had composed a tango that he played for Cahn at the beginning of every assignment. He liked the tune but also used it as a warm-up before he settled down to work. Cahn said that he "kept passing it by because it had a slightly Spanish flavor." Only after he read the script for *Romance*, which included a scene with Day and Jack Carson in a Latin nightclub, "did the song come into focus for me and I was able to do the lyrics."[20]

When a tune was working for Cahn, he would ask the composer to play it again and again, each time more slowly. This time, after the third playing, Cahn said, "Magic!" Styne had no idea what he meant. Cahn walked to the typewriter and began to peck with two fingers. The result was "It's Magic." The song was nominated for an Academy Award, as was their 1949 title song for "It's a Great Feeling." Cahn used to boast that he could turn any movie title into a love song. When someone asked what he would have done with the 1966 comedy, *The Russians Are Coming, The Russians Are Coming*, he sang:

The Russians are coming,
The Russians are coming,
So love me tonight!

*Romance on the High Seas* marked the end of Styne and Cahn's incredibly successful collaboration. Cahn wanted to continue living the good life in California while Styne had ambitions to write for the Broadway stage, but some ill-feeling and resentment had also grown up over the years. There was no argument, no formal break, says Styne, "It simply dissolved."[21]

### "Sleigh Ride" (1948)
Lyrics by Mitchell Parish (1900–1993), music by LeRoy Anderson (1908–1975)

LeRoy Anderson was a lifetime New Englander, and Mitchell Parish, born Michael Pashelinsky in Lithuania, grew up in Louisiana after his family migrated to the United States. One went to Harvard, the other to Tin Pan Alley, yet they collaborated on one of the twentieth century's most popular holiday songs even though they probably never met. In 2010, it received more radio play than any other song during the Christmas season.

An arranger for Arthur Fiedler's Boston Pops, Anderson wrote "Sleigh Ride" as an instrumental for Fiedler to introduce. It was typical of the short, light pieces he was known for: "Blue Tango" (1951), "The Syncopated Clock" (1945), and "The Typewriter" (1950), among them. His melody for "Sleigh Ride" is percussive and brisk, and uses the traditional sound effects that are so much a part of America's myth of Christmas—sleigh bells, the crack of a whip, and the whinnying of horses. It became a classic even though Anderson claimed that he wrote it during a beastly heatwave in the summer of 1946. He said that he was digging trenches, trying to find an abandoned pipe that could carry water to a dried-up well that served his cottage in Connecticut. As he dug in the heat, he thought back to the cold, snowy winters of his New England childhood. Although he didn't find the pipe, he went back inside with an idea in mind for a new piece of music.[22] It took him two years to finish, and Parish added lyrics two years after that.

### "Diamonds Are a Girl's Best Friend" (*Gentlemen Prefer Blondes*] (1949)
Lyrics by Leo Robin (1900–1984), music by Jule Styne (1905–1994)

In 1947, Jule Styne and Sammy Cahn wrote a successful stage musical, *High Button Shoes*, but Cahn wanted to return to California while Styne was eager to remain in New York. Before long, Cahn was writing movie songs with Jimmy Van Heusen, and Styne was at work on his next Broadway show with lyricist Leo Robin. The project began when the show's eventual set designer remarked to an acquaintance, "Wouldn't it be a great idea if someone made a musical out of Anita Loos' *Gentlemen Prefer Blondes*"?[23] In the 1925 comic novel, a Flapper named Lorelei Lee describes her madcap adventures as she travels through Europe. Eventually, she settles down and marries a wealthy American.

Once Styne agreed to write the music, he set out to find a lyricist. He had not written with anyone but Cahn for more than four years, and he had only one Broadway score to his credit, but he believed strongly that "you write as well as who you write with . . . If you can't be a collaborator, you don't belong in the theater." He once called himself, "the greatest collaborator that is."[24] Leo Robin, who had written most of his important songs for movies ("Beyond the Blue Horizon," "Thanks for the Memory"), had lost his collaborator, Ralph Rainger, in a plane crash in 1942. Since then, he had worked with several composers on one project at a time. He and Styne knew each other only casually even though they lived just two blocks apart. One morning, Styne rang his doorbell to ask if he'd like to write the lyrics for *Gentlemen Prefer Blondes*. Robin was not interested. His movie songs were earning him a good living and his previous shows had been flops. He was not eager to relive the bad old days on Broadway, but Styne persisted until Robin said, "Okay, as soon as I see a script, I'll see what I can do with it. I don't promise anything. Maybe I can; maybe I can't. Maybe I will; maybe I won't."[25] A week later, the two songwriters began their collaboration, and two weeks after that Styne and Robin called producer Herman Levin in a state of high excitement. They lay the phone on Styne's piano and sang their first song for Levin. He liked what he heard. Of course he did; it was "Diamonds Are a Girl's Best Friend."

### "Dear Hearts and Gentle People" [*Beyond the Purple Hills*] (1949)
Lyrics by Bob Hilliard (1918–1971), music by Sammy Fain (1902–1989)

Stephen Foster, America's first great songwriter, died at the age of 37 a penniless alcoholic, two weeks after he finished writing one of his greatest songs, "Beautiful Dreamer." Legend says that he had 40c in his pocket, along with a scrap of paper that read, "Dear hearts and gentle people." Many have speculated that he intended it as a title or a line in a lyric. That supposition came to fruition 185 years later, when lyricist Bob Hilliard said to Sammy Fain, "You've written a lot of beautiful songs, how would you like to write a country song with me?" Hilliard had a title in mind—"Dear Friends and Gentle Hearts"—and Fain started to hum a melody using the line. According to Fain, "We jockeyed around our own title and came up with the song, 'Dear Friends and Gentle People.'" They sent a demo to Dinah Shore, who loved it, but "she wanted to know if there was any way we could work the name 'Tennessee' into the verse. That didn't take very much effort. Dinah wanted the name of her home state in it. That's what Dinah wanted so that's what Dinah got!"[26]

Western singer Gene Autry also crooned the song in the Western *Beyond the Purple Hills*. Fain's gentle melody lacks the rich undertone of melancholy that deepens Foster's greatest work, but Hilliard's words about a wanderer who longs to return home to the good people he misses evoke the idealized rural America that was an important theme in Foster's work and also in the nostalgic songs that appealed so strongly to newcomers to America's cities in the years after the Civil War.

### "Enjoy Yourself (It's Later Than You Think)" (1950)
Lyrics by Herb Magidson (1906–1986), music by Carl Sigman (1909–2000)

### "Ballerina" (1947)
Lyrics by Bob Russell (1914–1970), music by Carl Sigman (1909–2000)

### "Civilization" (1947)
Lyrics by Bob Hilliard (1918–1971), music by Carl Sigman (1909–2000)

Carl Sigman was a composer who worked with lyricists and a lyricist who worked with composers. He said, "Anyone involved with songwriting will testify to the fact that each song, no matter how pure, or from the heart, has its own story, its own peculiar way of getting written. Some cases are more peculiar or paradoxical than others, but invariably some quirk or twist of luck enters the picture to prod a lyric or melody to its completion."[27] Sometimes it's frustration. Lyricist Herb Magidson, who had written a few hits ("Java Jive," "I'll Take Romance"), was working with composer Ben Oakland, who had little interest in finishing a song they had begun. They were going nowhere until Magidson asked if Oakland would mind if Carl Sigman stepped in to write the melody. Oakland was glad to agree. Magidson and Sigman wrote "Enjoy Yourself" over the telephone in thirty minutes. The frequently repeated title line underscored the importance of catchphrases in lyric writing.

The idea for Magidson's recurring phrase came from an old Chinese proverb (or was it a fortune cookie?), typical of the sort of thing a lyricist looks for. Sigman said of his own struggles to find the right words, "I was always listening, reading or looking for everyday expressions. I strive to make conversational lyrics—that's my strength—like 'Did anyone call?' or 'I'll never forgive myself.'"[28] In the process, he wrote some major hits as well as some very oddly titled flops: "I Left the One I Love on One of the Thousand Islands, But I Can't Remember Which One," "The Big High Mountain with Nothing on the Top," and "Our Horses Are Falling in Love." He also wrote the theme song for Mr. Kitzel on the Jack Benny radio show, "Pickle in the Middle with the Mustard on Top."

Sigman had a habit of writing as he played a round of golf. He almost never sat at a piano. When people asked his son what his father did, he answered, "He plays golf. In the winter, he bowls."[29] Wherever he was playing in 1947 and 1948, he got it right. In addition to "Enjoy Yourself," Sigman wrote "Crazy He Calls Me," "Civilization," "The Big Brass Band from Brazil," and "Ballerina." When he and lyricist Bob Russell gave "Ballerina" to publisher Redd Evans, Evans refused to give the song to the popular Vaughn Monroe because they weren't on speaking terms. Only after Jimmy Dorsey's recording flopped did the publisher beg Monroe to take it. His version soon rose to Number One.

In the same year, Sigman and lyricist Bob Hilliard wrote the wacky "Civilization" ("Bongo, bongo, bongo, / I don't want to leave the Congo") as special material for the famous Manhattan nightclub, the Copacabana. When The Copa turned it down, Sigman and Hilliard responded by mounting a Broadway revue of their own songs. Hilliard was known for being especially competitive. Record stores on Seventh Avenue near the Brill Building, the home of Tin Pan Alley, would try to draw customers through the doors by mounting speakers that blasted hit recordings out onto the sidewalk. When Hilliard heard his Number One "Ballerina" instead of his Number Two "Civilization," he would mutter, "I spit on those stores!"[30] He and Sigman were working together when the composer proposed to his wife. Not wanting to miss the chance to work during their two-week honeymoon, Hilliard accompanied them on their train trip to California.

### "When the World Was Young" (1950)
Lyrics by Angele Vannier (1917–1980), English lyrics by Johnny Mercer (1909–1976), music by M. Philippe-Gerard (1924–?)

Music publisher Mickey Goldsen asked Carl Sigman to set English lyrics to M. Philippe-Gerard's melody "Le Chevalier de Paris," and then turned down what Sigman wrote: "Carl came up with a light, romantic, workmanlike Tin Pan Alley ballad." Sigman was annoyed and said sarcastically, "If you want an important lyric, then get an important writer."[31] When Johnny Mercer listened to the song, he said, "Gee, I love this thing. I really feel it." Three days later, he had written three verses and three choruses, along with two versions of his lyric for a male or female singer—a reflection on aging by a no-longer-young man or woman. Reflecting on his joyful summers in rural Georgia, Mercer commented that the song "seemed to me just my way of remembering how it was in the old days . . . I just remembered all those things that I remembered as a boy."[32]

Only two years later, rock 'n' roll overwhelmed what later came to be called the Great American Songbook. Like many other songwriters and singers, Mercer would lose his bearings for a while, but he would find his way back with songs that were wistful and elegiac. Late in his career, in addition to "When the World Was Young," he also wrote "The Days of Wine and Roses," "Moon River," and "Autumn Leaves."

In 1955, pianist Bobby Troup released an album of Mercer's songs and asked him to write the liner notes. Instead, Mercer wrote a bit of wry doggerel: "I write because I love to write / And hope the words are not too trite . . . I do the best with what I have."[33] That's pretty straightforward, but on other occasions he offered a different kind of explanation. He once explained to his father: "Pop, to tell you the truth I simply get to thinking over the song, pondering over it in my mind and all of a sudden, I get in tune with the Infinite."[34]

But, the question remains, is getting in tune with the Infinite going to ensure the survival of the Great American Songbook beyond this generation and perhaps the next. Those raised on early rock 'n' roll remember Tony Bennett, Andy Williams, Frankie Laine, and Nat Cole, but then the 1960s swallowed everything that had come before—at least for a while. Jule Styne offers some hope. He once asked his son to play him a particular Billy Joel song that he liked. He answered, "Wait'll you hear the new one." Styne reacted: "The *new* one? The old one's only been around two months. So what happens? Songs that were big five years ago you don't even hear anymore. But I still hear Berlin, I still hear Gershwin. That's forever."[35]

## "Cold, Cold Heart" (1951)
Lyrics and music by Hank Williams (1922–1953)

In 1950, Hank Williams' wife Audrey had to be hospitalized after she had an illegal abortion at home without telling her husband. When Williams bent down to kiss her in her hospital bed, she turned away and said, "You sorry son of a bitch, it was you that caused me to suffer this." He later told their housekeeper that his wife had a "cold, cold heart."[36] That same night he wrote the song he called his favorite among the 100 songs he wrote. It was also in large part autobiographical, with references to his wife's first marriage and his adultery. He once told a TV audience that its success had bought him "quite a few beans and biscuits."[37]

Williams used to say that he wrote the song in about an hour, but he lifted the melody note for note from T. Texas Tyler's 1945 recording of "You'll Still Be in My Heart." It didn't matter that Williams lost the resulting lawsuit; he had died at the age of 29 under strange circumstances involving alcohol use, a morphine injection, and a vicious beating. Ironically, the song was supposed to be the B-side of a 78 r.p.m. recording of "Dear John" until the record producers heard Williams sing it and moved it to the A-side.

The song's success was uncommon: it rose to the number one spot on both the country and pop charts. After Williams recorded it in 1951, so did Tony Bennett. Bill Janovitz, a writer for *Allmusic*, said, "That a young Italian singing waiter from Queens could find common ground with a country singer from Alabama's backwoods is testament both to Williams' skills as a writer and to Bennett's imagination and artist's ear."[38] Bennett often tells the story about receiving a call from Williams that began, "Tony, why did you ruin my song"? It was a prank; Williams enjoyed Bennett's version. When Tony sang it at the Grand Old Opry in the 1960s, he brought his usual charts, but the house musicians who were accompanying him used different instrumentation. "You sing," they said, "and we'll follow you." And so they did.[39]

**"Inchworm"** [*Hans Christian Andersen*] (1951)
Lyrics and music by Frank Loesser (1910–1969)

Producer Samuel Goldwyn had spent ten years trying to get the right script for a movie to be based, however loosely, on the life and stories of Hans Christian Andersen. When Samuel Taylor, one of the thirty screenwriters he hired and fired, suggested hiring Frank Loesser to write the score, Goldwyn fired him, too. Eventually Goldwyn settled on playwright Moss Hart, who based his screenplay on a treatment written by Myles Connolly in 1938. The movie's casting history was even more bizarre. Goldwyn wanted Gary Cooper to play Andersen, but the success of the movie *The Red Shoes* led to the addition of ballet dancer Moira Shearer and then to Jimmy Stewart in the lead. Sylvia Fine, a songwriter and Danny Kaye's wife, thought that casting Stewart in a musical was odd. She asked, "Sam, why not use Danny?" Goldwyn agreed; he hired Kaye to play the lead and Fine to write the songs. But Hart wanted Frank Loesser because "he just did *Guys and Dolls*, and I'm sure he's got another great score coming up."[40] Goldwyn then dropped Fine, kept Kaye, and told Loesser to write eight songs. The movie is not a straight biography, even by Hollywood's loose "biopic" standards, but rather a fictional story in which Andersen is a cobbler who spends most of his time entertaining the children of his village with his stories. The movie's spoken introduction describes it as a "fairytale about a storyteller."[41]

Andersen considered his stories to be allegories. He said, "I seize an idea for older people and then tell it to the young ones, while remembering that father and mother are listening and must have something to think about."[42] Loesser wrote his songs in the same spirit. Their simple stories appeal to children, but their clever lyrics also charm adults. His favorite song from the score was the delightful "Inchworm," one of the contrapuntal duets that he, like Irving Berlin, liked to write. Children recite their multiplication tables in a classroom, while, just beyond the windows, Andersen watches the inchworm who serves as his inspiration. Two years after the movie opened, he received a letter—handwritten, his daughter wrote, "in a peculiar curvy, loopy, caterpillian script." It read:

> dear Loesser your song Inchworm makes me very happy; not only from an inchwormian point of view (I know you must realize that people will not be so repelled by us after this) but from the aspect of downright beauty . . . I'd like to send you a leaf or something in appreciation of the delight your song has given me, but since that probably wouldn't be the correct thing to do, I'll close by promising you that after this I'll try to admire the marigolds. Respectfully, a Kansas inchworm.

Loesser noticed a Lawrence, Kansas postmark on the envelope and placed an ad in the local paper, "INCHWORM F.L. SAYS THANKS FOR THE LETTER." The writer saw it and wired back, "gratitude gratefully and happily received" and followed with a letter that said her name was Emily Preyer, a kindergarten teacher who "always made up stories for children, so when I knew I had to write you about 'Inchworm' I just made up a story for you."[43]

### "Too Young" (1951)
Lyrics by Sylvia Dee (1914–1967), music by Sidney Lippman (1914–2003)

Sylvia Dee and Sidney Lippman had been collaborating for a long time when Dee mentioned that her brother was getting married, even though she thought he was too young. Lippman later remembered, "As she said that, she looked at me and I looked at her and we both said, 'Title?' "[44] The song they then wrote was on *Billboard Magazine*'s chart for twenty-nine weeks, twelve times in the top spot.

The simple, unambiguous words to "Too Young" touched a chord in adolescents, perhaps because the teenaged boy in the lyric wallows in self-pity as he affirms the depth and permanence of the love he and his girl feel for one another, and complains because adults don't take them seriously. Although "Too Young" precedes the rock 'n' roll tidal wave by a few years, it was the first song to become a hit by appealing directly and (some might say) shamelessly to what soon came to be known as the "youth market." Only four years later, James Dean would stir teenagers' deepest emotions as an inarticulate, alienated adolescent in such movies as *East of Eden* and *Rebel Without a Cause*. Anxiety roiled America as affluence increased during the post-war years. Young people wanted desperately to distinguish themselves from their parents and they had the money in their pockets to do it. They had indeed become a market and were becoming a commercial and cultural force.

Popular songs had always been about love, especially young love, but rarely so blatantly or sexually. Beginning in the early 1950s, popular music, like the larger world it reflected, was beginning to draw some lines in the cultural sand. "Too Young" lacked the defiance of the hard rock of the 1960s or even the generational tag line "Don't Trust Anyone Over Thirty," but

**FIGURE 12.1**    Nat "King" Cole records a mellow 1950s ballad. Courtesy of Photofest.

despite its soon-to-be-dated lyrics and Nat "King" Cole's sleek crooning on the hit recording, "Too Young" had begun the nation's accelerating slide into the future. The world that produced the Great American Songbook was coming to an end.

All those earlier songwriters, many of them immigrants or the children of immigrants, who had absorbed, translated, and given new voice to the "varied carols" of American life, were aging. Lorenz Hart, consumed by alcohol and his own inner demons, had already died, as had Jerome Kern of a heart attack at the age of 60. Those who remained would soon begin to lose their dominance over the music business and the nation's taste. What they represented continued for a while, though, in music as well as in the patterns of daily life. The best Broadway and Hollywood musicals were blessed with extraordinary scores in the 1950s, at the same time that rock and roll swept away the increasingly banal writing, bloated arrangements, and second-rate singers that characterized mainstream popular music after the War. Many of the same people who went to see *The King and I* and *My Fair Lady* on Broadway in the 1950s also bought recordings on the new long-playing discs by the likes of Joni James and Guy Mitchell.

As for the larger demands of life at home, even in 1945, as the War came to a close, a generation of new immigrants began to arrive:

> an immigrant ship occasionally docked on the West Side, and passers-by might glimpse its passengers from Europe, wide-eyed, shabby-clothed and emaciated from Europe, stumbling through the customs formalities in the echoing arrivals shed: out of the sea like so many before them, bewildered and tongue-tied, but ready to accept, as they stepped with their bags and blankets into the street outside, the island's limitless chance and bounty.[45]

And didn't the songwriters, mostly men in their 50s and 60s now, know about that. They were the musical chameleons who had mastered black syncopation—hot, sexy, loose, and lowdown—and made it an American birthright. Just as they had learned it from ragtime, the blues, and jazz, so these new Americans would learn it in turn, except it would soon be a different music.

With the end of the War in 1945, we had no idea that our desire to live a normal life would soon give way to dramatic changes. No Flaming Youth for these veterans, but rather college educations under the G.I. Bill, followed by careers, marriages, and mortgages in the suburbs. The golden age of the Broadway and Hollywood musical in the 1950s was a triumph of middle-class values, but it was accompanied by the explosion of rock 'n' roll. The early years of the decade gave us both *The King and I* and "Rock Around the Clock," as a new cultural split rocked America. It would soon become a different country, with many different kinds of music. But the songs of the previous half-century had served the nation so well and with such warmth and wit that Americans would continue to sing them for many years to come. The best of them had become part of our collective memory. What is remarkable is that so much of what we believed, celebrated, dreamed, and endured found its way into our popular songs. Regardless of the latest style or the most insistent craze, we could not imagine ourselves without remembering and singing the great songs that had given voice to America and its people for more than fifty years. As Irving Berlin wrote:

> What care I who makes the laws of a nation;
> Let those who will take care of its rights and wrongs.
> What care I who cares
> For the world's affairs
> As long as I can sing its popular songs.[46]

# Notes

(In some instances, newspaper and magazine articles from library clipping files were incompletely identified.)

## Preface

1. http://www.democratandchronicle.com/article/20120619/LIVING0105/ 306190031/water-street-music-hall-Kinky-Friedman?nclick_check=1

## Introduction

1. Letter to Abel Green, May 21, 1945, in Benjamin Sears, ed., *The Irving Berlin Reader* (New York: Oxford University Press, 2012), 194.
2. Gene Lees, *Portrait of Johnny: The Life of John Herndon Mercer* (New York: Pantheon Books, 2004), 294.
3. Anita Loos, *The Talmadge Girls* (New York: Viking Press, 1978), 40–41.
4. John F. Baker, "Sammy Cahn," *Publishers Weekly*. November 18, 1974.
5. John McClain, "Man about Manhattan," *The New York Journal-American*, June 29, 1948.
6. Michael Whorf, *American Popular Song Lyricists: Oral Histories, 1920s–1950s.* (Jefferson, NC: McFarland & Company, Inc., 2012), 151.
7. Irving Berlin, "All By Myself," Copyright © 1921 Irving Berlin, Inc., Copyright © renewed.
8. Mark Steyn, *Broadway Babies Say Goodnight: Musicals Then and Now* (New York: Routledge, 1999), 58.
9. John S. Wilson, "Harburg Roams World of Lyrics," *The New York Times*, December 15, 1970.
10. Cited in Gene Lees, *Singers and the Song II* (Oxford and New York: Oxford University Press, 1987, 1998), 45.

**1891–1895**

1. Thomas S. Hischak, *The Tin Pan Alley Song Encyclopedia* (Westport, CT: Green-wood Press, 2002), 4.
2. Cliff and Linda Hoyt, "Charles Hoyt, Popular Playwright of the Gay Nineties," http://choyt48.home.comcast.net/˜choyt48/chhoyt_run.htm
3. David Ewen, *The Life and Death of Tin Pan Alley* (New York: Funk and Wag-nell's Company, 1964), 77–8.
4. "Composer Tells of Sidewalks Song: Charles B. Lawlor, Now Blind, Wrote It 30 Years Ago and Got $5,000 for It," *New York Times* (June 28, 1924).
5. http://www.nytourgoddess.com/blog/2012/2/20/on-the-sidewalks-of-new-york.html

**1896–1900**

1. James J. Fuld, *Book of World-Famous Music: Classical, Popular and Folk* (New York: Crown Publishers, 1966), 278.
2. Fuld, 275–6.
3. Hischak, 144.
4. Ewen, 47.
5. Marva Carter, *Swing Along: The Musical Life of Will Marion Cook* (Oxford and New York: Oxford University Press, 2008), 41–2.
6. http://jass.com/wcook.html.
7. Edward B. Marks and Abbott J. Liebling, *They All Sang: From Tony Pastor to Rudy Vallee* (New York: Viking Press, 1934), 21.
8. David Ewen, *All the Years of American Popular Music* (Englewood, NJ: Prentice-Hall, Inc., 1977), 116–17, and Ewen, *Tin Pan Alley*, 62–3.
9. Hischak, 21.
10. B. Baldwin, "The Cakewalk: A Study in Stereotype and Reality," *Journal of Social History*, 15(2) (1981), 208.
11. Baldwin, 208.
12. Ewen, *All the Years*, 111.
13. Theodore Dreiser, "My Brother Paul," in *Twelve Men* (New York: Literary Classics of the United States, 1987), http://www.readbookonline.net/read/19482/55730/
14. Isaac Goldberg, *Tin Pan Alley: A Chronicle of American Popular Music* (New York: Frederick Unger Publishing Co., Inc., 1961), 121.
15. http://en.wikipedia.org/wiki/When_You_Were_Sweet_Sixteen
16. http://www.irishmusicforever.com/
17. http://www.frederickhodges.com/hellofriscolinernotes.html
18. http://en.wikipedia.org/wiki/A_Bird_in_a_Gilded_Cage
19. http://parlorsongs.com/issues/2004–2/thismonth/feature.php

**1901–1905**

1. Ewen, *Tin Pan Alley*, 172–3.
2. http://www.encyclopedia.com/topic/Lillian_Russell.aspx
3. Allen Churchill, *The Great White Way: A Re-Creation of Broadway's Golden Era of Theatrical Entertainment* (New York: E.P, Dutton Co. Inc., 1962), 33.

4. Armond Fields, *Lillian Russell: A Biography of "America's Beauty"* (Jefferson, NC: McFarland & Company, Inc., 2008), 132.

5. David A. Jasen, *Tin Pan Alley: The Composers, The Songs, The Performers, and Their Times* (New York: Donald I Fine, Inc., 1988), 37.

6. Robert E. Fleming, *James Weldon Johnson* (Boston: Twayne Publishers, 1987), 12.

7. Marks and Liebling, 96.

8. Marks and Liebling, 96.

9. Douglas Gilbert, *Lost Chords: The Diverting Story of America's Popular Songs* (Garden City, NY: Doubleday, Doran & Co., 1942), 274.

10. Al Jolson, 'The Parlor Songs Academy', at http://parlorsongs.com/bios/aljolson/aljolson.php

11. Ernest K. Emurian, *Living Stories of Favorite Songs* (Boston: W.A. Wilde Company, 1958), 86.

12. Ian Whitcomb, *After the Ball: Pop Music from Rag to Rock* (New York: Limelight Editions, 1986), 47.

13. David Ewen, *Great Men of American Popular Song* (Englewood Cliffs NJ: Prentice-Hall, Inc., 1970), 88.

14. http://www.music.umich.edu/performances_events/productions/past/01-02/uprod-tavern.html

15. Gerald Bordman, *Jerome Kern: His Life and Music* (New York and Oxford: Oxford University Press, 1980), 43.

16. Bordman, *Kern*, 57.

17. http://www.neh.gov/news/humanities/1999-09/popular_song.html

18. Philip Robert Dillson, "Shade of the Old Apple Tree: Princely Profits from Single Songs" *The Scrap Book*, 5(2) (August 2007), 185.

19. http://davecol8.tripod.com/id30.htm

20. http://justonesongmore.tumblr.com/post/5534447389/vi-1906

21. http://en.wikipedia.org/wiki/Bert_Williams

22. http://justonesongmore.tumblr.com/post/5534447389/vi-1906

23. http://parlorsongs.com/issues/2002-1/thismonth/featureb.php

24. Maxwell F. Marcuse, *Tin Pan Alley in Gaslight: A Saga of the Songs That Made the Gray Nineties "Gay"* (Watkins Glen, NY: Century House, 1959), 324.

25. http://www.archive.org/stream/storybehindpopul009092mbp/storybehindpopul009092mbp_djvu.txt

## 1906–1910

1. http://query.nytimes.com/gst/abstract.html?res=F40B16FE3B5916738DDDA10894D9415B848DF1D3

2. Gilbert, 319.

3. http://query.nytimes.com/gst/abstract.html?res=F40B16FE3B5916738DDDA10894D9415B848DF1D3

4. http://www.filmreference.com/Writers-and-Production-Artists-Ja-Kr/Kahn-Gus.html#b

5. Whorf, *Lyricists*, 130.

6. Whorf, *Lyricists*, 131.
7. Whorf, *Lyricists*, 129.
8. Whorf, *Lyricists*, 131.
9. http://www.archive.org/stream/storybehindpopul009092mbp/storybehindpopul009092mbp_djvu.txt
10. http://www.trackpads.com/forum/entertainment-celebrity-discussions/888437-cuddle-up-little-closer-shine-harvest-moon.html
11. Tom Prideaux, "Laureate of Sentiment," *Life*.
12. John McCabe, *George M. Cohan: The Man Who Owned Broadway* (New York: DaCapo Press, 1973), 51.
13. McCabe, 86–7.
14. http://www.trackpads.com/forum/entertainment-celebrity-discussions/888437-cuddle-up-little-closer-shine-harvest-moon.html
15. Richard and Paulette Ziegfeld, *The Ziegfeld Touch: The Life and Times of Florenz Ziegfeld, Jr.* (New York: Harry N. Abrams, Inc., Publishers, 1993), 41.
16. Andy Strasburg, Bob Thompson, and Tim Wiles, *Baseball's Greatest Hit: The Story of "Take Me Out to the Ballgame"* (New York: Hal Leonard, 2008), 8.
17. "Jack Norworth, Song Writer, Dies," *New York Times* (September 2, 1959).
18. http://www.ragpiano.com/comps/pwenrich.shtml
19. http://home.comcast.net/˜dvautier/book/songs/songs.htm
20. http://www.archive.org/stream/storybehindpopul009092mbp/storybehindpopul009092mbp_djvu.txt
21. http://parlorsongs.com/bios/cjbond/cjbond.php
22. http://parlorsongs.com/bios/cjbond/cjbond.php
23. http://parlorsongs.com/bios/cjbond/cjbond.php
24. Barnet, Richard D., Bruce Nemerov, and Mayo R. Taylor, *The Story Behind the Song: 150 Songs That Chronicle the 20th Century* (Westport, CT: Greenwood Press, 2004), 28–9.
25. Ewen, *Tin Pan Alley*, 100.
26. David A. Jasen and Gene Jones, *Spreadin' Rhythm Around: Black Popular Songwriters, 1880–1930* (New York: Routledge, 2006), 161.

**1911–1915**

1. http://www.traditionalmusic.co.uk/song-midis/I_Want_a_Girl_(Just_Like_the_Girl).htm#.UYho0pXqlgM
2. http://www2.sigmachi.org/article.phtml?iItemID=938&PHPSESSID=e56404f40e7d42c177e27fcd5ad2abb7
3. http://en.wikipedia.org/wiki/Ragtime_Cowboy_Joe
4. http://en.wikipedia.org/wiki/Harry_Cohn
5. http://www.songfacts.com/detail.php?id=15042
6. Hischak, 393.
7. "Alfred Bryan, 87, Writer of Lyrics," *New York Times* (April 2, 1958).
8. http://en.wikipedia.org/wiki/Harold_R._Atteridge
9. "Harold Atteridge, Broadway Author," *New York Times* (January 17, 1938).
10. http://www.openwriting.com/archives/2005/05/ivor_novello.php

11. Bill Crow, *Jazz Anecdotes: Second Time Around* (New York: Oxford University Press, 2005), 144.
12. Jasen and Jones, 288.
13. http://www.time.com/time/magazine/article/0,9171,796281,00.html

## 1916–1920

1. http://www.answers.com/topic/shelton-brooks#ixzz1htFREZPv
2. http://www.answers.com/topic/shelton-brooks#ixzz1htFREZPv
3. Howard Pollack, *George Gershwin: His Life and Work* (Berkeley: University of California Press, 2006), 49.
4. Shelton Brooks interviewed by Ian Whitcomb, 1969.
5. http://books.google.co.uk/books?id=tUYEAAAAMBAJ&pg=PA49&lpg=PA49&dq=lee+roberts+%26+will+callahan+smiles&source=bl&ots=zxmNmWNbst&sig=wDt4_LR1YydtkaiLtJQriKUPDCE&hl=en&ei=eQvwS7XrPIv80wTEnLDmBw&sa=X&oi=book_result&ct=result&resnum=8&ved=0CDIQ6AEwBzgK#v=onepage&q=lee%20roberts%20%26%20will%20callahan%20smiles&f=false
6. http://www.perfessorbill.com/pbmidi11.shtml
7. http://www.perfessorbill.com/pbmidi11.shtml
8. http://www.lanepl.org/scanned/BUTLER%20BIOS/butler%20bios%2025-30.pdf
9. http://www.lanepl.org/scanned/BUTLER%20BIOS/butler%20bios%2025-30.pdf
10. http://findarticles.com/p/articles/mi_m2342/is_1_35/ai_97074174/pg_3/
11. Arnold Shaw, *The Jazz Age: Popular Music in the 1920s* (New York: Oxford University Press, 1987), 95.
12. http://www.answers.com/topic/j-russell-robinson#ixzz1gv0OCCA7
13. Kathryn Kish Sklar, *Where Home Is: Life in Nineteenth Century Cincinnati*, New World Records, 80521.
14. Woolf, "What Makes a Song: A Talk with Irving Berlin," *New York Times* (July 28, 1940).
15. Laurence Bergreen, *As Thousands Cheer: The Life of Irving Berlin* (New York: Viking Press, 1990), 155.
16. Bergreen, 170–1.
17. Bergreen, 170.
18. Lees, 124.
19. Margaret Whiting and Will Holt, *It Might As Well Be Spring: A Musical Autobiography* (New York: William Morrow, 1987), 23–4.
20. http://en.wikipedia.org/wiki/Ted_Lewis_(musician)
21. Shaw, 100.

## 1921–1925

1. Letter from Jerome Kern to Alexander Woollcott, published 1925 by G.P. Putnam's Sons, © 1925 by Alexander Woollcott. Quoted in Sears, 83.

2. Sears, 165.

3. Michael Freedland, *A Salute to Irving Berlin* (London: W.H. Allen, 1986), 92–3.

4. Freedland, 92–3.

5. http://www.songfacts.com/detail.php?id=14397

6. Whitcomb, *After the Ball*, 42.

7. Joan Peyser, *The Memory of All That: The Life of George Gershwin* (Milwaukee: Hal Leonard, 2006), 143.

8. Michael Feinstein, *Nice Work if You Can Get It: My Life in Rhythm and Rhyme* (New York: Hyperion, 1995), 276.

9. William G. Hyland, *George Gershwin: A New Biography* (Westport, CT: Praeger, 2003), 32–3.

10. Deena Rosenberg, *Fascinating Rhythm: The Collaboration of George and Ira Gershwin* (New York: Dutton, 1991), a45.

11. Ira Gershwin, *Lyrics on Several Occasions* (New York: Alfred A. Knopf, 1959), 260.

12. Gershwin, 260.

13. Goldberg, 131.

14. http://songbook1.wordpress.com/pp/fx/features-2-older-2/focus-on-walter-donaldson/

15. Walter Rimler, *A Gershwin Companion: A Critical Inventory and Discography, 1916–1984* (Ann Arbor: Popular Culture, Inc., 1991), 47–9.

16. http://www.answers.com/topic/i-ll-build-a-stairway-to-paradise-song-from-george-white-s-scandals-of-1922#ixzz1eqIVwc3l

17. Rimler, 48.

18. Philip Furia, *Ira Gershwin: The Art of the Lyricist* (New York, Oxford University Press, 1996), 5.

19. Caryl Flinn, *Brass Diva: The Life and Legends of Ethel Merman* (Berkeley, University of California Press, 2007), 97.

20. Shaw, 132.

21. Shaw, 132–3.

22. Gilbert, 333–6.

23. Michael Whorf, *American Popular Song Composers: Oral Histories, 1920s–1950s* (Jefferson, NC: McFarland & Company, Inc., 2012), EBL, 149.

24. Whorf, 13.

25. Whorf, 15.

26. Irving Berlin, *The Complete Lyrics of Irving Berlin*, ed. Robert Kimball and Linda Emmett, (New York: Alfred A. Knopf, 2001), 225.

27. Richard Corliss, "That Old Feeling: A Berlin Bio-Pic," *Time* (December 30, 2001). http://www.time.com/time/arts/article/0,8599,190220,00.html

28. H Allen Smith, *A Short History of Fingers (And Other State Papers)* (Boston: Little, Brown and Company, 1943), 46.

29. Smith, 50.

30. Alyn Shipton, *I Feel a Song Coming on: The Life of Jimmy McHugh* (Urbana: University of Illinois Press, 2009), 61.

31. Billy Rose, *Wine, Women and Words* (New York: Simon and Schuster, 1946), 10.

32. Polly Rose Gottlieb, *The Nine Lives of Billy Rose* (New York: Crown Publishers, 1968), 78.
33. Earl Conrad, *Billy Rose: Manhattan Primitive* (Cleveland and New York: World Publishing Company, 1968), 46.
34. Untitled obituary, *New York Times* (February 11, 1966).
35. Patricia Dubin McGuire, *Lullaby of Broadway: Life and Times of Al Dubin, One of America's Great Lyricists* (Secaucus, NJ: Citadel Press, 1983), 193–4.

**1926–1930**

1. http://www.proincialthought.com/201105Iss20/Jazz%20Lines%2020/Jazz Lines20.html
2. Marshall Stearns, *Jazz Dance: The Story of American Vernacular Dance* (New York: Da Capo Press, 1994), 110.
3. http://en.wikipedia.org/wiki/Black_Bottom_(dance)
4. http://www.lorenzhart.org/enemy.htm
5. Stanley Green, *The World of Musical Comedy* (New York: Da Capo Press, 1980), 149.
6. Alec Wilder, *American Popular Song: The Great Innovators* (London, New York: Oxford University Press, 1972), 169.
7. Richard Rodgers, *Musical Stages: An Autobiography* (New York: Random House, 1975), 80.
8. Gary Marmorstein: *A Ship Without a Sail: The Life of Lorenz Hart* (New York: Simon & Schuster, 2012), 110.
9. Anonymous, "If You Must Write Lyrics," *New York Herald Tribune* (March 21, 1926), 5, 4, cited in Marmorstein, 110.
10. Gerald Bordman, *Days to Be Happy, Years to Be Sad: The Life and Music of Vincent Youmans* (Oxford and New York: Oxford University Press, 1982), 88.
11. Bordman, *Youmans,* 89.
12. Marks and Liebling, 177.
13. Gerald Bordman, *Youmans,* 88–96.
14. Meryle Secrest, *Somewhere for Me: A Biography of Richard Rodgers* (New York: Alfred A. Knopf, 2001), 79.
15. Michael Feinstein, *Nice Work If You Can Get It: My Life in Rhythm and Rhyme* (New York: Hyperion, 1995), 323.
16. Hyland, 115.
17. Rimler, 174–5.
18. Hyland, 115–17.
19. Kathleen Riley, *The Astaires: Fred and Adele* (Oxford and New York: Oxford University Press, 2012), 141.
20. Edward Jablonski, *Gershwin: A Biography* (New York: Doubleday, 1987), 145.
21. Rosenberg, 161–2.
22. Gershwin, 277–8.
23. Furia, 64.
24. Gershwin, 277–8.

25. Bordman, *Youmans*, 81–84.

26. Gershwin, 224–5.

27. Dennis McGovern and Deborah Grace Winer, *Sing Out, Louise! 150 Stars of the Musical Theatre Remember 50 Years on Broadway* (New York: Schirmer Books, 1993), 41.

28. ESS, "Musical Comedy Authors Tell Their Methods of Composition," *New York Herald Tribune* (August 29, 1926).

29. Bennett Cerf, *At Random: The Reminiscences of Bennett Cerf* (New York: Random House, 1977), 178.

30. Ira Gershwin, *The Complete Lyrics of Ira Gershwin*, ed. Robert Kimball, (New York: Alfred A. Knopf, 1993), 94.

31. http://www.uwosh.edu/home_pages/faculty_staff/earns/song.html

32. http://en.wikipedia.org/wiki/Nagasaki_(song)

33. Tony Thomas, *Harry Warren and the Hollywood Musical* (Secaucus, NJ: Citadel Press, 1975), 16.

34. Shaw, 200–1.

35. Ken Bloom, *The American Songbook: The Singers, the Songwriters, and the Songs* (New York: Black Dog & Leventhal, Publishers, 2005), 32.

36. Untitled obituary, *New York Times* (February 6, 1958).

37. John Lahr, *Notes on a Cowardly Lion: The Biography of Bert Lahr* (Berkeley: University of California Press, 2000), 98.

38. Philip Furia, "DeSylva, Brown & Henderson," in *American Song Lyricists, 1920–1960*, ed. Philip Furia, *Dictionary of Literary Biography* (Detroit: Gale, 2002), 265, 91.

39. Ewen, *All the Years*, 92–3.

40. David Ewen, cited in Mark White, "*You Must Remember This*": *Popular Songwriters 1900–1980* (New York: Charles Scribner's Song, 1985), 72.

41. Lahr, 99.

42. Lahr, 99.

43. Lahr, 100.

44. Philip Furia and Laurie Patterson. *The Songs of Hollywood* (New York: Oxford University Press, 2010), 30.

45. http://www.tcm.com/this-month/article/66966%7C0/The-Broadway-Melody.html

46. http://www.tcm.com/this-month/article/66966%7C0/The-Broadway-Melody.html

47. Jack Burton, cited in *http://books.google.com/books?id=l_UDAAAAMBAJ&pg=PA40&lpg=PA40&dq=%22honor+roll+of+popular+songwriters%22+billboard&source=bl&ots=jNTHT2Yr2d&sig=NS2p64Aq8BwzAAkzFr2cPO6qwq4&hl=en&sa=X&ei=tbPwTszDA-Ta0QGSk7HGAg&ved=0CCAQ6AEwAA#v=onepage&q=%22honor%20roll%20of%20popular%20songwriters%22%20billboard&f=false*

48. Richard Watts, Jr., cited in David Grafton, *Red, Hot & Rich! An Oral History of Cole Porter* (New York: Stein & Day, 1987), 73.

49. http://www.jazzstandards.com/compositions-0/loveforsale.htm

50. William McBrien, *Cole Porter: A Biography* (New York: Vintage Books, 2000), 137.

51. Grafton, 74.
52. http://www.jazzstandards.com/compositions-0/icoverthewaterfront.htm
53. http://www.popularsong.org/songwriter24.html
54. John Edward Hasse, *Beyond Category: The Life and Genius of Duke Ellington* (New York: Simon and Schuster, 1993), 134.
55. Ted Gioia, *The Jazz Standards: A Guide to the Repertoire* (New York: Oxford University Press, 2012), 272.
56. Harvey Cohen, *Duke Ellington's America* (Chicago: University of Chicago Press, 2010), 150.
57. Maurice Zolotow, *Never Whistle in a Dressing Room (Or Breakfast in Bedlam)*, (New York: E.P. Dutton & Company, Inc., 1944), 302.
58. http://songbook1.wordpress.com/pp/fx/features-2-older-2/1930-hits-and-standards/mood-indigo/
59. Mark Tucker, ed., *The Duke Ellington Reader* (New York: Oxford University Press, 1993), 269–70.
60. Nat Hentoff and Nat Shapiro, eds, *Hear Me Talkin' to Ya: The Story of Jazz by the Men Who Made It* (New York: Rinehart & Company, 1955), 224.
61. Gene Brown, *Duke Ellington: Genius! The Artist and the Process* (Englewood Cliffs, NJ: Silver Burdett Press, 1990), 54.
62. Hischak, 202.
63. Richard Sudhalter, *Stardust Melody: The Life and Music of Hoagy Carmichael* (Oxford and New York: Oxford University Press, 2002), 128–9.
64. http://robertcaseinpoint.com/?s=gentilea
65. Sudhalter, 128.
66. Thomas S. Hischak, "Howard Dietz," in *American Song Lyricists*, 103.
67. James Gavin, "Frankie & Jonathan," *New York Times* (March 7, 2004).
68. Jon Pareles, "Arthur Schwartz, Composer of Broadway Shows, Is Dead," *New York Times* (September 5, 1984).
69. Cited in Charlotte Greenspan, *Pick Yourself Up: Dorothy Fields and the American Musical* (New York: Oxford University Press, 2010), 120.
70. "1400 Pay Musical Tribute to Howard Dietz," *New York Times* (September 16, 1983).
71. "Howard Dietz," in *Current Biography Yearbook 1965*, ed. Charles Moritz (New York: H.W. Wilson Co., 1966), 120.
72. Greenspan, 120.
73. Howard Dietz, *Dancing in the Dark* (New York: Quadrangle, 1974), 132–3.
74. Conrad, 48–50.
75. Conrad, 48–9.
76. Whorf, 213.
77. Conrad, 63.
78. Thomas, 20.

## 1931–1935

1. White, 22.
2. Ken Bloom, 180.

3. http://www.steynonline.com/2350/dream-a-little-dream-of-me

4. Jeffrey Magee, *Irving Berlin's American Musical Theater* (Oxford and New York: Oxford University Press, 2012), 18.

5. http://www.songfacts.com/detail.php?id=6611

6. Sam Coslow, *Cocktails for Two: The Many lives of Giant Songwriter Sam Coslow* (New Rochelle NY: Arlington House Publishers, 1977), 111–14.

7. Kate Smith, *Upon My Lips a Song* (New York: Funk & Wagnalls, 1960), 89–90.

8. Kate Smith, *Living in a Great Big Way: The Life Story of Kate Smith* (New York: Blue Ribbon Books, 1938), 89.

9. http://www.network54.com/Forum/27140/message/1262982193/Speaking+ of+Bing+Crosby-+%26quot%3BWhere+the+Blue+of+the+Night%26quot %3B

10. http://en.wikipedia.org/wiki/Where_the_Blue_of_the_Night_(Meets_the_ Gold_of_the_Day)

11. "Jimmy McHugh, 74, Composer of 'Sunny Side of Street,' Dead," *New York Times* (May 24, 1969).

12. Shipton, 122.

13. Shipton, 122.

14. Mary Cleere Haran, cited by William Zinsser, *Easy to Remember: The Great American Songwriters and Their Songs* (Jaffrey, NH: David R. Godine, 2000), 47.

15. Zinsser, 257.

16. Bordman, *Youmans*, 153.

17. Ethel Merman, as told to Pete Martin, *Who Could Ask for Anything More: The Ethel Merman Story* (Garden City, NY: Doubleday & Company, 1955), 96.

18. Gerald Mast, *Can't Help Singin': The American Musical on Stage and Screen* (Woodstock, NY: Overlook Press, 1987), 109–15.

19. Rodgers, 152–3.

20. Thomas S. Hischak, *The Rodgers and Hammerstein Encyclopedia* (Westport, CT: Greenwood Press, 2007), 168.

21. Secrest, 299.

22. John S. Wilson, Interview with Peggy Lee, *New York Times*, July 31, 1981.

23. Secrest, 300.

24. Frank Ward O'Malley, "Irving Berlin Gives Nine Rules for Writing Popular Songs," *American Magazine*, 90 (October 1920), 36–7.

25. Author's conversation with Mary Ellin Barrett, November 29, 2012.

26. Bloom, 18.

27. http://www.cladriteradio.com/archives/2864

28. http://www.awn.com/mag/issue2.1/articles/kaufman2.1.html

29. Coslow, 141–2.

30. Coslow, 142.

31. Max Wilk, *They're Playing Our Song: From Jerome Kern to Stephen Sondheim— The Stories Behind the Words and Music of Two Generations* (New York: Athenaeum, 1973), 146.

32. Harold Meyerson and Ernie Harburg, *Who Put the Rainbow in the Wizard of Oz? Yip Harburg, Lyricist* (Ann Arbor: University of Michigan Press, 1993), 78.

33. John Lahr, "The Lemon-Drop Kid," *New Yorker* (September 30, 1996). http://www. newyorker.com/archive/1996/09/30/1996_09_30_068_TNY_CARDS_000375488 http://www.newyorker.com/archive/1996/09/30/1996_09_30_068_TNY_CARDS_ 000375488

34. Meyerson and Harburg, 76.

35. Meyerson and Harburg, 81.

36. Meyerson and Harburg, 94–9.

37. Thomas, 52.

38. http://www.michaelfeinsteinamericansongbook.org/songwriter.html?p=91

39. Thomas, 18.

40. http://www.anecdotage.com/articles/browse/page/13/tag/550?tag=550

41. http://www.michaelfeinsteinamericansongbook.org/songwriter.html?p=91

42. Thomas, 58.

43. McBrien, 238.

44. McBrien, 238–40.

45. Charles Schwartz, *Cole Porter: A Biography* (New York: Da Capo Press, 1979), 127–8.

46. Whiting and Holt, 35.

47. Theodore Taylor, *Jule: The Story of Composer Jule Styne* (New York: Random House, 1979), 67.

48. Whorf, *Lyricists*, 16.

49. Whorf, *Lyricists*, 17.

50. Thomas, 54.

51. Feinstein, 254–5.

52. Thomas, 68.

53. Thomas, 113.

54. Philip Furia, *Poets of Tin Pan Alley: A History of America's Great Lyricists* (New York: Oxford University Press, 1990), 232.

55. Secrest, 183.

56. http://www.lorenzhart.org/toes.htm

57. Secrest, 384.

58. Ben Brantley, "The Sound of His Music," *New York Times* (May 17, 1998), at http://www.nytimes.com/books/98/05/17/reviews/980517.17brantlt.html

59. Edward Jablonski, *Harold Arlen: Rhythm, Rainbows, and Blues* (Boston: Northeastern University Press, 1996), 99.

60. Meyerson and Harburg, 94.

61. Meyerson and Harburg, 94–9.

62. Jablonski, *Arlen*, 99.

**1936–1940**

1. McBrien, 201–2.

2. Schwartz, 169.

3. Grafton, 90.

4. Brooks Atkinson, "The Play: 'Red, Hot and Blue,'" *New York Times* at http:// www.nytimes.com/books/98/11/29/specials/porter-red.html

5. McBrien, 202.

6. Gilbert Millstein, "Words Anent Music by Cole Porter," *New York Times* (February 20, 1955), at http://www.nytimes.com/books/98/11/29/specials/porter-words.html

7. Margaret Case Harriman, "Words and Music," *New Yorker* (November 23, 1940), 24.

8. http://www.americanmusicpreservation.com /billyhill.htm

9. http://www.jazzstandards.com/compositions-0/inasentimentalmood.htm

10. Tucker, 34.

11. Tucker, 34.

12. http://songbook1.wordpress.com/pp/fx/features-2-older-2/1935-standards/in-a-sentimental-mood/

13. Lees, 97.

14. Philip Furia, *Skylark: The Life and Times of Johnny Mercer* (New York: St. Martin's Press, 2003), 88.

15. Freedland, *Salute to Berlin*, 162.

16. Fred Astaire, *Steps in Time* (New York, Harper, 1959), 216.

17. Cited in Sears, 138.

18. http://www.charliechaplin.com/en/biography/articles/26-Chaplin-Music

19. Gershwin, 135–6.

20. Feinstein, 327–8.

21. Saul Chaplin, *The Golden Age of Movie Musicals and Me* (Norman, OK: University of Oklahoma Press, 1994), 35–7.

22. Sammy Cahn, *I Should Care: The Sammy Cahn Story* (New York: Arbor House, 1974), 64.

23. Wilk, 176.

24. Chaplin, 35–7.

25. Joe Smith, *Off the Record: An Oral History of Popular Music*, ed. Mitchell Fink (New York: Warner Books, 1988), 16.

26. Yip Harburg, "From the Lower East Side to 'Over the Rainbow,'" in Bernard Rosenberg and Ernest Goldstein, *Creators and Disturbers: Reminiscences by Jewish Intellectuals of New York* (New York: Columbia University Press, 1982), 117.

27. Harburg, in Rosenberg and Goldstein, 149.

28. Eric Page, "Harold Arlen, Composer of Song Standards," *New York Times* (April 24, 1986), at http://www.nytimes.com/1986/04/24/obituaries/harold-arlen-composer-of-song-standards.html

29. Harburg, in Rosenberg and Goldstein, 146.

30. Harburg, in Rosenberg and Goldstein, 146.

31. Gerald Morris, "Broadway Morris," *New York Herald Tribune.*

32. http://www.benandbrad.com/docs/harburg

33. Stephen Citron, "Oscar Hammerstein," in *American Song Lyricists, 1920–1960*, 206–7.

34. Hugh Fordin, *Getting to Know Him: A Biography of Oscar Hammerstein* (New York: Random House, 1977), 148.

35. Fordin, 148.
36. Hyland, 200–1.
37. Gershwin, 371.
38. Furia, *Ira Gershwin*, 153–5.
39. Gershwin, *Complete Lyrics*, 139.
40. Gershwin, *Complete Lyrics*, 139.
41. http://www.mouseplanet.com/8664/_Some_Day_My_Lawsuit_Will_Come
42. http://www.mouseplanet.com/8664/_Some_Day_My_Lawsuit_Will_Come
43. http://www.jazzstandards.com/compositions-0/theycanttakethatawayfromme. htm, and Gershwin, *Complete Lyrics*, 266.
44. Gerald Clarke, "George Gershwin: The Celebrated Composer's Manhattan Penthouse," *Architectural Digest* (November 1929), 52, 193.
45. Peyser, 30.
46. Peyser, 29–30.
47. Unnamed author, "Reborn in the USA," *New York Herald Tribune* (September 6, 1987), 5.
48. Rosenberg, 344–5.
49. Rimler, 354–5.
50. Zinsser, 85.
51. http://en.wikipedia.org/wiki/Flat_Foot_Floogie_%28with_a_Floy_Floy%29
52. http://www.pocreations.com/slimbio1.html
53. Tom Dalzell, *Flappers 2 Rappers: American Young Slang* (Springfield, MA: Merriam-Webster, 1967), 59.
54. Michael Zwerin, *The Parisian Jazz Chronicles: An Improvisational Memoir* (New Haven and London: Yale University Press, 2005), 159.
55. Sudhalter, 128.
56. Thomas L. Riis, *Frank Loesser* (New Haven and London: Yale University Press, 2008), 34.
57. Susan Loesser, *A Most Remarkable Fella: Frank Loesser and the Guys and Dolls in His Life* (New York: Donald I. Fine, 1993), 30.
58. Tucker, 341.
59. Tucker, 72–3.
60. Bloom, 218.
61. Cohen, 149.
62. Cohen, 150.
63. Chuck Denison, *The Great American Songbook: The Stories Behind the Standards* (Bandon, OR: Robert D. Reed Publishers, 2004), 10.
64. Denison, 9–11, and David Hadju, *Lush Life: A Biography of Billy Strayhorn* (New York: Farrar, Straus, Giroux, 1996), 56–8.
65. Hischak, *Tin Pan Alley*, 355–6.
66. Furia, *Skylark*, 109.
67. Furia, *Skylark*, 111.
68. Furia, *Skylark*, 111.
69. http://www.jacklawrencesongwriter.com/songs/if_i_didnt_care.html
70. http://www.jacklawrencesongwriter.com/songs/if_i_didnt_care.html

71. Walter Winchell, cited in Sudhalter, 213.
72. http://en.wikipedia.org/wiki/Deep_Purple_(song)
73. http://www.jazzstandards.com/compositions-2/deeppurple.htm
74. David Margolick, "Strange Fruit," at http://www.ladyday.net/stuf/vfsept98.html
75. Jack Lawrence, "The Story Behind the Song," at http://www.jacklawrencesongwriter.com/songs/all_or_nothing_at_all.html
76. Jack Lawrence, "The Story Behind the Song," at http://www.jacklawrencesongwriter.com/songs/all_or_nothing_at_all.html
77. http://www.songfacts.com/detail.php?id=2078
78. http://www.songfacts.com/detail.php?id=2078
79. http://www.johnnymercerfoundation.org/FrankLoesserLyricNotes.pdf
80. http://www.michaelfeinsteinsamericansongbook.org/songwriter.html?p=258
81. Feinstein, 68–9.
82. Jasen and Jones, 217.
83. Barnet, Nemerov, and Taylor, 97–8.
84. Freedland, 183–4.
85. Berlin, *Complete Lyrics*, 359.
86. Whorf, *Composers*, 153.
87. http://trochilustales.blogspot.com/2009/08/well-meet-again.html
88. Whorf, *Composers*, 30.

**1941–1945**

1. http://www.mikelief.com/archives/002179.html
2. Whorf, *Lyricists*, 178.
3. Whorf, *Composers*, 211.
4. Thomas, 17.
5. Thomas, 17.
6. http://www.talkinbroadway.com/cabaret/whiting.html
7. http://www.jazzstandards.com
8. http://articles.latimes.com/1986–11–07/entertainment/ca-15556_1_matt-dennis
9. http://articles.latimes.com/1986–11–07/entertainment/ca-15556_1_matt-dennis
10. http://articles.latimes.com/1986–11–07/entertainment/ca-15556_1_matt-dennis
11. Chaplin, 175–6.
12. Lees, *Portrait of Johnny*, 141.
13. Lees, *Portrait of Johnny,* 142.
14. Furia, *Skylark*, 145.
15. http://www.jazzstandards.com/compositions-1/irememberyou.htm
16. www.jazzstandards.com/compositions-2/tangerine.htm
17. http://www.tcm.com/this-month/article/253205|0/Featured-Films.html
18. Furia, *Skylark*, 145.
19. Ewen, *Great Men*, 112.

20. Lees, *Portrait of Johnny*, 143.
21. Lees, *Portrait of Johnny*, 143.
22. Lees, *Portrait of Johnny*, 143–4.
23. Furia, *Skylark*, 144.
24. Thomas, 187.
25. Thomas, 187–8.
26. http://www.michaelfeinsteinsamericansongbook.org/songwriter.html?p=104
27. http://www.michaelfeinsteinsamericansongbook.org/songwriter.html?p=104
28. http://www.michaelfeinsteinsamericansongbook.org/songwriter.html?p=91
29. Frederick Nolan, "Johnny Burke," in *Dictionary of Literary Biography*, 45.
30. Whorf, *Lyricists*, 46.
31. David Ewen, *Great Men*, 326.
32. Shipton, 171.
33. Shipton, 171–2.
34. http://disney.go.com/disneyinsider/history/legends/oliver-wallace
35. http://disney.go.com/disneyinsider/history/legends/oliver-wallace
36. Thomas S. Hischak and Mark A. Robinson, *The Disney Song Encyclopedia* (Lanham, MD: Scarecrow Press, Inc., 2009).
37. Harriet Hyman Alonso, *Yip Harburg: Legendary Lyricist and Human Rights Activist* (Middletown, CT, Wesleyan University Press, 2012), 100.
38. John S Wilson, "Harold Arlen Dead at 81," *New York Times* (April 24, 1986).
39. Whorf, *Composers*, 28–9.
40. Cited in Meyerson and Harburg, 176.
41. Meyerson and Harburg, 176–7.
42. Meyerson and Harburg, 181.
43. Shipton, 175.
44. http://www.kwf.org/kurt-weill/weill-works/389-one-touch-of-venus-an-appreciation.html
45. Ronald Sanders, *The Days Grow Short: The Life and Music of Kurt Weill* (New York: Holt, Rinehart and Winston, 1980), 323.
46. Sanders, 323.
47. Mary Martin, *My Heart Belongs* (New York: William Morrow and Company, Inc., 1976), 108.
48. Sanders, 326.
49. Cited in Foster Hirsch, *Kurt Weill on Stage: From Berlin to Broadway* (New York: Alfred A. Knopf, 2002), 228.
50. Ed O'Brien with Robert Wilson, *Sinatra 101: The 101 Best Recordings and the Stories Behind Them* (New York: Boulevard Books, 1996), 22.
51. Unnamed writer, "Johnny Burke, 55, Lyricist Is Dead," *New York Times* (February 26, 1964).
52. Frederick Nolan, "Johnny Burke," in *Dictionary of Literary Biography*, 45.
53. Frederick Nolan, "Johnny Burke," in *Dictionary of Literary Biography*, 45.
54. http://georgiamusicmag.com/johnny-mercer-music-master/
55. http://www.star1400.com/johnnymercer.html

56. Lees, *Portrait of Johnny,* 157.
57. Furia, *Skylark*, 44.
58. Cahn, 97.
59. Eleanor Blau, "Jule Styne, Bountiful Creator of Song Favorites, Dies at 88," *New York Times* (September 21, 1994).
60. Taylor, 105.
61. Taylor, 105–8.
62. Taylor, 98.
63. Blau, "Jule Styne."
64. Taylor, 98–9.
65. http://www.thegreatamericansongbook.net/2010_02_01_archive.html
66. Taylor, 426.
67. Taylor, 103.
68. Whorf, *Composers*, 191.
69. Sammy Cahn, *Sammy Cahn's Rhyming Dictionary* (Milwaukee, WI: Hal Leonard Corporation, 1983), xxxviii.
70. Jerry Tallmer, "What Made Sammy Fun," *New York Post* (January 18, 1993).
71. Whorf, *Composers*, 30.

## 1946–1951

1. Furia, *Skylark*, 160.
2. Jablonski, *Arlen*, 139.
3. http://en.wikipedia.org/wiki/St._Louis_Woman
4. Furia, *Skylark*, 159.
5. http://livingstonandevans.com/index.html
6. http://livingstonandevans.com/index.html
7. http://livingstonandevans.com/index.html
8. Graham Wood, "Ray Evans and Jay Livingston," in *Dictionary of Literary Biography*, 127.
9. http://www.upenn.edu/gazette/0597/0597pro1.html
10. http://livingstonandevans.com/20SNGbuttonsandbows.html
11. http://www.johnnymercerfoundation.org/FrankLoesserLyricNotes.pdf
12. Taylor, 112.
13. http://en.wikipedia.org/wiki/Sammy_Cahn
14. Frederick Nolan, "Sammy Cahn," in *Dictionary of Literary Biography*, 69.
15. http://www.michaelfeinsteinamericansongbook.org/songwriter.html?p=151
16. Bloom, 105.
17. Bloom, 105.
18. Philip Furia, *Irving Berlin: A Life in Song* (New York: Schirmer Books, 1998), 151.
19. Edward Jablonski, *Irving Berlin: American Troubadour* (New York: Holt, 1999), 250–1.
20. http://www.michaelfeinsteinamericansongbook.org/songwriter.html?p=151
21. Taylor, 127.

22. http://www.hymnsandcarolsofchristmas.com/Hymns_and_Carols/sleigh_ride.htm
23. Taylor, 131.
24. Blau, "Jule Styne."
25. Taylor, 144.
26. Whorf, *Composers*, 81.
27. http://www.americansongwriter.com/2009/05/american-icons-carl-sigman/
28. Carl Sigman, *The Carl Sigman Songbook* (New York: Amsco Publications, 2007), 16–17.
29. http://www.huffingtonpost.com/michael-sigman/field-notes-from-a-songwr_b_278777.html
30. http://www.ascap.com/playback/2009/11/ACTION/Carl_Sigman.aspx
31. Lees, 216.
32. Furia, *Skylark*, 177–8.
33. Tim Smith, "Mercer's 'Marvelous' Words," in *Baltimore Sun* (December 30, 2010), at http://articles.baltimoresun.com/2010–12–30/entertainment/bs-ae-arts-story-1231–20101230_1_howard-breitbart-songs-johnny-mercer
34. http://georgiamusicmag.com/johnny-mercer-music-master/
35. Steyn, 227.
36. http://www.songfacts.com/detail.php?id=11794
37. en.wikipedia.org/wiki/Hank_Williams
38. en.wikipedia.org/wiki/Cold,_Cold_Heart
39. http://www.songfacts.com/detail.php?id=11794
40. Loesser, 122–3.
41. en.wikipedia.org/wiki/Hans_Christian_Andersen_(film)
42. http://www.answers.com/topic/hans-christian-anderson-film-score
43. Loesser, 129–30.
44. en.wikipedia.org/wiki/Too_Young, en.wikipedia.org/wiki/Sidney_Lippman, Hischak, *Tin Pan Alley*, 373.
45. Jan Morris, *Manhattan '45* (New York: Oxford University Press, 1987), 268.
46. Irving Berlin, "Let Me Sing and I'm Happy," Copyright © 1928, 1929 Irving Berlin, Inc. Copyright Renewed. International Copyright Secured All Rights Reserved Reprinted by Permission.

# Bibliography

Alonso, Harriet Hyman. *Yip Harburg: Legendary Lyricist and Human Rights Activist*. Middletown, CT: Wesleyan University Press, 2012.

Astaire, Fred. *Steps in Time*. New York: Harper & Brothers, Publishers, 1959.

Banfield, Stephen. *Jerome Kern*. New Haven: Yale University Press, 2006.

Barnet, Richard D., Bruce Nemerov and Mayo R. Taylor. *The Story Behind the Song: 150 Songs That Chronicle the 20th Century*. Westport, CT: Greenwood Press, 2004.

Barrett, Mary Ellin. *Irving Berlin: A Daughter's Memoir*. New York: Simon and Schuster, 1994.

Bennett, Robert Russell. *The Broadway Sound: The Autobiography and Selected Essays of Robert Russell Bennett*. George J. Ferencz, ed. Rochester, NY: University of Rochester Press, 1999.

Bergreen, Laurence. *As Thousands Cheer: The Life of Irving Berlin*. New York: Viking, 1990.

Berlin, Irving. *The Complete Lyrics of Irving Berlin*. Robert Kimball and Linda Emmet, eds. New York: Alfred A. Knopf, 2001.

Bloom, Ken. *The American Songbook: The Singers, the Songwriters, and the Songs*. New York: Black Dog & Leventhal, Publishers, 2005.

Boller, Paul F., Jr. and Ronald L. Davis. *Hollywood Anecdotes*. New York: William Morrow and Company, Inc., 1987.

Bond, Carrie Jacobs. *The Roads of Melody*. New York, London: D. Appleton, 1927.

Bordman, Gerald. *American Musical Theatre: A Chronicle*. New York, Oxford: Oxford University Press, 1978.

_____. *Days to Be Happy, Years to Be Sad: The Life and Music of Vincent Youmans*. Oxford and New York: Oxford University Press, 1982.

_____. *Jerome Kern: His Life and Music*. New York, Oxford: Oxford University Press, 1980.

Brown, Gene. *Duke Ellington: Genius! The Artist and the Process*. Englewood Cliffs, NJ: Silver Burdett Press, 1990.

Cahn, Sammy. *I Should Care: The Sammy Cahn Story*. New York: Arbor House, 1974.

_____. *Sammy Cahn's Rhyming Dictionary*. Milwaukee, WI: Hal Leonard Corporation, 1983.

Cantor, Eddie with Jane Kesner Ardmore. *Take My Life*. Garden City, NY: Doubleday & Company, 1957.

Carter, Marva. *Swing Along: The Musical Life of Will Marion Cook*. Oxford and New York: Oxford University Press, 2008.

Cerf, Bennett. *At Random: The Reminiscences of Bennett Cerf*. New York: Random House, 1977.

Chaplin, Saul. *The Golden Age of Movie Musicals and Me*. Norman, OK: University of Oklahoma Press, 1994.

Clarke, Donald. *The Rise and Fall of Popular Music*. New York: St. Martin's Griffin, 1995.

Cohen, Harry G. *Duke Ellington's America*. Chicago: University of Chicago Press, 2010.

Collins, Ace. *Stories Behind the Best-Loved Songs of Christmas*. Grand Rapids, MI: Zondervan, 2001.

Conrad, Earl. *Billy Rose: Manhattan Primitive*. Cleveland and New York: World Publishing Company, 1968.

Coslow, Sam. *Cocktails for Two: The Many Lives of Giant Songwriter Sam Coslow*. New Rochelle, NY: Arlington House Publishers, 1977.

Crow, Bill. *Jazz Anecdotes: Second Time Around*. New York: Oxford University Press, 2005.

Dalzell, Tom. *Flappers 2 Rappers: American Young Slang*. Springfield, MA: Merriam-Webster, 1967.

Davis, Lee. *Bolton and Wodehouse and Kern: The Men Who Made Musical Comedy*. New York: Joseph H. Heinseman, Inc., 1993.

Denison, Chuck. *The Great American Songbook: The Stories Behind the Standards*. Bandon, OR: Robert D. Reed Publishers, 2004.

Dennison, Sam. *Scandalize My Name: Black Imagery in American Popular Music*. New York: Garland Publishing Co., 1982.

Dietz, Howard. *Dancing in the Dark*. New York: Quadrangle, 1974.

Dreiser, Theodore. "My Brother Paul," in *Twelve Men*. New York: Literary Classics of the United States, 1987.

Emurian, Ernest K. *Living Stories of Favorite Songs*. Boston: W.A. Wilde Company, 1958.

Engel, Lehman. *Their Words Are Music: The Great Theatre Lyricists and Their Lyrics*. New York: Crown Publishers, Inc., 1975.

Ewen, David. *All the Years of American Popular Music*. Englewood Cliffs, NJ: Prentice-Hall, Inc. 1977.

_____. *The Life and Death of Tin Pan Alley*. New York: Funk and Wagnell's Company, 1964.

_____. ed. *Songs of America*. Chicago: Ziff-Davis Publishing Company, 1947.

_____. *Great Men of American Popular Song*. Englewood Cliffs, NJ: Prentice-Hall, 1970.

Feinstein, Michael. *Nice Work if You Can Get It: My Life in Rhythm and Rhyme*. New York: Hyperion, 1995.

Fields, Armond. *Lillian Russell: A Biography of "America's Beauty."* Jefferson, NC: McFarland & Company, Inc., 1999.

Fleming, Robert E. *James Weldon Johnson*. Boston: Twayne Publishers, 1987.

Flinn, Caryl. *Brass Diva: The Life and Legends of Ethel Merman*. Berkeley: University of California Press, 2007.

Fordin, Hugh. *Getting to Know Him: A Biography of Oscar Hammerstein*. New York: Random House, 1977.

Freedland, Michael. *Irving Berlin*. New York: Stein and Day, 1974.

_____. *Jerome Kern: A Biography*. New York: Stein and Day, 1978.

_____. *A Salute to Irving Berlin*. London: W.H. Allen, 1986.

Fuld, James J. *The Book of World-Famous Music: Classical, Popular and Folk*. New York: Crown Publishers, Inc., 1966.

Furia, Philip, ed. *Dictionary of Literary Biography: American Song Lyricists, 1920–1960*. Detroit, New York: Gale, 2002.

_____. *Ira Gershwin: The Art of the Lyricist*. New York: Oxford University Press, 1996.

_____. *Irving Berlin: A Life in Song*. New York: Schirmer Books, 1998.

_____. *Poets of Tin Pan Alley: A History of America's Great Lyricists*. New York: Oxford University Press, 1990.

_____. *Skylark: The Life and Times of Johnny Mercer*. New York: St. Martin's Press, 2003.

Furia, Philip and Michael Lasser. *America's Songs: The Stories Behind the Songs of Broadway, Hollywood, and Tin Pan Alley*. New York: Routledge, 2006.

Furia, Philip and Laurie Patterson. *The Songs of Hollywood*. New York: Oxford University Press, 2010.

Gershwin, Ira. *The Complete Lyrics of Ira Gershwin*. Robert Kimball, ed. New York: Alfred A. Knopf, 1993.

_____. *Lyrics on Several Occasions*. New York: Alfred A. Knopf, 1959.

Giddins, Gary. *Bing Crosby: A Pocket Full of Dreams: The Early Years, 1903–1940*. Boston and New York: Little, Brown and Company, 2001.

Gilbert, Douglas. *Lost Chords: The Diverting Story of American Popular Songs*. Garden City NY: Doubleday, Doran and Co., 1942.

Gioia, Ted. *The Jazz Standards: A Guide to the Repertoire*. New York: Oxford University Press, 2012.

Goldberg, Isaac. *Tin Pan Alley: A Chronicle of American Popular Music*. New York: Frederick Ungar Publishing Co., Inc., 1961.

Goldman, Herbert G. *Fanny Brice: The Original Funny Girl*. New York: Oxford University Press, 1992.

Gottlieb, Polly Rose. *The Nine Lives of Billy Rose*. New York: Crown Publishers, 1968.

Grafton, David. *Red, Hot & Rich! An Oral History of Cole Porter*. New York: Stein & Day, 1987.

Green, Stanley. *The World of Musical Comedy*. New York: Da Capo Press, 1980.

Greenspan, Charlotte. *Pick Yourself Up: Dorothy Fields and the American Musical*. New York: Oxford, 2010.

Griffin, Mark. *A Hundred or More Hidden Things: The Life and Films of Vincente Minnelli*. Cambridge, MA: Da Capo Press, 2010.

Grossman, Barbara. *Funny Woman: The Life and Times of Fanny Brice*. Bloomington and Indianapolis: Indiana University Press, 1992.

Hadju, David. *Lush Life: A Biography of Billy Strayhorn*. New York: Farrar, Straus, Giroux, 1996.

Harburg, Yip. "From the Lower East Side to 'Over the Rainbow,'" in Bernard Rosenberg and Ernest Goldstein, eds. *Creators and Disturbers: Reminiscences by Jewish Intellectuals of New York*. New York: Columbia University Press, 1982.

Haskins, James and N.R. Mitgang. *Mr. Bojangles: The Biography of Bill Robinson*. New York: William Morrow & Company, Inc., 1988.

Hasse, John Edward. *Beyond Category: The Life and Genius of Duke Ellington*. New York: Simon & Schuster, 1993.

Hentoff, Nat and Nat Shapiro, eds. *Hear Me Talkin' To Ya: The Story of Jazz by the Men Who Made It*. New York: Rinehart & Company, Inc., 1955.

Hirsch, Foster. *Kurt Weill on Stage: From Berlin to Broadway*. New York: Alfred A. Knopf, 2002.

Hischak, Thomas S. *The Rodgers and Hammerstein Encyclopedia*. Westport, CT: Greenwood Press, 2007.

_____. *The Tin Pan Alley Song Encyclopedia*. Westport, CT: Greenwood Press, 2002.

Hischak, Thomas S. and Mark A. Robinson. *The Disney Song Encyclopedia*. Lanham, MD: The Scarecrow Press, Inc., 2009.

Hyland, William G. *George Gershwin: A New Biography*. Westport, CT: Praeger, 2003.

Jablonski, Edward. *Harold Arlen: Rhythm, Rainbows, and Blues*. Boston: Northeastern University Press, 1996.

_____. *Irving Berlin: American Troubadour*. New York: Holt, 1999.

_____. *Gershwin: A Biography*. New York: Doubleday, 1987.

Jasen, David A. *Tin Pan Alley: The Composers, the Songs, the Performers, and Their Times: The Golden Age of American Popular Music from 1886 to 1956*. New York: Donald I. Fine, 1988.

Jasen, David A. and Gene Jones. *Spreadin' Rhythm Around: Black Popular Songwriters, 1880–1930*. New York: Routledge, 2006.

Johnson, James Weldon. "NAACP Testimonial Dinner Speech," in Sondra Kathryn Wilson, ed., *The Selected Writings of James Weldon Johnson*, Vol. 2. New York: Oxford University Press, 1995.

Kaplan, James. *Sinatra: The Voice*. New York: Doubleday, 2010.

Kashner, Sam and Nancy Schoenberger. *A Talent for Genius: The Life and Times of Oscar Levant*. New York: Villard Books, 1994.

Kellow, Brian. *Ethel Merman: A Life*. New York: Viking, 2007.

Lahr, John. *Notes on a Cowardly Lion: The Biography of Bert Lahr*. Berkeley: University of California Press, 2000.

Lees, Gene. *Portrait of Johnny: The Life of John Herndon Mercer*. New York: Pantheon Books, 2004.

_____. *Singers and the Song*. New York: Oxford, 1987.

_____. *Singers and the Song II*. Oxford and New York: Oxford University Press, 1987, 1998.

Loesser, Susan. *A Most Remarkable Fella: Frank Loesser and the Guys and Dolls in His Life*. New York: Donald I. Fine, 1993.

Lyons, Jeffrey. *Stories My Father Told Me: Notes from "The Lyons Den."* New York: Abbeville Press, 2011.

Magee, Jeffrey. *Irving Berlin's American Musical Theater*. Oxford and New York: Oxford University Press, 2012.

Marcuse, Maxwell F. *Tin Pan Alley in Gaslight: A Saga of the Songs That Made the Gray Nineties "Gay."* Watkins Glen, NY: Century House, 1959.

Marks, Edward B and Abbott J. Liebling. *They All Sang: From Tony Pastor to Rudy Valèe*. New York: Viking, 1934.

Marx, Samuel and Jan Clayton. *Rodgers and Hart*. New York: G.P. Putnam's Sons, 1976.

Marmorstein, Gary. *A Ship without a Sail: The Life of Lorenz Hart*. New York: Simon & Schuster, 2012.

Martin, Mary. *My Heart Belongs*. New York: William Morrow and Company, Inc., 1976.

Mast, Gerald. *Can't Help Singin': The American Musical on Stage and Screen*. Woodstock, NY: Overlook Press, 1987.

McBrien, William. *Cole Porter: A Biography*. New York: Vintage Books, 2000.

McCabe, John. *George M. Cohan: The Man Who Owned Broadway*. New York: Da Capo Press, 1973.

McGovern, Dennis and Deborah Grace Winer. *Sing Out, Louise! 150 Stars of the Musical Theatre Remember 50 Years on Broadway*. New York: Schirmer Books, 1993.

McGuire, Patricia Dubin. *Lullaby of Broadway: Life and Times of Al Dubin, One of America's Great Lyricists*. Secaucus, NJ: Citadel Press, 1983.

Mercer, Johnny. Edited by Bob Bach and Ginger Mercer. *Johnny Mercer: The Life, Times and Song Lyrics of Our Huckleberry Friend*. Secaucus, NY: Lyle Stewart, 1982.

Merman, Ethel, as told to Pete Martin. *Who Could Ask for Anything More: The Ethel Merman Story*. Garden City, NY: Doubleday & Company, 1955.

Meyerson, Harold and Harburg, Ernie. *Who Put the Rainbow in the Wizard of Oz? Yip Harburg, Lyricist*. Ann Arbor: University of Michigan Press, 1993.

Montgomery, Elizabeth Rider. *The Story Behind Popular Songs*. New York: Dodd, Mead, 1953.

Mordden, Ethan. *Love Song: The Lives of Kurt Weill and Lotte Lenya*. New York: St. Martin's Press, 2012.

Morgan, Thomas L. and William Barlow. *From Cakewalks to Concert Halls: An Illustrated History of African American Popular Music from 1895 to 1930*. Washington, DC: Wlliott & Clark Publishing, 1992.

Morris, Jan. *Manhattan '45*. New York: Oxford University Press, 1987.

O'Brien, Ed with Robert Wilson. *Sinatra 101: The 101 Best Recordings and the Stories Behind Them*. New York: Boulevard Books, 1996.

Peyser, Joan. *The Memory of All That: The Life of George Gershwin*. Milwaukee: Hal Leonard, 2006.

Pollack, Howard. *George Gershwin: His Life and Work*. Berkeley: University of California Press, 2006.

Riis, Thomas L. *Frank Loesser*. New Haven and London: Yale University Press, 2008.

Riley, Kathleen. *The Astaires: Fred and Adele*. Oxford and New York: Oxford University Press, 2012.

Rimler, Walter. *George Gershwin: An Intimate Portrait*. Urbana and Chicago: University of Illinois Press, 2009.

_____. *A Gershwin Companion: A Critical Inventory and Discography, 1916–1984*. Ann Arbor: Popular Culture, Inc., 1991.

Rodgers, Richard. *Musical Stages: An Autobiography*. New York: Random House, 1975.

Rose, Billy. *Wine, Women and Words*. New York: Simon and Schuster, 1946.

Rosenberg, Deena. *Fascinating Rhythm: The Collaboration of George and Ira Gershwin*. New York: Dutton, 1991.

Sanders, Ronald. *The Days Grow Short: The Life and Music of Kurt Weill*. New York: Holt, Rinehart and Winston, 1980.

Sanjek, Russell. *American Popular Music and Its Business: The First Four Hundred Years*. New York: Oxford University Press, 1988.

Schwartz, Charles. *Cole Porter: A Biography*. New York: Da Capo Press, 1979.

Schwartz, Jonathan. *All in Good Time*. New York: Random House, 2004.

Sears, Benjamin, ed. *The Irving Berlin Reader*. New York: Oxford University Press, 2012.

Secrest, Meryle. *Somewhere for Me: A Biography of Richard Rodgers*. New York: Alfred A. Knopf, 2001.

Shaw, Arnold. *The Jazz Age: Popular Music in the 1920s*. New York: Oxford University Press, 1987.

Sheed, Wilfrid. *The House That George Built: With a Little Help from Irving, Cole, and a Crew of About Fifty*. New York: Random House, 2007.

Shipton, Alyn. *I Feel a Song Coming on: The Life of Jimmy McHugh*. Urbana: University of Illinois Press, 2009.

Sigman, Carl. *The Carl Sigman Songbook*. New York: Amsco Publications, 2007.

Singer, Barry. *Black and Blue: The Life and Lyrics of Andy Razaf*. New York: Schirmer, 1992.

Smith, H. Allen. *A Short History of Fingers (And Other State Papers)*. Boston: Little, Brown and Company, 1943.

Smith, Joe. *Off the Record: An Oral History of Popular Music*. Mitchell Fink, ed. New York: Warner Books, 1988.

Smith, Kate. *Living in a Great Big Way: The Life Story of Kate Smith*. New York: Blue Ribbon Books, 1938.

_____. *Upon My Lips a Song*. New York: Funk & Wagnalls, 1960.

Stearns, Marshall. *Jazz Dance: The Story of American Vernacular Dance.* New York: Da Capo Press, 1994.

Steyn, Mark. *Broadway Babies Say Goodnight: Musicals Then and Now.* New York: Routledge, 1999.

Strasberg, Andy, Bob Thompson and Tim Wiles. *Baseball's Greatest Hit: The Story of Take Me Out to the Ballgame.* New York: Hal Leonard, 2008.

Studwell, William E. *The Popular Song Reader: A Sampler of Well-Known Twentieth-Century Songs.* New York: Harrington Park Press, 1994.

Studwell, William E. and Mark Baldin. *The Big Band Reader: Songs Favored by Swing Era Orchestras and Other Popular Ensembles.* New York: The Haworth Press, 2000.

Sudhalter, Richard M. *Stardust Melody: The Life and Music of Hoagy Carmichael.* Oxford and New York: Oxford University Press, 2002.

Taylor, Theodore. *Jule: The Story of Composer Jule Styne.* New York: Random House, 1979.

Thomas, Tony. *Harry Warren and the Hollywood Musical.* Secaucus, NY: Citadel Press, 1975.

Tolbert-Rouchaleau, Jane. *James Weldon Johnson.* New York: Chelsea House Publishers, 1988.

Tucker, Mark, ed. *The Duke Ellington Reader.* New York: Oxford University Press, 1993.

Vance, Joel. *Fats Waller: His Life and Times.* Chicago: Contemporary Books, Inc., 1977.

Whitcomb, Ian. *After the Ball: Pop Music from Rag to Rock.* New York: Limelight Editions, 1986.

_____. *Irving Berlin and Ragtime America.* London: Century-Hutchinson, 1987.

White, Mark. *"You Must Remember This": Popular Songwriters 1900–1980.* New York: Charles Scribner's Song, 1985.

Whiting, Margaret and Will Holt. *It Might As Well Be Spring: A Musical Autobiography.* New York: William Morrow, 1987.

Whorf, Michael. *American Popular Song Composers: Oral Histories, 1920s–1950s.* Jefferson, NC: McFarland & Company, Inc., 2012.

_____. *American Popular Song Lyricists: Oral Histories, 1920s–1950s.* Jefferson, NC: McFarland & Company, Inc., 2012.

Wilder, Alex. *American Popular Song: The Great Innovators, 1900–1950.* London and New York: Oxford University Press, 1972.

Wilk, Max. *They're Playing Our Song: from Jerome Kern to Stephen Sondheim—The Stories Behind the Words and Music of Two Generations.* New York: Athenaeum, 1973.

Williams, William H.A. *'Twas Only an Irishman's Dream: The Image of Ireland and the Irish in American Popular Song Lyrics, 1800–1920.* Champaign, IL: University of Illinois Press, 1996.

Wondrich, David. *Stomp and Swerve: American Music Gets Hot, 1842–1924.* Chicago: A Cappella Books, 2003.

Ziegfeld, Richard and Paulette Zinsser. *The Ziegfeld Touch: The Life and Times of Florenz Ziegfeld, Jr.* New York: Harry N. Abrams, Inc., Publishers, 1993.

Zinsser, William. *Easy to Remember: The Great American Songwriters and Their Songs*. Jaffrey, NH: David R. Godine, 2000.

Zolotow, Maurice. *Never Whistle in a Dressing Room (Or Breakfast in Bedlam)*. New York: E.P. Dutton & Company, Inc., 1944.

Zwerin, Michael. *The Parisian Jazz Chronicles: An Improvisational Memoir*. New Haven, CT: Yale University Press, 2005.

# Credits

(Songs published before 1923 are in the Public Domain)

## 1921–1925

"**Do, Do, Do**" music by George Gershwin, lyrics by Ira Gershwin. Copyright © WARNER BROTHERS MUSIC CORP. "**That Old Gang of Mine**" music by Ray Henderson, lyrics by Billy Rose and Mort Dixon. Copyright © 1923 by Bourne Co. Ray Henderson Music and Olde Clover Leaf Music. Copyright Renewed. All rights for the extended term administered by Fred Ahlert Music Corporation on behalf of Olde Clover Leaf Music. International Copyright Secured. All Rights Reserved. "**(The Gang That Sang) Heart of My Heart**" music and lyrics by Ben Ryan. Copyright © 1926 (renewed 1946 ROBBINS MUSIC CORPORATION). "**Wedding Bells (Are Breaking Up That Old Gang of Mine)**" music by Sammy Fain, lyrics by Irving Kahal and Willie Raskin. Copyright © 1929 MILLS MUSIC, INC. Copyright Renewed RYTVOC, INC. and FAIN MUSIC CO. All Rights Reserved. "**Yes! We Have No Bananas**" music and lyrics by Frank Silver and Irving Cohn. Copyright © 1923 SKIDMORE MUSIC CO., INC. Copyright Renewed 1950 and Assigned to Skidmore music Co., Inc. All Rights Reserved. "**Hard Hearted Hannah**" music by Milt Ager, lyrics by Jack Yellen, Bob Bigelow, and Charles Bates. Copyright © 1924 Ager, Yellen & Bornstein Incorporated, USA. Lawrence Wright Music Company Limited. All Rights Reserved. International Copyright Secured. "**Lazy**" music and lyrics by Irving Berlin. Copyright © 1924 IRVING BERLIN MUSIC CORP. "**When My Sugar Walks Down the Street**" music by Jimmy McHugh, lyrics by Irving Mills and Gene Austin. Copyright © 1924 (Renewed 1954) EMI MILLS MUSIC, INC. Rights for the Extended Term of Copyright in the U.S. Assigned to COTTON CLUB PUBLISHING (Adm. By UNIVERSAL-MCA MUSIC PUBLISHING, A Division of UNIVERSAL STUDIOS, INC. and EMI MILLS MUSIC, INC. Print Rights for EMI MILLS MUSIC, INC. Administered by WARNER BROS. PUBLICATIONS US. INC. All Rights Reserved. "**I Can't Believe That You're in Love with Me**" music by Jimmy McHugh, lyrics by Clarence Gaskill. Copyright © 1926 (Renewed 1954) EMI MILLS MUSIC, INC. Rights for the Extended Term of Copyright

249

in the U.S. Assigned to COTTON CLUB PUBLISHING (adm. By UNIVERSAL-MCA MUSIC PUBLISHING, A Division of UNIVERSAL STUDIOS, INC. and EMI MILLS MUSIC, INC. All Rights Reserved. "**A Cup of Coffee, A Sandwich And You**" music by Joseph Meyer, lyrics by Al Dubin and Billy Rose. Copyright © 1925 Harms T B Company. CHAPPEL MUSIC LIMITED (75%)/REDWOOD MUSIC LIMITED (25%). All Rights Reserved. International Copyright Secured.

## 1926–1930

"**The Birth of the Blues**" music by Ray Henderson, lyrics by B.G. DeSylva and Lew Brown. Copyright © 1926 STEPHEN BALLENTINE MUSIC, WARNER BROS. INC. and RAY HENDERSON MUSIC. Copyright Renewed. All Rights for STEPHEN BALLENTINE Administered by THE SONGWRITERS GUILD OF AMERICA. "**Black Bottom**" music by Ray Henderson, lyrics by B.G. DeSylva and Lew Brown. Copyright © Publishers/Administrators STEPHEN BALLENTINE MUSIC PUBL CO., RAY HENDERSON MUSIC CO, INC. WARNER BROS INC. (WARNER BROS. MUSIC DIVISION). "**The Blue Room**" music by Richard Rodgers, lyrics by Lorenz Hart. Copyright © 1926 WARNER BROS. INC. Copyright Renewed. Rights for the Extended Renewal Term in the United States Controlled by THE ESTATE OF LORENZ HART (Administered by WB music Corp) and FAMILY TRUST U/W RICHARD RODGERS AND THE ESTATE OF DOROTHY F. RODGERS (Administered by WILLIAMSON MUSIC). This Arrangement © 1997 by THE ESTATE OF LORENZ HART (Administered by WB music Corp) and FAMILY TRUST U/W RICHARD RODGERS AND THE ESTATE OF DOROTHY F. RODGERS (Administered by WILLIAMSON MUSIC). All Rights Reserved. "**I Know That You Know**" music by Vincent Youmans, lyrics by Anne Caldwell. Copyright © 1926 WARNER BROS., INC. (Renewed). All Rights Reserved. "**Mountain Greenery**" music by Richard Rodgers, lyrics by Lorenz Hart. Copyright © 1926 by CHAPPELL CO. Rights for the Extended Renewal Term in the U.S. Controlled © by WILLIAMSON MUSIC, a Division of RODGERS & HAMMERSTEIN: an Imagam Company and WB MUSIC CORP. a/b/o THE ESTATE OF LORENZ HART. International Copyright Secured. All Rights Reserved. "**Among My Souvenirs**" music by Horatio Nicholls, lyrics by Edgar Leslie. Copyright © 1927 and 1947 LAWRENCE WRIGHT MUSIC COMPANY LIMITED. REDWOOD MUSIC LIMITED (50%)/EMI MUSIC PUBLISHING LIMITED (50%). All Rights Reserved. International Copyright Secured. "**Funny Face**" music by George Gershwin, lyrics by Ira Gershwin. Copyright © 1927 WB MUSIC CORP. (Renewed). All Rights Reserved. "**The Babbitt and the Bromide**" music by George Gershwin, lyrics by Ira Gershwin. Copyright © 1927 IRA GERSHWIN MUSIC, NEW WORLD MUSIC COMPANY LTD. "**How Long Has This Been Going On?**" music by George Gershwin, lyrics by Ira Gershwin. Copyright © 1927 WB MUSIC CORP. (Renewed). All Rights Reserved. "**Sometimes I'm Happy**" music by Vincent Youmans, lyrics by Irving Caesar. Copyright © 1927 WARNER BROS. INC. Copyrights Renewed. All Rights Reserved. "**Strike Up the Band**" music by George Gershwin, lyrics by Ira Gershwin. Copyright © 1927 WB MUSIC CORP. (Renewed). All Rights Reserved. "**Doin' the**

New Low Down" music by Jimmy McHugh, lyrics by Dorothy Fields. Copyright © 1928 (Renewed 1956) EMI MILLS MUSIC, INC. Rights for the Extended Term of Copyright in the U.S. Assigned to COTTON CLUB PUBLISHING (adm. By UNIVERSAL-MCA PUBLISHING, A Division of UNIVERSAL STUDIOS, INC.) and ALDI MUSIC CO. (adm. By THE SONGWRITERS GUILD OF AMERICA). All Rights Reserved. "**Hooray for Captain Spaulding**" music by Harry Ruby, lyrics by Bert Kalmar. Copyright © 1936 WARNER BROS. INC. (Renewed). All Rights Reserved. "**I'd Rather Be Blue**" music by Fred Fisher, lyrics by Billy Rose. Copyright © 1928 BOURNE, INC. Original Proprietor IRVING BERLIN, INC., name changed to BOURNE, INC. © Arrangement Copyright 1968 BOURNE CO. Copyright Renewed. All Rights Reserved including the Right of Public Performance for profit. International Copyright Secured. "**I've Got a Crush on You**" music by George Gershwin, lyrics by Ira Gershwin. Copyright © 1930 WB MUSIC CORP. (Renewed). All Rights Reserved. "**Nagasaki**" music by Harry Warren, lyrics by Mort Dixon. Copyright © 1928 FOUR JAYS MUSIC CO. OLDE CLOVER LEAF MUSIC. "**Sonny Boy**" music by Ray Henderson, lyrics by B.G. DeSylva and Lew Brown. Copyright © 1928 DESYLVA, BROWN & HENDERSON INCORPORATED, USA. REDWOOD MUSIC LIMITED (75%)/CAMPBELL, CONNELLY & COMPANY LIMITED (25%). All Rights Reserved. International Copyright Secured. "**Sweet Lorraine**" music by Cliff Burwell, lyrics by Mitchell Parish. Copyright © 1928 (Renewed 1956) EMI MILLS MUSIC INC. All Rights Controlled by EMI MILLS MUSIC, INC. All Rights Controlled by EMI MILLS MUSIC, INC. (Publishing) and WARNER BROS. PUBLICATIONS U.S. INC. (Print). All Rights Reserved. "**You're the Cream in My Coffee**" music by Ray Henderson, lyrics by B.G. DeSylva and Lew Brown. Copyright © 1928 DESYLVA, BROWN & HENDERSON INC. Copyright Renewed. Rights for the Extended Renewal Term in the United States Controlled by RAY HENDERSON MUSIC COMPANY, CHAPPELL & CO. and STEPHEN BALLENTINE MUSIC. Rights for Canada Controlled by CHAPPELL & CO. All Rights Reserved. "**Broadway Melody**" music by Nacio Herb Brown, lyrics by Arthur Freed. Copyright © 1929 (Renewed) EMI ROBBINS CATALOG INC. All Rights Controlled by EMI CATALOG INC (Publishing) and ALFRED PUBLISHING CO., INC. (Print). All Rights Reserved. "**Love for Sale**" music and lyrics by Cole Porter. Copyright © 1930 (Renewed) WARNER BROS. INC. This Arrangement © 2001 WARNER BROS. INC. All Rights Reserved. "**I Cover the Waterfront**" music by John Green, lyrics by Edward Heyman. Copyright © 1933 WARNER BROS, INC (WARNER BROS. MUSIC DIV). "**Mood Indigo**" music by Duke Ellington and Barney Bigard, lyrics by Irving Mills. Copyright © 1931 (Renewed 1958) and Assigned to FAMOUS MUSIC CORPORATION, EMI MILLS MUSIC INC. and INDIGO MOOD MUSIC. c/o THE SONGWRITERS GUILD OF AMERICA in the U.S.A. Rights for the world outside the U.S.A. Controlled by EMI MILLS MUSIC INC. (Publishing) and WARNER BROS. PUBLICATIONS INC. (Print). "**Rockin' Chair**" music and lyrics by Hoagy Carmichael. Copyright © 1929 by HOAGY PUBLISHING COMPANY. Copyright Renewed. All Rights Administered by PSO Limited. "**Something To Remember You By**" music by Arthur Schwartz, lyrics by Howard Dietz. Copyright © 1930 WARNER BROS. INC. (Renewed). All Rights Reserved. "**Would You Like To Take a Walk**" music by Harry Warren, lyrics by

Billy Rose and Mort Dixon. Copyright © 1930 WARNER BROS, INC. (Renewed). All Rights Reserved. "**Cheerful Little Earful**" music by Harry Warren, lyrics by Billy Rose and Ira Gershwin. Copyright © 1930 WARNER BROS. INC. Copyright Renewed and Assigned to WB MUSIC CORP. and WARNER BROS. INC. This arrangement © 1999 WB MUSIX CORP. and WARNER BROS. INC. All Rights Reserved. "**I Found a Million Dollar Baby**" Copyright © 1931 (Renewed 1958) OLDE CLOVER LEAF MUSIC (ASCAP) Adminstered by BUG MUSIC and WARNER BROS. INC. (ASCAP). All Rights Reserved.

## 1931–1935

"**Between the Devil and the Deep Blue Sea**" music by Harold Arlen, lyrics by Ted Koehler. Copyright © 1931 (Renewed 1959) MILLS MUSIC, INC., c/o EMI MUSIC PUBLISHING. All Rights Reserved. "**I Love a Parade**" music by Harold Arlen, music by Ted Koehler. Copyright © 1931 WARNER BROS. INC. (Renewed). All Rights Reserved. "**Dream a Little Dream of Me**" music by Fabian Andre and Wilbur Schwandt, lyrics by Gus Kahn. Copyright © 1931 WORDS AND MUSIC INCORPORATED, USA. FRANCIS DAY & HUNTER, London/EMI MUSIC PUBLISHING, London. All Rights Reserved. International Copyright Secured. "**It Don't Mean a Thing (If It Ain't Got That Swing)**" music by Duke Ellington, lyrics by Irving Mills. Copyright © 1932 (Renewed 1960) EMI MILLS MUSIC, INC. and FAMOUS MUSIC CORPORATION in the U.S.A. All Rights outside the USA. Controlled by EMI MILLS MUSIC INC. (Publishing) and WARNER BROS. PUBLICATIONS U.S. Inc. (Print). All Rights Reserved including Public Performance for Profit. "**Just One More Chance**" music by Arthur Johnston, lyrics by Sam Coslow. Copyright © 1931 (Renewed 1958) by FAMOUS MUSIC CORPORATION. "**When the Moon Comes Over the Mountain**" music and lyrics by Harry Woods, Howard Johnson, and Kate Smith. Copyright © 1931 (Renewed 1959) METRO-GOLDWYN-MAYER, INC. All Rights Controlled and Administered by ROBBINS MUSIC CORPORATION. All rights for ROBBINS MUSIC CORPORATION Assigned to EMI CATALOGUE PARTNERSHIP, and contained and administered by EMI ROBBINS CATALOG INC. Rights on Behalf of Harry Woods for the Extended Renewal Term in the United States controlled by CALLICOON MUSIC and administered by THE SONGWRITERS GUILD OF AMERICA. All Rights Reserved. "**Where the Blue of the Night (Meets the Gold of the Day)**" music by Fred E. Ahlert, lyrics by Roy Turk and Bing Crosby. Copyright © 1931 (Renewed) CROMWELL MUSIC, INC. New York. CHAPPELL & Co., Los Angeles. The FRED AHLERT MUSIC GROUP/Administered by BUG MUSIC, and PENAL MARK MUSIC, Inc, Bronxville. International Copyright Secured. All Rights Reserved including Public performance for Profit. "**Don't Blame Me**" music by Jimmy McHugh, lyrics by Dorothy Fields. Copyright © 1932, 1933 METRO-GOLDWYN-MAYER INC. Renewed 1960, 1961 EMI ROBBINS CATALOG INC. Rights to the Extended Term of Copyright in the U.S. Assigned to COTTON CLUB PUBLISHING (adm. by UNIVERSAL-MCA MUSIC PUBLISHING, a Division of UNIVERSAL STUDIOS INC. and EMI ROBBINS CATALOGING. Print Rights for EMI CATALOG INC. Administered by WARNER BROS. PUBLICATIONS U.S. INC. All Rights Reserved.

"**Eadie Was a Lady**" music by Nacio Herb Brown and Richard A. Whiting, lyrics by B.G., DeSylva. Copyright © 1932 STEPHEN BALLENTINE MUSIC PUBL CO., DE LA PRADE MUSIC, HIGHCOURT MUSIC, MARKFLITE, WARNER BROS. INC. (WARNER BROS. MUSIC DIV). "**Lover**" music by Richard Rodgers, lyrics by Lorenz Hart. Copyright © 1933 (Renewed 1961). FAMOUS MUSIC CORPORATION (ASCAP). All Rights Reserved. "**Soft Lights and Sweet Music**" Music and Lyrics by Irving Berlin. Copyright © 1932 IRVING BERLIN MUSIC CORPORATION. "**The Carioca**" music by Vincent Youmans, lyrics by Edward Eliscu and Gus Kahn. Copyright © 1932 TB HARMS COMPANY. CHAPPELL MUSIC LIMITED. All Rights Reserved. International Copyright Secured. "**Did You Ever See a Dream Walking**" music by Harry Revel, lyrics by Mack Gordon. Copyright © 1933 SONY/ ATV HARMONY, CHAPPELL CO, INC. "**With My Eyes Wide Open, I'm Dreaming**" music by Harry Revel, lyrics by Mack Gordon. Copyright © 1934 CHAPPELL-CO INC, WB MUSIC CORP. "**Who's Afraid of the Big Bad Wolf?**" music and lyrics by Frank Churchill, Additional lyrics by Ann Ronell. Copyright © 1933 by IRVING BERLIN INC., now BOURNE CO. Copyright renewed. International Copyright Secured. All Rights Reserved. "**Cocktails for Two**" music by Arthur Johnston, lyrics by Sam Coslow. Copyright © 1934 (Renewed 1961) by FAMOUS MUSIC CORPORATION. International Copyright Secured. All Rights Reserved. "**The Continental**" music by Con Conrad, lyrics by Herb Magidson. Copyright © 1934 (Renewed) WB MUSIC CORP and BERNHARDT MUSIC. All Rights Administered by WB MUSIC CORP. All Rights Reserved. "**Fun to Be Fooled**" music by Harold Arlen, lyrics by Ira Gershwin and E.Y. Harburg. Copyright © 1934 NEW WORLD MUSIC CORPORATION. Copyright Renewed. All Rights Reserved. "**I'll String Along with You**" music by Harry Warren, lyrics by Al Dubin. Copyright © 1934 WARNER BROS. INC. (Renewed). All Rights Reserved. "**Miss Otis Regrets**" music and lyrics by Cole Porter. Copyright © 1934 WARNER BROS. INC (WARNER BROS. MUSIC DIV). "**On the Good Ship Lollipop**" music by Richard A. Whiting, lyrics by Sidney Clare. Copyright © 1934 (Renewed 1962) MOVIETONE MUSIC CORPORATION. All Rights for MOVIETONE MUSIC CORPORATION Assigned to WB MUSIC CORP. All Rights for the Extended Term in the U.S. Administered by SHIP LOLLIPOP PUBLISHING. All Rights Reserved. "**Stompin' at the Savoy**" music by Benny Goodman, Edgar Sampson, and Chick Webb, lyrics by Andy Razaf. Copyright © 1936 (Renewed 1964) and Assigned to RAZAF MUSIC CO., JEWEL MUSIC PUBLISHING CO., INC. and EMI ROBBINS CATALOG INC. in the U.S.A. All Rights outside the USA controlled by EMI ROBBINS CATALOG INC. (Printing) and WARNER BROS. PUBLICATIONS U.S. INC (Print). "**What a Diff'rence a Day Makes**" Music by Maria Grever, Lyrics by Stanley Adams. Copyright © EDWARD B. MARKS MUSIC COMPANY. Copyright Renewed and Assigned to Stanley Adams Music, Inc. and Grever Music Publishing. All rights for Stanley Adams Music Inc. Administered by The Songwriters Guild of America. All rights for Grever Music Publishing Administered by Zorea Enterprises, Inc. "**About a Quarter To Nine**" music by Harry Warren, lyrics by Al Dubin. Copyright © 1935 WARNER BROS. INC. Copyright Renewed. All Rights Reserved. "**It's Easy To Remember**" music by Richard Rodgers, lyrics by Lorenz Hart. Copyright © 1934, 1935 (Renewed 1961, 1962) FAMOUS MUSIC CORPORATION. "**Last Night When We Were Young**" music by Harold Arlen, lyrics by Yip Harburg.

1937 (Renewed) GLOCCA MORRA MUSIC and S.A. MUSIC CO. All Rights for GLOCCA MORRA MUSIC Controlled and Administered by NEXT DECADE ENTERTAINMENT, INC. All Rights for Canada Controlled by BOURNE CO. All Rights Reserved.

## 1936–1940

"**Down in the Depths**" music and lyrics by Cole Porter. Copyright © 1936 CHAPPELL & CO. INC. Copyright Renewed. International Copyright Secured. All Rights Reserved. "**Glory of Love**" music and lyrics by Billy Hill. Copyright © 1936 by SHAPIRO, BERNSTEIN & CO. INC. Copyright Renewed. International Copyright Secured. All Rights Reserved. "**The Last Round-Up**" music and lyrics by Billy Hill. Copyright © 1933 by SHAPIRO, BERNSTEIN & CO. INC. Copyright Renewed. International Copyright Secured. All Rights Reserved. "**In a Sentimental Mood**" music by Duke Ellington. lyrics by Irving Mills and Manny Kurtz. Copyright © 1935 (Renewed 1963) and Assigned to FAMOUS MUSIC CORPORATION in the USA. Rights for the world outside the USA controlled by EMI MILLS MUSIC INC and CPP/BELWIN, INC. International Copyright Secured. All Rights Reserved. "**Goody Goody**" music by Matt Malneck, lyrics by Johnny Mercer. Copyright © 1935, 1936 by DESYLVA, BROWN AND HENDERSON, INC. Copyrights Renewed and Assigned to WB MUSIC CORP. and MALNECK MUSIC. All Rights Reserved. "**Bob White (Whatcha Gonna Swing Tonight?)**" music by Bernie Hanighen, lyrics by Johnny Mercer. Copyright © 1937 by WARNER BROS. INC. and WB MUSIC CORP. (Renewed). All Rights Reserved. "**Let's Face the Music and Dance**" music and lyrics by Irving Berlin. Copyright © 1936 by IRVING BERLIN/ WB MUSIC CORP. WARNER CHAPPELL MUSIC LTD. "**Let Yourself Go**" music and lyrics by Irving Berlin. Copyright © 1936 Irving Berlin Music Corp. "**Smile**" music by Charles Chaplin, lyrics by John Turner and Geoffrey Parsons. Copyright © 1954 Bourne Co. All Rights Reserved. International Copyright Secured. Copyright Renewed. "**(I've Got) Beginner's Luck**" music by George Gershwin, lyrics by Ira Gershwin. Copyright © 1937 GEORGE GERSHWIN MUSIC, IRA GERSHWIN MUSIC, WB MUSIC CORP. "**Bei Mir Bist Du Schoen**" music by Sholom Secunda, original lyrics by Jacob Jacobs, English version by Sammy Cahn and Saul Chaplin. Copyright © 1937 WARNER BROS. INC. (Renewed). All Rights Reserved. "**Down with Love**" music by Harold Arlen, lyrics by E.Y. Harburg. Copyright © 1937 CHAPPELL & CO., INC. Copyright Renewed. International Copyright Secured. All Rights Reserved. "**Buds Won't Bud**" music by Harold Arlen lyrics by E.Y. Harburg. Copyright © 1937 GLOCCA MORRA MUSIC CORP., SA MUSIC CORP. "**The Folks Who Live on the Hill**" music by Jerome Kern, lyrics by Oscar Hammerstein II. Copyright © 1937 by UNIVERSAL-POLYGRAM INTERNATIONAL PUBLISHING, INC. Copyright Renewed. International Copyright Secured. All Rights Reserved. "**Love Walked in**" music by George Gershwin, lyrics by Ira Gershwin. Copyright © 1937, 1938 (Renewed 1964–1965). GEORGE GERSHWIN MUSIC and IRA GERSHWIN MUSIC. All Rights Administered by WB MUSIC CORP. All Rights Reserved. "**Some Day My Prince Will Come**" music by Frank Churchill, lyrics by Larry Morey. Copyright © 1937 by IRVING BERLIN, INC., now BOURNE CO. Copyright Renewed. International Copyright Secured. All Rights Reserved. "**They Can't Take That Away from Me**" music by George Gershwin, lyrics by Ira Gershwin. Copyright © 1936, 1937 (Renewed 1963, 1964) GEORGE GERSHWIN MUSIC and IRA GERSHWIN MUSIC. All Rights Administered by WB MUSIC CORP. All Rights Reserved. "**Flat Foot Floogie (with a Floy Floy)**" music and lyrics by Slim Gaillard, Slam Stewart, and Bud Green. Copyright © 1938 HOLLIDAY PUBLISHING, JEWEL MUSIC PUBLISHING CO., INC. O'VOUTI PUBLISHING, OPTISSIMO PUBLISHING, SPLOGHM MUSIC, TOO LATE BLUES MUSIC. "**Heart and Soul**" music by Hoagy Carmichael, lyrics by Frank Loesser. Copyright © 1938 SONY/ATV MUSIC PUBLISHING L.L.C. Copyright Renewed. All Rights Administered by SONY/ATV MUSIC PUBLISHING L.L.C. and MUSIC SQUARE WEST. International Copyright Secured. All Rights Reserved. "**I Let a Song Go Out of My Heart**" music by Duke Ellington, lyrics by Henry Nemo, John Redmond, and Irving Mills. Copyright © 1938 (Renewed 1966) FAMOUS MUSIC CORPORATION (ASCAP) MILLS MUSIC INC. (ASCAP). All Rights Reserved. "**Take the 'A' Train**" music and lyrics by Billy Strayhorn. Copyright © 1941 TEMPO MUSIC INCORPORATED, USA. CAMPBELL CONNELLY & COMPANY LIMITED. International Copyright Secured. All Rights Reserved. "**Day in, Day Out**" music by Rube Bloom, lyrics by Johnny Mercer. Copyright © 1939 WB MUSIC CORP. (Renewed). All Rights Reserved. "**Fools Rush in**" music by Rube Bloom, lyrics by Johnny Mercer. Copyright © 1940 WB MUSIC CORP. (Renewed) All Rights Reserved. "**If I Didn't Care**" music and lyrics by Jack Lawrence. Copyright © 1939 CHAPPELL & CO. INC. Copyright renewed. Extended term of Copyright Deriving from Jack Laurence Assigned and Effective April 11, 1995 to RANGE ROAD MUSIC, INC. International Copyright Secured. All Rights Reserved. "**I Get Along Without You Very Well**" music and lyrics by Hoagy Carmichael. Copyright © 1938, 1939 by FAMOUS MUSIC CORPORATION. Copyright renewed 1965, 1966 and Assigned to FAMOUS MUSIC CORPORATION. All Rights Reserved. "**Stairway to the Stars**" music by Matt Malneck and Frank Signorelli, lyrics by Mitchell Parish. Copyright © 1935, 1939 (Renewed 1962, 1966) ROBBINS MUSIC CORPORATION. All Rights Reserved. "**Deep Purple**" music by Peter DeRose, lyrics by Mitchell Parish. Copyright © 1934, 1939 ROBBINS MUSIC CORPORATION, INC. Copyright Renewed 1962, 1967 ROBBINS MUSIC CORPORATION. International Copyright Secured. All Rights Reserved. "**Strange Fruit**" music and lyrics by Lewis Allen. Copyright © 1939 EDWARD B. MARKS MUSIC CO. CARLIN MUSIC CORP. "**All or Nothing at All**" music by Arthur Altman, lyrics by Jack Lawrence. Copyright © 1939 by UNIVERSAL-MCA MUSIC PUBLISHING, a Division of UNIVERSAL STUDIOS, INC. Copyright Renewed. Extended term of Copyright from Jack Lawrence and Arthur Altman Assigned and Effective June 20, 1995 to RANGE ROAD MUSIC, INC. "**Blueberry Hill**" music by Vincent Rose, lyrics by Al Lewis and Larry Stock. Copyright © 1940 CHAPPELL & COMPANY INCORPORATED USA. REDWOOD MUSIC LIMITED (66.67%) CHAPPELL MORRIS LIMITED (33.33%). International Copyright Secured. All Rights Reserved. "**I Hear Music**" music by Burton Lane, lyrics by Frank Loesser. Copyright © 1940 (Renewed 1967) by FAMOUS MUSIC CORPORATION. "**Dancing on a Dime**" music by Burton Lane, lyrics by Frank Loesser. Copyright © 1940 SONY ATV HARMONY. "**In the Mood**" music by Joe Garland, lyrics by Andy

Razaf. Copyright © 1939, 1960 SHAPIRO, BERNSTEIN & CO. INC. Copyright Renewed International Copyright Secured. All Rights Reserved. "**Moonlight Serenade**" music by Glenn Miller, lyrics by Mitchell Parish. Copyright © 1939 (Renewed 1967) EMI ROBBINS CATGALOGING. All Rights Controlled by EMI ROBBINS CATALOG INC. (Publishing) and WARNER BROS. PUBLICATIONS U.S. INC (Print). All Rights Reserved. "**One O'Clock Jump**" music by Count Basie. Copyright © 1938 (Renewed 1965) EMI FEIST CATALOG INC. All Rights Controlled EMI FEIST CATALOG INC. (Publishing) and WARNER BROS. PUBLICATIONS U.S. INC. (Print). All Rights Reserved. "**Let's Dance**" music by Josef Bonime and Gregory Stone, lyrics by Fanny Baldridge. Copyright © 1934. EDWARD B. MARKS. "**It's a Lovely Day Tomorrow**" music and lyrics by Irving Berlin. Copyright © 1939 IRVING BERLIN MUSIC CORP. WARNER CHAPPELL MUSIC LTD. All Rights Reserved. "**Java Jive**" music by Milton Drake, lyrics by Ben Oakland. Copyright © 1940 SNY/ATV TUNES LLC, WARNER BROS INC (WARNER BROS MUSIC DIV.) "**We'll Meet Again**" music by Ross Parker, lyrics by Hughie Charles. Copyright © 1939 DASH MUSIC COMPANY LIMITED. International Copyright Secured. All Rights Reserved. "**A Nightingale Sang in Berkeley Square**" music by Manning Sherwin, lyrics by Eric Maschwitz. Copyright © 1940 by THE PETER MAURICE MUSIC CO. LTD. Sole Selling Agents—SHAPIRO, BERNSTEIN & CO. INC. All Rights Reserved. "**(There'll Be Blue Birds Over) The White Cliffs of Dover**" music by Walter Kent, lyrics by Nat Burton. Copyright © 1941 (Renewed) by SHAPIRO, BERNSTEIN & CO. INC. International Copyright Secured. All Rights Reserved. "**When the Lights Go on Again (All Over the World)**" music by Sol Marcus and Eddie Seiler, lyrics by Bennie Benjamin. Copyright © 1942 PORGIE MUSIC INCORPORATED/DUCHESS MUSIC CORPORATION USA. DASH MUSIC COMPANY LIMITED International Copyright Secured. All Rights Reserved.

## 1941–1945

"**Boogie Woogie Bugle Boy**" music and lyrics by Don Raye and Hughie Prince. Copyright © 1940, 1941 UNIVERSAL MUSIC CORP. Copyright Renewed. This arrangement Copyrighted © 1966 UNIVERSAL MUSIC CORP. All Rights Reserved. "**I'll Remember April**" music by Don Raye, lyrics by Gene de Paul and Patricia Johnston. Copyright © 1941, 1942 by MCA MUSIC PUBLISHING, A Division of MCA INC. and PIC CORPORATION. Copyright Renewed. International Copyright Secured. All Rights Reserved. "**Don't Sit Under the Apple Tree (With Anyone Else But Me)**" music by Sam H. Stept, lyrics by Charles Tobias and Lew Brown. Copyright © 1942 EMI ROBBINS CATALOG INC. © Renewed and Assigned to CHED MUSIC CORPORATION and EMI ROBBINS CATALOG INC in the U.S.A. and EMI. ROBBINS CATALOG INC elsewhere throughout the world. Print Rights on behalf of EMI ROBBINS CATALOG INC. Administered by WARNER BROS PUBLICATIONS U.S. INC. All Rights Reserved. "**Chattanooga Choo Choo**" music by Harry Warren, lyrics by Mack Gordon. Copyright © 1941 (Renewed 1969) TWENTIETH CENTURY MUSIC CORPORATION. All Rights

Reserved by LEO FEIST INC. All rights of LEO FEIST INC. Assigned to SBK CATALOGUE PARTNERSHIP. All rights administered by SBK FEIST CATALOG INC. International Copyright Secured. All Rights Reserved. "**Everything Happens to Me**" music by Matt Dennis, lyrics by Tom Adair. Copyright © 1941 (Renewed 1968) DORSEY BROTHERS MUSIC INCORPORATED, a division of MUSIC SALES CORPORATION, USA. MAC MUSIC LIMITED. International Copyright Secured. All Rights Reserved. "**Let's Get Away from It All**" music by Matt Dennis, lyrics by Tom Adair. Copyright © 1941 (Renewed) by MUSIC SALES CORPORATION (ASCAP). International Copyright Secured. All Rights Reserved. "**Violets for Your Furs**" music by Matt Dennis, lyrics by Tom Adair. Copyright © 1941 (Renewed) by DORSEY BROS. MUSIC, A DIVISION OF MUSIC SALES CORPORATION. International Copyright Secured. All Rights Reserved. "**This Time the Dream's on Me**" music by Harold Arlen, lyrics by Johnny Mercer. Copyright ©1941 WARNER BROS INC. (Renewed) All Rights Reserved. "**Hit the Road to Dreamland**" music by Harold Arlen, lyrics by Johnny Mercer. Copyright © 1942 SONY/ATV MUSIC PUBLISHING LLC. Copyright Renewed. All Rights Administered by SONY/ATV MUSIC PUBLISHING LLC. International Copyright Secured. All Rights Reserved. "**I Remember You**" music by Victor Schertzinger, lyrics by Johnny Mercer. Copyright © 1948 (Renewed 1969) by PARAMOUNT MUSIC CORPORATION. "**Tangerine**" music by Victor Schertzinger, lyrics by Johnny Mercer. Copyright © 1948 (Renewed 1969) by FAMOUS MUSIC CORPORATION. "**(I Left My Heart at) The Stage Door Canteen**" music and lyrics by Irving Berlin. Copyright © 1942 by IRVING BERLIN. Copyright Renewed. Copyright Assigned to the TRUSTEES OF THE GOD BLESS AMERICA FUND. International Copyright Secured. All Rights Reserved. "**I'm Old-Fashioned**" music by Jerome Kern, lyrics by Johnny Mercer. Copyright © 1942) LERNER MUSIC, MARBLE MUSIC CO., THE JOHNNY MERCER FOUNDATION, UNIVERSAL POLYGRAM INTERNATIONAL PUBLISHING INC. "**(I've Got a Gal in) Kalamazoo**" music by Harry Warren, lyrics by Mack Gordon. Copyright © 1942 by MUSIC CORP (Renewed). All Rights Reserved. "**Road to Morocco**" music by Jimmy Van Heusen, lyrics by Johnny Burke. Copyright © 1942 (Renewed 1968) by PARAMOUNT MUSIC CORPORATION. International Copyright Secured. All Rights Reserved. "**Comin' in on a Wing and a Prayer**" music by Jimmy McHugh, lyrics by Harold Adamson. Copyright © 1943 (Renewed 1971) EMI ROBBINS CATALOG INC. and JIMMY MCHUGH MUSIC. Rights for the Extended Term in the US. Assigned to COTTON CLUB PUBLISHING (Administered by UNIVERSAL-MCA MUSIC PUBLISHING, a Division of UNIVERSAL STUDIOS INC. and HAROLD ADAMSON MUSIC (Adm. by THE SONGWRITERS GUILD OF AMERICA). All Rights Reserved. "**Der Fuehrer's Face**" music and lyrics by Oliver G. Wallace. Copyright © 1943 SOUTHERN MUSIC PUBLISHING CO., INC. "**Mairzy Doats**" music and lyrics by Jerry Livingston, Milton Drake and Al Hoffman. Copyright © 1943 EMI MILLER CATALOG INC. Copyright Renewed and Assigned to HALLMARK MUSIC CO., INC., AL HOFFMAN/ SONY TUNES INC. in the United States. Rights Elsewhere Controlled by EMI MILLER CATALOGING INC. (Publishing) WARNER BROS. PUBLICATIONS U.S. INC. (Print). All Rights Reserved. "**Happiness Is Just a Thing Called Joe**" music by Harold Arlen, lyrics by E.Y. Harburg. Copyright © 1942 (Renewed 1970)

METRO-GOLDWYN-MAYER INC. All Rights Controlled and Administered by LEO FEIST INC. All Rights of LEO FEIST, INC Assigned to CBS CATALOGUE PARTNERSHIP and Controlled and Administered by CBS FEIST CATALOG, INC. International Copyright Secured. All Rights Reserved. "**I Couldn't Sleep a Wink Last Night**" music by Jimmy McHugh, lyrics by Harold Adamson. Copyright © 1943 (Renewed 1973) UNIVERSAL-POLYGRAM INTERNATIONAL PUBLISHING, INC. Rights for the Extended Term of Copyright in the U.S. Assigned to COTTON CLUB PUBLISHING (Adm. by UNIVERSAL-MCA MUSIC PUBLISHING, a Division of UNIVERSAL STUDIOS, INC. and HAROLD ADAMSON MUSIC (Adm. by THE SONGWRITERS GUILD OF AMERICA). All Rights Reserved. "**I'll Be Home for Christmas**" music and lyrics by Kim Gannon, Buck Ram and Walter Kent. Copyright © 1943, 1956 by KIM GANNON-WALTER KENT. International Copyright Secured. All Rights Reserved. "**Speak Low**" music by Kurt Weill, lyrics by Ogden Nash. Copyright © 1943 (Renewed 1971) HAMPSHIRE HOUSE PUBLISHING CORP. and CHAPPELL & CO. All Rights Reserved. "**That's Him**" music by Kurt Weill, lyrics by Ogden Nash. Copyright © 1943 (Renewed 1971) HAMPSHIRE HOUSE PUBLISHING CORP. and CHAPPELL & CO. All Rights Reserved. "**Straighten Up and Fly Right**" music by Nat K. Cole, lyrics by Irving Mills. Copyright © 1944 AMERICAN ACADEMY OF MUSIC INC. USA. WARNER CHAPPELL MUSIC LTD, LONDON. "**Sunday, Monday, or Always**" music by Jimmy Van Heusen, lyrics by Johnny Burke. Copyright © 1943 BOURNE CO., MUSIC SALES CORP. "**Dream**" music and lyrics by Johnny Mercer. Copyright © 1945 (Renewed) THE JOHNNY MERCER FOUNDATION. All Rights Administered by WB MUSIC CORP. All Rights Reserved. "**It's Been a Long, Long Time**" music by Jule Styne, lyrics by Sammy Cahn. Copyright © 1945 MORLEY MUSIC CO. Copyright Renewed, Assigned to MORLEY MUSIC CO. and CAHN MUSIC COMPANY. All Rights outside the United States Controlled by MORLEY MUSIC CO. All Rights Reserved. "**Saturday Night Is the Loneliest Night in the Week**" music by Jule Styne, lyrics by Sammy Cahn. Copyright © 1944 BARTON MUSIC CORP. Copyright Renewed and Assigned to JULE STYNE & CAHN MUSIC COMPANY. Jule Styne's Interest Controlled in the U.S.A. by PRODUCERS MUSIC PUB. CO., INC. and Administered by CHAPPELL & CO. All Rights Reserved. "**Swinging on a Star**" music by James Van Heusen, lyrics by Johnny Burke. Copyright © 1944 (Renewed) by MUSIC SALES CORPORATION and BOURNE CO. International Copyright Secured. All Rights Reserved. "**I Fall in Love Too Easily**" music by Jule Styne, lyrics by Sammy Cahn. Copyright © 1944 METRO-GOLDWYN-MAYER INC. (Renewed) All Rights Controlled by EMI CATALOG INC. (Publishing) and WARNER BROS. PUBLICATIONS U.S. INC. (Print). All Rights Reserved. "**I'll Buy That Dream**" music by Allie Wrubel, lyrics by Herb Magidson. Copyright © 1945 EDWIN H. MORRIS & CO., INC. "**Oh! What It Seemed To Be**" music and lyrics by Bennie Benjamin, George David Weiss and Frankie Carle. Copyright © 1945 by CHAPPELL & CO. Copyright Renewed, Assigned to CHAPPELL & CO. CLAUDE A MUSIC and ABILENE MUSIC INC. All rights for CLAUDE A MUSIC Administered by CHAPPELL & CO. All Rights for ABILENE MUSIC INC. Administered by THE SONGWRITERS GUILD OF AMERICA. International Copyright Secured. All Rights Reserved.

## 1946–1951

"**Any Place I Hang My Hat Is Home**" music by Harold Arlen, lyrics by Johnny Mercer. Copyright © 1946 by A-M MUSIC CORPORATION. Copyright Renewed. CHAPPELL & CO., INC. Sole Selling Agent. International Copyright Secured. All Rights Reserved. "**Route 66**" music and lyrics by Bobby Troup. Copyright © 1946, Renewed 1973. Assigned 1974 to LONDONTOWN MUSIC. All Rights Outside the U.S.A. Controlled by EMI MORRIS & COMPANY. "**To Each His Own**" music by Jay Livingston and Ray Evans, lyrics by Ray Evans. Copyright © 1946 (Renewed 1973) by PARAMOUNT MUSIC CORPORATION. International Copyright Secured. All Rights Reserved. "**Buttons and Bows**" music by Jay Livingston and Ray Evans, lyrics by Ray Evans. Copyright © 1948 (Renewed) 1975) FAMOUS MUSIC CORPORATION (ASCAP). All Rights Reserved. "**I Wish I Didn't Love You So**" music and lyrics by Frank Loesser. Copyright © 1947 SONY/ATV MUSIC PUBLISHING LLC. Copyright Renewed. Administered by SONY/ATV MUSIC PUBLISHING LLC, & MUSIC SQUARE WEST. music by Jay Livingston and Ray Evans, lyrics by Ray Evans. "**Time After Time**" music by Jule Styne, lyrics by Sammy Cahn. Copyright © 1947 SINATRA SONGS INC. Copyright Renewed and Assigned to SANDS MUSIC CORP. All Rights Reserved. "**Five Minutes More**" music by Jule Styne, lyrics by Sammy Cahn. Copyright © 1946 MORLEY MUSIC CO. Copyright Renewed, Assigned to MORLEY MUSIC CO. and CAHN MUSIC COMPANY. All Rights Outside the United States Controlled by MORLEY MUSIC CO. All Rights Reserved. "**A Couple of Swells**" music and lyrics by Irving Berlin. Copyright © 1947 IRVING BERLIN MUSIC CORP. WARNER/CHAPPELL MUSIC LTD. "**It's Magic**" music by Jule Styne, lyrics by Sammy Cahn. Copyright © 1948 WARNER BROS. INC. Copyright Renewed and Assigned to WARNER BROS. INC. and JULE STYNE. Jule Styne's Interest Controlled by PRODUCERS MUSIC PUB. CO. and Administered by CHAPPELL & CO. All Rights Reserved. "**Sleigh Ride**" music by LeRoy Anderson, lyrics by Mitchell Parish. Copyright © 1948, 1950 (Renewed 1976, 1978) EMI MILLS MUSIC, INC. Print Rights on behalf of EMI MILLS MUSIC, INC. Administered by WARNER BROS. PUBLICATIONS U.S. INC. All Rights Reserved. "**Diamonds Are a Girl's Best Friend**" music by Jule Styne, lyrics by Leo Robin. Copyright © 1949 (Renewed) CONSOLIDATED MUSIC PUBLISHERS INCORPORATED / MUSIC SALES CORPORATION / DORSEY BROTHERS MUSIC USA. DORSEY BROTHERS MUSIC LIMITED. International Copyright Secured. All Rights Reserved. "**Dear Hearts and Gentle People**" music by Sammy Fain, lyrics by Bob Hilliard. Copyright © 1949 WARNER/CHAPPELL MUSIC LIMITED (50%) / BOURNE MUSIC LIMITED (50%). International Copyright Secured. All Rights Reserved. "**Enjoy Yourself (It's Later Than You Think)**" music by Carl Sigman, lyrics by Herb Magidson. Copyright © 1950 CHAPPELL MORRIS LIMITED. International Copyright Secured. All Rights Reserved. "**Ballerina**" music by Carl Sigman, lyrics by Bob Russell. Copyright © 1947 (Renewed 1975) CROMWELL MUSIC, INC. and HARRISON MUSIC CORP. All Rights Reserved. "**Civilization**" music by Carl Sigman, lyrics by Bob Hilliard. Copyright © 1948 BOURNE MUSIC LIMITED (50%)/EDWIN H. MORRIS & COMPANY LIMITED (50%). International Copyright Secured. All Rights Reserved. "**When the World Was Young**" music by M. Philippe-Gerard, lyrics by Angele Vannier, English lyrics by Johnny

# Index